Huskey's Study Notes on Historical Theology

Huskey's Study Notes on Historical Theology

MICHAEL HUSKEY

RESOURCE *Publications* • Eugene, Oregon

HUSKEY'S STUDY NOTES ON HISTORICAL THEOLOGY

Copyright © 2020 Michael Huskey. All rights reserved. Except for brief quotations in critical publications or reviews, no part of this book may be reproduced in any manner without prior written permission from the publisher. Write: Permissions, Wipf and Stock Publishers, 199 W. 8th Ave., Suite 3, Eugene, OR 97401.

Resource Publications
An Imprint of Wipf and Stock Publishers
199 W. 8th Ave., Suite 3
Eugene, OR 97401

www.wipfandstock.com

PAPERBACK ISBN: 978-1-7252-7866-0
HARDCOVER ISBN: 978-1-7252-7867-7
EBOOK ISBN: 978-1-7252-7868-4

Manufactured in the U.S.A. 10/02/20

Contents

Introduction to Huskey's Study Notes | ix
    Using This Guide for Small Groups or Sunday School | x
    Using This for Personal Study | xi

Introduction | 1
    Why Should You Study Church History? | 1

The Apostolic Church: First Century | 7

The Disciples of the Apostles: First Century | 13
    Clement of Rome (Not to Be Confused with Clement of Alexandria) | 13
    Polycarp of Smyrna (AD 69–155) | 18
    Ignatius of Antioch (AD 35–?) | 23
    Papias of Hierapolis (AD 60–155) | 26
    The Shepherd of Hermas | 27
    The Epistle of Barnabas | 29
    The Didache (The teaching of the Twelve) | 30

An Introduction to Historic Heresies | 33
    First Century Heresies | 33
    Second Century Heresies | 36
    Third Century Heresies | 39
    Fourth Century Heresies | 41
    Fifth Century Heresies | 43

The Apologists: The Apologetics and Polemics of the Church Fathers: Second Century | 47
    Justin Martyr AD 100–165 | 48

  Tatian AD 110–72 | 51
  Athenagoras of Athens AD 133–90 | 52
  Clement of Alexandria AD 150–215 (Egypt) | 55
  Tertullian AD 155–240 (North Africa) | 58

The Ante-Nicene Fathers: Third Century | 62
  Irenaeus AD 130–202 (Greece-France) | 62
  Origen AD 184–253 | 64
  Cyprian of Carthage AD 200–258 | 66

Are the Solas Something New? | 70

Nicene Christianity | 77
  The Council of Nicaea | 80

The Nicene Fathers: Fourth Century | 86
  Athanasius (296–373) | 86
  The Cappadocian Fathers (335–95) | 92
  Ambrose of Milan (339–97) | 93
  Jerome (347–420) | 95
  John Chrysostom (347–407) The Bishop of Constantinople | 97
  Augustine (354–430) The Bishop of Hippo | 99
  Pelagius (360–420) | 101

The History of Eschatology | 105

Controversies and Councils | 117
  Jesus of the Scriptures is Truly God and Truly Man. | 118
  The Council of Nicaea in AD 325 (The First Council) | 119
  The Council of Constantinople in AD 381 (The Second Council) | 119
  The Council of Ephesus in AD 431 (The Third Council) | 120
  The Council of Chalcedon in AD 451 (The Fourth Council) | 121
  The Second Council of Constantinople in AD 553 (The Fifth Council) | 123
  The Third Council of Constantinople in AD 680 (The Sixth Council) | 124
  The Second Council of Nicaea in AD 787 (The Seventh Council) | 125

The Fall of Western Rome: Middle Ages | 127
    The Rise of Islam | 128
    Three Great Signs | 131

The Canon | 135

The Middle Ages | 140
    Leo the Great (400–461) | 141
    Justinian the Great (Eastern Rome 527–65) | 145
    Gregory the Great (Western Rome 540–604) | 146
    The Iconoclast Controversy (730–842) | 146
    The Donation of Constantine | 149
    The Great Schism (1054) | 151
    The Crusades | 153
    Scholarship during The Crusades (1095–1290) | 160
    Divine Proofs | 162
    Peter Abelard (1079–1142) | 166
    Peter Lombard (1096–1160) | 166
    Thomas Aquinas (1225–1274) | 167
    Corruption in the Papacy Continues | 169
    The Babylonian Captivity (1305–1377) | 169
    The Papal Schism (1378–1417) | 170
    The Council of Constance (1414–1418) | 171

An Introduction to The Reformation | 174
    Forerunners to the Reformation | 176
    Reformers | 185
    The English Reformation | 209
    The Scottish Reformation | 210
    Other Important Events during This Time | 212

An Introduction to The Puritans: 1559–1688 | 217
    Puritan Pastors to Be Familiar With | 221
    Other Important Events Alongside the Puritans | 226

The Great Awakening | 239
    The Age of Enlightenment | 240
    Solomon Stoddard Became the Pastor of the Church in Northampton, Massachusetts. | 243

John Wesley (1703–1791) (England) | 245
George Whitefield (1714–1770) (England) | 245
Jonathan Edwards (1703–1758) | 250

The Second Great Awakening: 1792–1820s | 258

Liberalism and The Higher Critics | 268
Johann Gottfried Eichhorn (1753–1827) (Germany) | 269
Friedrich Schleiermacher (1768–1834)
    The Father of Liberal Theology | 270
David Friedrich Strauss (1808–1874) | 272
Albrecht Ritschl (1822–1889) | 272
Julius Wellhausen (1844–1918) | 273
Adolf von Harnack (1851–1930) | 273

The Cults and Heretics of the Nineteenth and Twentieth Centuries | 276
The Restorationist Movement | 276

The Keswick Movement and its Theology | 284

The Charismatic Movement | 289
Is Hindu Worship Similar to Charismatic Worship? | 292
Classical Pentecostalism (The First Wave) | 293
Charismatic Renewal (The Second Wave) (1960) | 300
Signs and Wonders (The Third Wave) (1980s) | 302
Continuationism, Cessationism, and Restorationism | 311

Fundamentalism and Evangelicalism in America | 315
Major Issues the Church Faced | 315
The Niagara Creed (1878) | 317
Modernism vs. Fundamentalism Was at the Center of
    Evolution vs. Biblical Creationism | 319
Indifferentists | 321
Evangelicalism | 324

Bibliography | 331
Subject Index | 337
Index of Quotes | 340

Introduction to Huskey's Study Notes

"What aim should we set ourselves in life? To know God."

J. I. Packer

THESE ARE MY PERSONAL study notes to help teach small groups and Sunday school classes. I wanted to make these available to anyone that is looking to either grow in their knowledge and understanding of God's Word or teach God's Word to others.

This study will be concerning the history of theology and how it was forced to better define biblical doctrine as well as heresies that crept into the church.

Some of the resources used in this study are from Dr. Nathan Busenitz. Others will be mentioned as we progress.

There are basic notes, questions, and expositions throughout this study. The intention is to either bring to remembrance the things you have already studied in order to expound upon them, or to help engage conversation among those you are teaching.

The Bible version selected for this study was the NASB. The subpoints have been staggered in order to help you keep your place when you look away. Space has been included for you to add your personal notes.

In addition to the questions included, you may present any statement or point into a question format if you are trying to get the group of students to better engage with the topic.

I cannot stress the importance of learning and using critical thinking when going through a study like this. You must learn to compare all things to what Scripture says, including the comments made by myself on various expositions. A secondary intention of this study is to help you learn how to critically think. Keep this in mind as questions are presented. Some of the questions have basic answers and some have no answers at all. This is intentional to help you learn to think critically.

I hope that this study is beneficial in helping you to grow in your understanding of Scripture and the character of God, as well as aiding you to teach others the richness of God's holy Word. The Gospel is the most important thing for us to understand. We need to hear it daily because our nature wants to turn us inwardly. We need to learn to articulate it well. I pray this study will help deepen your understanding of what Jesus has done to set us free and his completed work on our behalf at Calvary.

USING THIS GUIDE FOR SMALL GROUPS OR SUNDAY SCHOOL

Read ahead. If you read the material ahead of time you will be able to transition from point to point smoother. As you read and study feel free to add notes between the lines or in the margins. The way this study is designed is meant to trigger you to expound on the point being made.

Be punctual. It is important to start on time because of the nature of discussion that is prompted by the questions in this guide. Time will truly get away from you.

Open in prayer. Pray that God will bless you as you teach, that his word is handled correctly, that those you are teaching will understand God in a greater way and be challenged to grow in Christ. Pray that if any are lost God will open their eyes as his word is being read and taught. Thank Jesus for his sacrifice to make us righteous before a holy God.

Stay God centered. In today's self-absorbed world it is easy to get people to insert themselves into the Scriptures and make it all about them. When conversations turn to personal matters, that is okay, sometimes people need to get something out that they are struggling with. Make sure you take the focus back to God and how that all Scripture is about him and the work he has done.

Ask questions. There are questions in this study to help guide the direction you are going or to further expound upon certain points. Feel free to turn any point into a question or add your own. If you do not know the answer to someone's question tell them that. Let them know that you will research their question and get back with them either personally or next time you meet.

I also like to ask questions to see if anyone else has anything beneficial to say about a particular point.

Don't get in a hurry. The church growth movement has done much damage to the way we handle classes. Secular research has been done that indicates that people can only handle six to eight-week studies. This may be true for those who do not have the indwelling Holy Spirit who aids us in walking in the Fruit of the Spirit. I can assure you that the slower you move the deeper and richer both you and your class's understanding and amazement of God will become. Don't get caught up thinking you have to finish in six to eight weeks. You will be robbing both yourself and your class. It is good to plan what you think you can cover, but due to the nature of the questions associated with this study, be prepared to not make it as far as you would like. You can easily pick up where you left off with a quick overview. I discourage skipping over material or rushing through this study.

Give glory to God. We were created to give glory to God. Give glory to God for how he has preserved his church and developed our understanding of him over the last two thousand years. Give glory to God for helping our brothers draw a line in the sand when heresies were spreading like infectious disease. His goodness, kindness, and mercy point to his worth not to ours. That he loves us is a profound mystery. That he loves us is clearly seen but not clearly understood. We may not understand why he has ordained all things, but we must understand that all things will ultimately give glory to him.

Pray again. If you have time and a smaller group go around the room and have everyone pray. If this isn't possible, ask your class if there is anything specific that you can pray about.

USING THIS FOR PERSONAL STUDY

Suggestions for using this study guide for personal growth and understanding.

This applies to people in a classroom setting going through this study as well.

Pray. You should always pray before you begin studying God's Word. We are studying the way God's Word has been handled over the last two thousand years of church history. Ask him to help open your eyes and understand what you are reading.

Glorify God. Not only in this book, but any theological book you read, always be asking the question . . . how does this help me understand God in a greater way? You will be exposed to many ideas of who God is. This knowledge should lead you to a greater understanding of the true nature of God and how holy and mighty he truly is.

Share what you learn. The Gnostics gloried in having a secret knowledge. Other religions take joy in withholding information in order to esteem themselves higher than others. Christians, on the other hand, want to share every detail of what we learn. We desperately want others to come to faith in the maker and ruler of all things. We also want those who are in Christ to grow deeper and deeper in their love and understanding. A Christian's goal isn't to withhold any information, but to grow those around us to be a better Christian than we are.

Pray again. Pray that what you have learned will be lived out in day to day life. That this isn't just knowledge but life. Pray that God will give you a hunger for his word and a desire to tell everyone you know about the God you serve and what he has done.

Michael Huskey

Introduction

WHY SHOULD YOU STUDY CHURCH HISTORY?

1. God has continued to work sovereignly since the canon was closed with the last word of the book of Revelation.
    i. Church history helps us better understand the nature of God.
    ii. God was actively bringing the dead to eternal life, actively convicting the believer of their sins, and actively drawing the saint to himself. It is good to learn from what has been recorded.
2. Polemics/discernment
    - What are Polemics? Being inwardly focused on the church in a critical manner. Think of it as apologetics, which outwardly focuses on defending what we believe, turned inwardly. Polemics is a sheepdog guarding the sheep from wolves.
    - Are there any new heresies today?
        - The majority of the epistles are written to battle heresy by bringing clarity to the gospel. We are clearly instructed to be discerning and test all things according to the Scriptures. You cannot test all things if you have no knowledge of what Scripture teaches. Our Christian forefathers have already fought against every conceivable heresy. It is important to understand the battles they fought so you too can be equipped to understand when God's word is being twisted, or you have been taught

something wrong. The same heresies we will study continue to show up again and again.

Malachi 3:18 *So you will again distinguish between the righteous and the wicked, between one who serves God and one who does not serve Him.*

   i. Church history teaches us how to distinguish between truth and error.

3. Jesus said he would build his church in **Matthew 16:18**. To see Jesus's prophecy unfold to his glory over the last two thousand years despite Satan attempting to stomp it out.

   i. This isn't just the history of some ancient and foreign people; this is the history of the bride of Christ . . . our brothers and our sisters.

   ii. You are part of church history if you are in Christ.

4. The truth has been preserved and passed down through history.

   i. When you are exegeting Scripture and come to an understanding of what you are studying, it is best to look at what others have taught throughout all of church history in order to be sure you are correct. Don't only look at modern commentaries or a study Bible, look at how the church fathers understood the passage, how the reformers understood the passage, how the Puritans understood the passage, etc. If your understanding is different from the collective historical view, who is in error?

   There are secondary issues such as baptism and eschatology that are much more difficult because the historical church has been divided over these for a long time.

- What is exegesis (exegeting Scripture)? Drawing the true meaning out of the verse using proper context. This is the opposite of eisegesis.

- What is eisegesis? Reading your own ideas or what you have been taught into the text.

"When we study church history, we not only confirm the fact that what we believe today is what the apostolic church believed, but we also see how the truth was preserved throughout history." Nathan Busenitz

2 Timothy 2:2 *The things which you have heard from me in the presence of many witnesses, entrust these to faithful men who will be able to teach others also*

5. Church history gives us motivation to persevere. Learning what our brothers and sisters in Christ suffered will make many of our complaints seem petty.
    i. We will learn of the sacrifices made in both major and what we would consider minor doctrinal matters. (Those who were martyred would probably disagree that anything is minor.)
    ii. We can be motivated by seeing the faithfulness of these saints such as Polycarp and others.
6. We will see an eagerness for Jesus to return, the same eagerness that we should have today.
    - Do you have an eagerness to see Jesus return? Everyone should be ready for it no matter what time period you live in.
        i. It is by design and purpose that Jesus's second coming is always lurking in immanency.
7. We can learn from others' failures.
    i. Small compromises by men who should have known better have opened up a can of worms that has led to entire false religions.
8. Ignorance is not bliss.
    i. Even though we live in the most advanced society, our ignorance of church history itself is historical.
    ii. Better understanding of church history gives us better understanding of theology which gives us our true and living God and not a false god that we have created in our own minds.
    iii. Church leaders must be able to defend and protect the church from false teachers.

What is theology?

Theology is the study of the nature of God.

- Why is studying theology important?

1. Because we love God
    i. If you love someone you want to learn everything there is to know about that person.
2. To better understand God's attributes
    i. The attributes of God are truly amazing. In better understanding God's attributes, you will better understand yourself and the relationship that you have with him.
    ii. This will bring you to an overwhelming sense of the vastness of God. The more you understand God's attributes, the larger your view of God becomes and the smaller your view becomes of man. This is truly humbling.
3. To better understand God's nature
    i. Understanding the nature of the Trinity and the nature of Christ can be a lifetime undertaking and can never be fully comprehended. However, it is vital to at least have an elementary understanding of in order to avoid the many heretical teachings floating around concerning the nature of God. The greater your understanding of God's nature, the greater your understanding and appreciation of the gospel will become.
4. To learn to be pleasing to God
    i. If we truly love God, we want to be pleasing to him. You cannot be pleasing to him unless you know who he is. The study of theology helps us understand all of the things mentioned above in order for our love of him to grow and to help us better understand how to be pleasing to him.

Introduction

"Every time we mention God we become theologians, and the only question is whether we are going to be good ones or bad ones." J.I. Packer[1]

There are three distinct ways that theology has been framed: Biblical Theology, Historical Theology, and Systematic Theology. Each of these methods of study are important and should closely be examined by all Christians.

Note: When the church fathers used the word "catholic" it means the whole church, not Roman Catholic as is known today. We are all catholic who are in the body of Christ . . . not Roman Catholic!!!

It is a misconception that church history is equal to the Bible. The Bible alone is our authority. Sola Scriptura.

---

1. Packer. *Knowing God*

NOTES

The Apostolic Church
First Century

- This will be a quick recap of the way the New Testament Church began and how it spread.
    i. We will be establishing a timeline to help us understand the situation and world view that the church fathers were in as soon as the last apostle died.
    ii. For this recap we will be in the book of Acts.
    iii. Once we complete the foundation of the New Testament Church as laid down in Scripture, we will spend the remainder of this study focusing on the church and development of doctrine and theology of the church after the last word of Scripture was penned.
    iv. Open your Bible to the book of Acts.
    - When did the New Testament Church start?

- In Acts chapter 2 the church begins just ten days after the ascension of Jesus. It is in the year **30 AD** and is on the day of Pentecost. Read **verses 1–13.**
    i. The book of Acts is the start of the New Testament church, which is something new and requires authentication. Just as Jesus's ministry was authorized by many supernatural signs and wonders, so was the beginning of the church.

- The Apostles receive the indwelling Holy Spirit in chapter 2.

- Post-Pentecost preaching, persecution, and revival are found in chapters 2 and 3.
- Deacons are chosen in chapter 6 in order that the apostles may (Verse 4) *"devote ourselves to prayer and to the ministry of the word."*
- Stephen preaches and is martyred in chapter 7.
    i. This is significant because it is the start of the persecution that causes the church to flee Jerusalem and spread out across the nation.
    - How does the start of persecution in Jerusalem show the sovereignty of God found in the Great Commission? (Matthew 28:19)
        - Jesus commands that the gospel be taken to all of the world.
        - It is very likely that Jesus allowed persecution to force the disciples out of Jerusalem in order to fulfill the Great Commission.
    i. In Acts 8:4 the gospel was taken to Samaria.
    ii. In Acts 8:26 the gospel was taken to Ethiopia.
    iii. In Acts 11:19–20 the gospel was taken to the Jews and Gentiles in Asia Minor.
- We find the conversion of Saul in Chapter 9 around the year **AD 34**.
- In Acts 9:23: *"When many days had elapsed"* refers to three or four years according to Galatians 1:15–19. Luke (the author of Acts) picks up in Acts 9:23–25 where Paul is forced to flee Damascus.

Read Acts 9:23–31

- Chapter 10 is where the first gentile convert was made which is a major turning point. This occurred after **AD 37**.
- The gentile Pentecost happened in chapter 10:44–46. In chapter 11 Peter goes back to Jerusalem and reports to the Jewish leaders that a gentile had been converted and they *"took issue with him."*
    i. Many gentiles were saved. (probably in the early AD forties) Read Acts 11:10–21.

The Apostolic Church

- a. These were saved by the gospel spread by Jewish Christians who fled the persecution led by Saul.
  - ii. There were probably people in the church at Antioch who fled Jerusalem because of Saul's persecution who would now be pastored by him.

- In Acts 11:22-30 Saul ministers with Barnabas for a year around **AD 45**, before going to support the church in Jerusalem due to the coming famine around **AD 46**.
  - i. Historical and archeological facts indicate that the famine was in the mid AD forties.

- Paul's missionary journeys begin in chapter 13.
  - How many missionary journeys did Paul have? Four

- They traveled first to Cyprus where Saul begins using his Greek name Paul.
  - i. They are joined by John Mark who wrote the book of Mark.
  - ii. The persecution proved too much for Mark and he returned home, which damaged the relationship between himself and Paul. They later restored that relationship and Mark became useful to Paul again.

- Acts 13:38-39 lays the foundation of the gospel which should be carried through church history. However, it gets distorted as we shall see.

- Acts 15 deals with whether or not a gentile convert should keep the Law. This is a major point and further clarifies the foundation of the gospel that our doctrine and theology must be built upon.
  - Is salvation by faith alone or is it faith plus works?
    - i. This is still a dividing line today.
  - What stands out in verses 9 and 11? *"By faith, through grace"*
    - i. Paul gives more details concerning this council in Galatians 2.

    ii. The book of Galatians is a response to the Judaizers adding Law to the gospel (faith + works = redemption). It was probably written on Paul's first missionary journey.

- Paul's second missionary journey is found in Acts 15 and was between **AD 50–52**.
    i. The canonical books that were written: 1 and 2 Thessalonians
        - What does the word canonical or canon refer to and what does it mean?
            - The authoritative sixty-six books of the Bible. It is the Greek word for measuring stick.

- Paul's third missionary journey is found in Acts 18. It was somewhere between **AD 53–56**.
    i. The canonical books that were written: 1 and 2 Corinthians and Romans

- Paul was arrested in Jerusalem in **AD 56–58**. (Acts 20:22–23 and Acts chapters 21–22)

- In Acts 28 Paul traveled to Rome and was arrested and placed under house arrest for two years. (verse 30) This occurred in **AD 59**.
    i. The canonical books that were written: Ephesians, Colossians, Philemon, and Philippians

- Paul's fourth missionary journey is in **AD 62–66** and is found in 1 Timothy 1:3 and 2 Timothy 4:13–20. (It is also referenced in Clement of Rome's writings.)

- Paul is arrested in Rome again in **AD 66–67**. This time he is placed in the dungeon because Christians had become an enemy of the state after Nero's fire in AD 64.

Note: Nero constructed a palace in the part of the city that burned which caused people to think that he started the fire, though this is unlikely because he was reportedly in Antium at the time. Nero blamed Christians for the fire to get the public to turn against them in order to get the heat off himself. Some of the most cruel torture was dealt out at this time to Christians, including being wrapped in animal skin and either torn by wild dogs or soaked in oil then hung on a post and set on fire . . . reportedly to light the garden of Nero. (Source: Tacitus, a non-Christian historian who lived during this time)

    i. The canonical books that were written: 1 and 2 Timothy and Titus

- In **AD 68** Peter goes to Rome and is arrested. Both he and his wife are executed by being crucified upside down.

    i. Paul is also beheaded around this time under Nero.

- The book of Hebrews is written in **AD 68-69.**
- The fall of Jerusalem occurred in **AD 70** when Titus invaded with over twenty thousand Roman soldiers.
- The only New Testament books written after **AD 70** are by the Apostle John. He wrote the books of John, 1, 2, and 3 John, and Revelation.

    i. Revelation is written near the end of a second wave of Christian persecution under the rule of Domitian who ruled from AD **81-96.**

- John continues to pastor and disciple churches in Asia Minor for close to thirty years after the death of Peter and Paul. Some of the churches he was involved in are the seven mentioned in the book of Revelation.

    i. This is significant because many of the second wave church leaders, known as the church fathers, were discipled by John.

NOTES

The Disciples of the Apostles
First Century

- All of the apostles are gone. We are now introduced to the next generation of church leaders known as the Apostolic Fathers.
  - Can you name any of the Apostolic Fathers?

    Clement of Rome

    Ignatius of Antioch (discipled by Peter and John)

    Barnabas of Alexandria (not the Barnabas of the Bible)

    Papias of Hierapolis

    Polycarp of Smyrna (discipled by John)

    The authors of the Didache, The Shepherd of Hermas, and The Letter to Diognetus.

- These men are known as pastors, elders, and bishops.

Note: Don't think of bishops during this time period as the ones of the Roman Catholic Church today.

  i. Each of these men were personally discipled by an Apostle.

CLEMENT OF ROME (NOT TO BE CONFUSED WITH CLEMENT OF ALEXANDRIA)

- Clement of Rome was discipled by the Apostle Paul.
- He was the fourth pastor of the church in Rome from AD 90–100.

    i. The first was Peter, the second Linus and the third was Anacletus.

- He is mentioned in **Philippians 4:3** *Indeed, true companion, I ask you also to help these women who have shared my struggle in the cause of the gospel, together with Clement also and the rest of my fellow workers, whose names are in the book of life.*

- He wrote one letter that has survived. **Clement's 1st epistle to the Corinthians** is concerning division in the church.

    i. He has been falsely attributed to other letters.

- Significant theology found in his letter:

    i. The proof of our justification which we will look at first.

    ii. The nature of justification which we will look at second.

The Proof of our Justification

- The proof of our justification is found in how a person lives and not just in what a person says.

    i. A mere profession is meaningless if it is not backed up by the fruit of a righteous life.

    ii. Today this is referred to as Lordship Salvation.

        a. Lordship Salvation is a term that came along after the idea of the carnal Christian. It was introduced in the late 1800s.

- We will read an excerpt from Clement's writings. Though the big picture here is the proof of our justification, look for other biblical doctrines.

"Every kind of honor and happiness was bestowed upon you, and then was fulfilled that which is written, *'My beloved did eat and drink, and was enlarged and became fat, and kicked.'* Hence flowed emulation and envy, strife and sedition, persecution and disorder, war and captivity. So, the worthless rose up against the honored, those of no reputation

The Disciples of the Apostles

against such as were renowned, the foolish against the wise, the young against those advanced in years."

- What is the antecedent or cause of the discontentment that Clement is referring to in this section that we just read?
    i. It seems like the Corinthian church had everything that the world had to offer to make them happy, but the world only made them "*fat*"; because true happiness is not found in the world.
    ii. All that the world had to offer only drove them deeper into their depravity. This caused them to rise up against people who should be honored.

"For this reason righteousness and peace are now far departed from you, inasmuch as **everyone abandons the fear of God, and is become blind in His faith, neither walks in the ordinances of His appointment, nor acts a part becoming a Christian, but walks after his own wicked lusts, resuming the practice of an unrighteous and ungodly envy, by which death itself entered into the world**. These things, beloved, we write unto you, not merely to admonish you of your duty, but also to remind ourselves. For we are struggling on the same arena, and the same conflict is assigned to both of us."

- According to Clement, what brings us righteousness and peace? The fear of God
- What is the result of not fearing God in this section?

"Wherefore let us give up vain and fruitless cares, and approach to the glorious and venerable rule of our holy calling. Let us attend to what is good, pleasing, and acceptable in the sight of Him who formed us. Let us look steadfastly to the blood of Christ, and see how precious that blood is to God, which, having been shed for our salvation, has set the grace of repentance before the whole world. Let us turn to every age that has passed, and learn that, from generation to generation, the Lord has granted a place of repentance to all such as would be converted unto Him. "The ministers of the grace of God have, by the Holy Spirit, spoken of repentance; and the Lord of all things has himself declared with an oath regarding it, "As I live, saith the Lord, I desire not the death of the sinner, but rather his repentance; " adding, moreover, this gracious declaration Repent O house of

Israel, of your iniquity. Say to the children of My people, though your sins reach from earth to heaven, and though they be redder than scarlet, and blacker than sackcloth, yet if ye turn to Me with your whole heart, and say, Father! I will listen to you, as to a holy people." And in another place He speaks thus: "Wash you, and become clean; put away the wickedness of your souls from before mine eyes; cease from your evil ways, and learn to do well; seek out judgment, deliver the oppressed, judge the fatherless, and see that justice is done to the widow; and come, and let us reason together. He declares, though your sins be like crimson, I will make them white as snow; though they be like scarlet, I will whiten them like wool."

- What are some of the things that Clement is dealing with in this section?
    - The vanity of worldly pursuits.
    - The work of Christ and the value of what he has done.
    - The major theme is repentance.

"And if ye be willing and obey Me, ye shall eat the good of the land; but if ye refuse, and will not hearken unto Me, the sword shall devour you, for the mouth of the Lord hath spoken these things." Desiring, therefore, that all His beloved should be partakers of repentance, He has, by His almighty will, established [these declarations]." Take heed, beloved, lest His many kindnesses lead to the condemnation of us all. [For thus it must be] unless we walk worthy of Him, and with one mind do those things which are good and well-pleasing in His sight. For [the Scripture] saith in a certain place, "The Spirit of the Lord is a candle searching the secret parts of the belly." Let us reflect how near He is, and that none of the thoughts or reasonings in which we engage are hid from Him."

- What is the main idea of the above passage from Clement?
    - A believer walks worthy or bears fruit. Self-examination is something all believers should use to be sure they are in the faith.
- What else do we find in this section?
    - To not take advantage of God's grace.

The Nature of Justification.

- The basis for our justification is found solely in God's grace through faith in Christ.

"And we, too, being called by His will in Christ Jesus, are not justified by ourselves, nor by our own wisdom, or understanding, or godliness, or works which we have wrought in holiness of heart; but by that faith through which, from the beginning, Almighty God has justified all men; to whom be glory for ever and ever. Amen." Clement of Rome

- Clement distinguishes between the <u>root</u> of justification and the <u>fruit</u> of justification.
    - In the Bible, is Paul preaching a different gospel than James?
        - No, Paul focuses on the root of justification and James on the fruit of justification, but they are preaching the same gospel.

"Why was our father Abraham blessed? Was it not because he wrought righteousness and truth through faith?"[1] Clement of Rome

- This fundamental understanding of justification was lost somewhere in church history. Getting back to this understanding (biblical truth) is what the Reformation was about.

Martin Luther "When we have thus taught faith in Christ, then do we teach also good works? Because thou hast laid hold upon Christ by faith, through whom thou art made righteous, being now to work well. Love God and thy neighbor, call upon God, give thanks unto him, praise him, confess him. Do good to thy neighbor and serve him: fulfill thine office. These are good works indeed, which flow out of this faith."[2]

John Calvin "We dream not of a faith which is devoid of good works . . . Would ye then obtain justification in Christ? You must previously possess Christ. But you cannot possess him without being made a partaker of his sanctification: for Christ cannot be divided."

---

1. Clement. *The Epistles of Clement*
2. Luther. *Commentary on Galatians*. P. 85

"We deny that good works have any share in justification, but we claim full authority for them in the lives of the righteous . . . It is obvious that gratuitous (grace-wrought) righteousness is necessarily connected with regeneration."[3]

John MacArthur "The genuineness of a profession of Jesus Christ as Savior and Lord is evidenced more by what a person does than by what he claims . . . It cannot be stressed too often that no one can be saved by works (Eph 2:8–9). But neither can it be stressed too often that, as James declares in the present passage, "faith, if it has no works, is dead, being by itself" (James 2:17). Genuine, transforming faith not only should, but will, produce genuine works, notably repentance and obedient submission to Christ's lordship."[4]

- Because of the impact of Clement's ministry, Emperor Trajan had him tied to an iron anchor and thrown overboard at sea.

POLYCARP OF SMYRNA (AD 69–155)

- Polycarp was discipled by the Apostle John.
- He was the teacher of Irenaeus who we will study later.
- He wrote one letter that has survived: *Letter to the Philippians*
- Polycarp was the pastor at Smyrna which is one of the seven churches addressed in the Book of Revelation.

"The Martyrdom of Polycarp" is the recorded details of what is considered to be one of the earliest genuine accounts of Christian martyrdom outside of Scripture. There seems to be some legend and folklore that has been added but the overall picture is believed to be accurate. Polycarp had become a wanted man for preaching the gospel.

> "But the most admirable Polycarp, when he first heard [that he was sought for], was in no measure disturbed, but resolved to stay in the city. However, in deference to the wish of many, he was persuaded to leave it. He departed, therefore, to a country house not far distant from the city. There he stayed with a few

---

3. Calvin. *Institutes*. P. 386
4. McArthur. *N.T. Commentary: James*. P. 122

[friends], engaged in nothing else night and day than praying for all men, and for the Churches throughout the world, according to his usual custom. And while he was praying, a vision presented itself to him three days before he was taken; and, behold, the pillow under his head seemed to him on fire. Upon this, turning to those that were with him, he said to them prophetically, I must be burnt alive. And when those who sought for him were at hand, he departed to another dwelling, whither his pursuers immediately came after him. And when they found him not, they seized upon two youths [that were there], one of whom, being subjected to torture, confessed. It was thus impossible that he should stay hidden, since those that betrayed him were of his own household. The Irenarch then (whose office is the same as that of the Cleronomus), by name Herod, hastened to bring him into the stadium. [This all happened] that he might fulfil his special lot, being made a partaker of Christ, and that they who betrayed him might undergo the punishment of Judas himself. His pursuers then, along with horsemen, and taking the youth with them, went forth at suppertime on the day of the preparation with their usual weapons, as if going out against a robber. And having come about evening [to the place where he was], they found him lying down in the upper room of a certain little house, from which he might have escaped into another place; but he refused, saying, The will of God be done. So when he heard that they had come, he went down and spoke with them. And as those that were present marveled at his age and constancy, some of them said. Was so much effort made to capture such a venerable man? Immediately then, in that very hour, he ordered that something to eat and drink should be set before them, as much indeed as they cared for, while he besought them to allow him an hour to pray without disturbance. And on their giving him leave, he stood and prayed, being full of the grace of God, so that he could not cease for two full hours, to the astonishment of those who heard him, insomuch that many began to repent that they had come forth against so godly and venerable an old man. Now, as soon as he had ceased praying, having made mention of all that had at any time come in contact with him, both small and great, illustrious and obscure, as well as the whole Catholic Church throughout the world, the time of his departure having arrived, they set him upon an ass, and conducted him into the city, the day being that of the great Sabbath. And the Irenarch Herod, accompanied by his father Nicetes (both riding in a chariot), met him, and taking him up into the chariot, they seated themselves beside him, and

endeavored to persuade him, saying, What harm is there in saying, Lord Cæsar, and in sacrificing, with the other ceremonies observed on such occasions, and so make sure of safety? But he at first gave them no answer; and when they continued to urge him, he said, I shall not do as you advise me. So they, having no hope of persuading him, began to speak bitter words unto him, and cast him with violence out of the chariot, insomuch that, in getting down from the carriage, he dislocated his leg [by the fall]. But without being disturbed, and as if suffering nothing, he went eagerly forward with all haste, and was conducted to the stadium, where the tumult was so great, that there was no possibility of being heard. Now, as Polycarp was entering into the stadium, there came to him a voice from heaven, saying, Be strong, and show yourself a man, O Polycarp! No one saw who it was that spoke to him; but those of our brethren who were present heard the voice. And as he was brought forward, the tumult became great when they heard that Polycarp was taken. And when he came near, the proconsul asked him whether he was Polycarp. On his confessing that he was, [the proconsul] sought to persuade him to deny [Christ], saying, Have respect to your old age, and other similar things, according to their custom, [such as], Swear by the fortune of Caesar; repent, and say, Away with the Atheists. But Polycarp, gazing with a stern countenance on all the multitude of the wicked heathen then in the stadium, and waving his hand towards them, while with groans he looked up to heaven, said, Away with the Atheists. Then, the proconsul urging him, and saying, Swear, and I will set you at liberty, reproach Christ; Polycarp declared, Eighty and six years have I served Him, and He never did me any injury: how then can I blaspheme my King and my Savior? And when the proconsul yet again pressed him, and said, Swear by the fortune of Caesar, he answered, *Since you are vainly urgent that, as you say, I should swear by the fortune of Caesar, and pretend not to know who and what I am, hear me declare with boldness, I am a Christian. And if you wish to learn what the doctrines of Christianity are, appoint me a day, and you shall hear them.*

The proconsul replied, Persuade the people. But Polycarp said, *To you I have thought it right to offer an account [of my faith]; for we are taught to give all due honour (which entails no injury upon ourselves) to the powers and authorities which are ordained of God. But as for these, I do not deem them worthy of receiving any account from me.* The proconsul then said to him, I have wild beasts at hand; to these will I cast you, unless you repent.

But he answered, Call them then, for we are not accustomed to repent of what is good in order to adopt that which is <u>evil</u>; and it is well for me to be changed from what is evil to what is righteous.

But again the proconsul said to him, I will cause you to be consumed by fire, seeing you despise the wild beasts, if you will not repent.

But Polycarp said, You threaten me with fire which burns for an hour, and after a little is extinguished, but are ignorant of the fire of the coming judgment and of eternal punishment, reserved for the ungodly. But why do you tarry? Bring forth what you will. While he spoke these and many other like things, he was filled with confidence and <u>joy</u>, and his countenance was full of grace, so that not merely did it not fall as if troubled by the things said to him, but, on the contrary, the proconsul was astonished, and sent his herald to proclaim in the midst of the stadium thrice, Polycarp has confessed that he is a Christian. This proclamation having been made by the herald, the whole multitude both of the heathen and Jews, who dwelt at Smyrna, cried out with uncontrollable fury, and in a loud voice, This is the teacher of Asia, the father of the Christians, and the overthrower of our gods, he who has been teaching many not to sacrifice, or to worship the gods. Speaking thus, they cried out, and besought Philip the Asiarch to let loose a lion upon Polycarp. But Philip answered that it was not lawful for him to do so, seeing the shows of wild beasts were already finished. Then it seemed good to them to cry out with one consent, that Polycarp should be burnt alive. For thus it behooved the vision which was revealed to him in regard to his pillow to be fulfilled, when, seeing it on fire as he was praying, he turned about and said prophetically to the faithful that were with him, I must be burnt alive. This, then, was carried into effect with greater speed than it was spoken, the multitudes immediately gathering together wood and fagots out of the shops and baths; the Jews especially, according to custom, eagerly assisting them in it. And when the funeral pile was ready, Polycarp, laying aside all his garments, and loosing his girdle, sought also to take off his sandals—a thing he was not accustomed to do, inasmuch as every one of the faithful was always eager who should first touch his skin. For, on account of his good behavior he was, even before his martyrdom, adorned with every kind of good. Immediately then they surrounded him with those substances which had been prepared for the funeral pile. But when they were about also to fix him with nails, he said, Leave me as I am; for He that gives me strength to endure the fire, will also enable me, without your securing me by nails, to remain without moving in the pile. They did not nail him then, but simply bound him. And he, placing his hands behind him, and being bound like a distinguished ram [taken] out of a great flock for sacrifice, and prepared to be an acceptable burnt-offering unto God, looked up to heaven, and said,

"O Lord God Almighty, the Father of your beloved and blessed Son Jesus Christ, by whom we have received the knowledge of You, the God of angels and powers, and of every creature, and of the whole race of the righteous who live before you, I give You thanks that You have counted me, worthy of this day and this hour, that I should have a part in the number of Your martyrs, in the cup of your Christ, to the resurrection of eternal life, both of soul and body, through the incorruption [imparted] by the Holy Ghost. Among whom may I be accepted this day before You as a fat and acceptable sacrifice, according as You, the ever-truthful God, have foreordained, have revealed beforehand to me, and now have fulfilled. Wherefore also I praise You for all things, I bless You, I glorify You, along with the everlasting and heavenly Jesus Christ, Your beloved Son, with whom, to You, and the Holy Ghost, be glory both now and to all coming ages. Amen." *Ante-Nicene Fathers, Vol. 1* P. 40–41[5]

- Notice the clear reference to the Trinity in his prayer.

    i. This will become important as we get into the Arian heresy.

- The last paragraph of *The Martyrdom of Polycarp* also holds key theological distinctions:

"For, having through patience overcome the unjust governor, and thus acquired the crown of immortality, he now, with the apostles and all the righteous (in heaven), rejoicingly glorifies God, even the Father, and blesses our Lord Jesus Christ, the Savior of our souls . . ."

    i. There is no mention of "soul sleep" or "purgatory."
    ii. Notice he isn't considered an apostle but joining the apostles.

---

5. Polycarp. *The Apostolic Fathers Vol. 1: Epistle Concerning the Martyrdom of.* P. 39–42

- What did Polycarp believe? The below quotes are from *Letter to the Phillipians*:

Chapter 1 "and because the strong root of your faith, spoken of in days long gone by, endures even until now, and brings forth fruit to our Lord Jesus Christ, **who for our sins suffered even unto death**, [but] whom **God raised from the dead, having loosed the bands of the grave.** In whom, though now you see Him not, you believe, and **believing, rejoice with joy unspeakable and full of glory**; into which joy many desire to enter, knowing that **by grace you are saved, not of works.**"

Chapter 2 "He comes as **the Judge** of the living and the dead. His blood will God require of those who do not believe in Him. But He who raised Him up from the dead will raise up us also"

Chapter 4 "But the love of money is the root of all evils. Knowing, therefore, that as **we brought nothing into the world, so we can carry nothing out,** let us arm ourselves with the armor of righteousness, and let us teach, first of all, ourselves to walk in the commandments of the "Lord. Next, [teach] your wives [to walk] in the faith given to them, and in love and purity tenderly loving their own husbands in all truth, and loving all [others] equally in all chastity; and to **train up their children in the knowledge and fear of God.**"[6]

- What are some of the doctrinal points Polycarp made in these excerpts?

IGNATIUS OF ANTIOCH (AD 35-?)

- Ignatius was discipled by two apostles, Peter and John.
- He was the pastor of the church in Syrian Antioch.
- He wrote seven letters that have survived.
- He was killed as a martyr in Rome between AD 98–117.
- Ignatius coined the term "bishop" which was a response to quarreling church leaders. Ignatius wanted one person as the leader among equals to resolve issues that arose. His intention was to unify.

6. Polycarp. *The Apostolic Fathers Vol. 1: The Epistle of Polycarp.* P. 33–66

          i. Over time this role was problematically elevated higher and higher to the point of having bishops over entire countries who claim to be the spokesperson of Christ himself.

- He taught the biblical concept that the Sabbath had been replaced by the Lord's day.

    - How do we know that we should worship on Sunday (the Lord's day) rather than Saturday (the Sabbath)?

        ◆ First, the Law was entirely fulfilled by Jesus. Gathering on Sunday shows that Jesus fulfilled the Law of Moses at the cross. (**Matthew 5:17**)

        ◆ Second, the apostles worshiped on Sunday. (**Acts 20:7**)

        ◆ Third, and most importantly, it was the day Jesus was resurrected!
        (See quote from Justin Martyr on page 24)

Letter to the Magnesians 9. "Consequently, if the people who were given to obsolete practices faced the hope of a new life, and if these no longer observe the Sabbath, but regulate their calendar by the Lord's Day, the day, too, on which our Life rose by His power and through the medium of His death—though some deny this; and if to this mystery we owe our faith and because of it submit to sufferings to prove ourselves disciples of *Jesus Christ, our only Teacher*: how, then, can we possibly live apart from Him of whom, *by the working of the Spirit, even the Prophets were disciples and to whom they looked forward as their Teacher*? And so *He, for whom they rightly waited, came and raised them from the dead*.

10. Let us not, then, be insensible to His loving kindness. Certainly, *if He were to imitate our way of acting, we should be done for instantly. We must, therefore, prove ourselves His disciples and learn to live like Christians*. Assuredly whoever is called by a name other than this, is not of God. Hence, put away the deteriorated leaven, a leaven stale and sour, and turn to the new leaven, that is, Jesus Christ. *Be salted in Him to keep any among you from being spoiled, for by your odor you will be tested*. It is absurd to have Jesus Christ on the lips, and at the same time live like a Jew. No; Christianity did not believe in Judaism, but Judaism believed in Christianity, and in its bosom was assembled everyone professing faith in God.

11. As one who is not your superior, I merely wish to warn you betimes *not to yield to the bait of false doctrine*, but to believe most steadfastly in the birth, the Passion, and the Resurrection, which took place during the procuratorship of Pontius Pilate.

12. May you be my joy in all respects, if indeed I deserve it! For, though I am in chains, compared with one of you who are free, *I am nothing*. I know that you are not conceited, for you have Jesus Christ in you.

13. *Be zealous, therefore, to stand squarely on the decrees of the Lord and the Apostles*, that in all things whatsoever *you may prosper, in body and in soul, in faith and in love, in the Son and the Father and the Spirit, in the beginning and the end*, together with your most reverend bishop and with your presbytery—that fittingly woven spiritual crown!—and with your deacons, men of God. Submit to the bishop and to each other›s rights, just as did Jesus Christ in the flesh to the Father, and as the Apostles did to Christ and the Father and the Spirit, *so that there may be oneness both of flesh and of spirit*.

14. Knowing that you are steeped in God, I am exhorting you but briefly. Remember me in your prayers that I may happily make my way to God. Remember, too, the Church in Syria, of which I am an unworthy member. Yes, I do stand in need of your God-inspired prayer and your love. Thus the Church in Syria will be privileged through your Church to be quickened with refreshing dew.

15. The Ephesians at Smyrna—the place from which I am writing to you—send their greetings. Like yourselves, *they have come here for the glory of God*. They have revived my spirits in every way, as does Polycarp, the bishop of Smyrna. The rest of the Churches, too, beg to be remembered in honor of Jesus Christ. Farewell—you who, being of one mind with God, possess an unflinching spirit—which is to be like Jesus Christ."[7]
Ignatius of Antioch

- Discuss the emphasized portions of the above letter from Ignatius and how this can help us with our walk with God?

---

7. Ignatius. Ancient Christian Writers: To the Magnesians. P. 72–74

PAPIAS OF HIERAPOLIS (AD 60–155)

- Papias was discipled by John and he was a companion of Polycarp.
- There is one known set of books written by Papias: *Interpretations of the Sayings of the Lord*. These books were lost, however.
    i. Irenaeus and Eusebius refer to this five-volume set in their writings.
- Papias is who noted that the Gospel of Mark was written under the direction or influence of Peter.

> Fragments of his writing: "And the presbyter said this. Mark having become the interpreter of Peter, wrote down accurately whatsoever he remembered. It was not, however, in exact order that he related the sayings or deeds of Christ. For he neither heard the Lord nor accompanied Him. But afterwards, as I said, he accompanied Peter, who accommodated his instructions to the necessities [of his hearers], but with no intention of giving a regular narrative of the Lord's sayings. Wherefore Mark made no mistake in thus writing some things as he remembered them. For of one thing he took especial care, not to omit anything he had heard, and not to put anything fictitious into the statements."[8]

- He was pre-millennial in his eschatology and believed in a literal millennium according to Eusebius.
    i. Eusebius writes concerning Papias: "To these belong his statement that **there will be a period of some thousand years after the resurrection of the dead**, and that the **kingdom of Christ will be set up in material form on this very earth.**"[9]

Fragment of Papias's writing: "For I did not, like the multitude, take pleasure in those who spoke much, but in those who taught the **truth**; nor in those who related strange commandments, but in those who rehearsed the commandments given by the Lord to *faith*, and proceeding from **truth** itself."[10]

---

8. *Eusebius, Ecclesiastical History* 3.39.14–17
9. *Ecclesiastical History*, 3.39.12
10. *Eusebius, Hist. Eccl. iii.* P 39

The Disciples of the Apostles

- What is our ultimate source of truth?

THE SHEPHERD OF HERMAS

- The Shepherd of Hermas is considered to be written by an apostolic father, however it is unknown which apostle, if any, truly discipled him.
- Some scholars have placed this writing in the first century, while others in the second.
- It was more than likely written by Hermas the brother of Pius. Pius was the tenth Bishop of Rome.
- It should be looked at as allegorical much like the *Pilgrim's Progress*.
    i. There are five visions, twelve mandates, and ten parables in this book.
    ii. It is unclear, yet highly improbable, that the writer claimed these as "visions." This was more than likely added at a later time when the writings were divided and put into a systematic framework with chapters and verses.

Vision 1 3:4 "Behold, the God of Hosts, Who by **His invisible and mighty power** and by **His great wisdom created the world**, and by **His glorious purpose** clothed His creation with comeliness, and **by His strong word fixed the heaven, and founded the earth upon the waters**, and **by His own wisdom and providence formed His holy Church**, which also He blessed-behold, He removeth the heavens and the mountains and the hills and the seas, and all things are made level for His elect, **that He may fulfill to them the promise which He promised with great glory and rejoicing**, if so be that they shall keep the ordinances of God, which they received, with great faith."

Vision 4 2[23]:3 She answered and said unto me, "Did nothing meet thee? "I say unto her, Lady, such a huge beast, that could have destroyed whole peoples: but, by the power of the Lord and by His great mercy, I escaped it."

2[23]:4 "***Thou didst escape it well***," saith she, "**because thou didst cast thy care upon God, and didst open thy heart to the Lord, believing that thou canst be saved by nothing else but by His great and glorious Name**. Therefore, the Lord sent His angel, which is over the beasts, whose name is Segri, and *shut his mouth that it might not hurt thee.* Thou hast **escaped a great tribulation by reason of thy faith,** and because, though thou sawest so huge a beast, thou didst not doubt in thy mind.

2[23]:5 *Go* therefore **and declare to the elect of the Lord His mighty works** and tell them that this beast is a type of the great tribulation which is to come. *If* therefore *ye prepare yourselves beforehand, and repent (and turn) unto the Lord with your whole heart, ye shall be able to escape it, if your heart be made pure and without blemish,* and *if for the remaining days of your life ye serve the Lord blamelessly. Cast your cares upon the Lord and He will set them straight.*

2[23]:6 **Trust ye in the Lord, ye men of doubtful mind, for He can do all things,** yea, He both turneth away His wrath from you, and again He sendeth forth His plagues upon you that are of doubtful mind. **Woe to them that hear these words and are disobedient; it were better for them that they had not been born."**

3[24]:1 I asked her concerning the four colors, which the beast had upon its head. Then she answered me and said, "Again thou art curious about such matters." "Yes, lady," said I, "make known unto me what these things are."

3[24]:2 "Listen," said she; "the black is this world in which ye dwell;

3[24]:3 and the fire and blood color showeth that this world must perish by blood and fire;

3[24]:4 and the golden part are ye that has escaped from this world. For as the gold is tested by the fire and is made useful, so ye also [that dwell in it] are being tested in yourselves. **Ye then that abide and pass through the fire will be purified by it.** For as the old loses its dross. so Ye also shall cast away all sorrow and tribulation, and shall be purified, and shall be useful for the building of the tower.

3[24]:5 But the white portion is the coming age, in which the elect of God shall dwell; because the elect of God shall be without spot and pure unto life eternal.

3[24]:6 Wherefore cease not thou to speak in the ears of the saints. Ye have now the symbolism also of the tribulation which is coming in power. But if ye be willing, it shall be nought. Remember ye the things that are written beforehand."

3[24]:7 With these words she departed, and I saw not in what direction she departed; for a noise was made: and I turned back in fear, thinking that the beast was coming.[11]

- Discuss the emphasized portions and how they can help us understand God in a greater way.

    - Does God still give people visions today?

THE EPISTLE OF BARNABAS

- The Epistle of Barnabas was written by an unknown author. It is considered to be written by an apostolic father, though that is hard to prove since the author is unknown.
- It was written between AD 70–132 from Alexandria, Egypt.
- It is highly allegorical.

    i. It introduces an allegorical hermeneutic which dominates Alexandria later.

        a. Using an allegorical hermeneutic, the writer begins to distance himself from Israel which can lead to replacement theology . . . even though he was a premillennialist.

- Below is a helpful excerpt from the Epistle of Barnabas:

    "But the way of the Black One is crooked and full of a curse. For it is a way of eternal death with punishment wherein are the things that destroy men's souls—idolatry, boldness, exhalation of power, hypocrisy, doubleness of heart, adultery, murder, plundering, pride, transgression, treachery, malice, stubbornness, witchcraft, magic, covetousness, absence of the fear of God; persecutors of good men, hating the truth, loving lies, not perceiving the reward of righteousness, not *cleaving to the good* nor to the righteous judgment, paying no heed to the widow and the orphan, wakeful not for the fear of God but for that which is evil; men from whom gentleness and forbearance stand aloof

---

11. Hermas. *The Shepherd of Hermas*. Translated by J. B. Lightfoot

and far off; loving vain things, pursuing a recompense, not pitying the poor man, not toiling for him that is oppressed with toil, ready to slander, not recognizing Him that made them murderers of children, corrupters of the creatures of God, turning away from him that is in want, oppressing him that is afflicted, advocates of the wealthy, unjust judges of the poor, sinful in all things. It is good therefore to learn the ordinances of the Lord, as many as have been written above, and to walk in them. For he that doeth these things [19:2—19:12] shall be glorified in the kingdom of God; whereas he that chooseth their opposites shall perish together with his works. For this cause is the resurrection, for this the recompense."[12]

- How can this excerpt help us better understand depravity?
- How can this excerpt help a believer better understand God?

THE DIDACHE (THE TEACHING OF THE TWELVE)

- The Didache was written late first to early second century.
- This was a summary of the teaching of the Twelve Apostles.
    i. Some attribute the apostles as its author, yet this has never been proven. The author is unknown.

Chapter 2 "And the second commandment of the Teaching; You shall not commit murder, you shall not commit adultery, you shall not commit pederasty [man and boy], you shall not commit fornication, you shall not steal, you shall not practice magic, you shall not practice witchcraft, **you shall not murder a child by abortion nor kill that which is begotten.**"

- What are some of the doctrines that stand out in chapter 2?

Chapter 7 "And concerning baptism, baptize this way: Having first said all these things**, baptize into the name of the Father, and of the Son, and of the Holy Spirit**, Matthew 28:19 **in living water**. But if you have not living water, baptize into other water; and if you cannot in cold, in warm. But if you have not either, pour out water thrice upon the head into the name of Father and

---

12. Unknown. *The Epistle of Barnabas*. Translated by J.B. Lightfoot

Son and Holy Spirit. But before the baptism let the baptizer fast, and the baptized, and whatever others can; but you shall order the baptized to fast one or two days before."

Chapter 16 "Watch for your life's sake. Let not your lamps be quenched, nor your loins unloosed; but be ready, for you know not the hour in which our Lord comes. Matthew 24:42 But often shall you come together, seeking the things which are befitting to your souls: for the whole time of your faith will not profit you, if you be not made perfect in the last time. For in the last days false prophets and corrupters shall be multiplied, and the sheep shall be turned into wolves, and love shall be turned into hate; Matthew 24:11–12 for when lawlessness increases, they shall hate and persecute and betray one another, Matthew 24:10 and then shall appear the world-deceiver as the Son of God, and shall do signs and wonders, and the earth shall be delivered into his hands, and he shall do iniquitous things which have never yet come to pass since the beginning. Then shall the creation of men come into the fire of trial, and many shall be made to stumble and shall perish; but they that endure in their faith shall be saved from under the curse itself. And then shall appear the signs of the truth; first, the sign of an outspreading in heaven; then the sign of the sound of the trumpet; and the third, the resurrection of the dead; yet not of all, but as it is said: The Lord shall come and all His saints with Him. Then shall the world see the Lord coming upon the clouds of heaven."[13]

- Discuss some of the doctrines that stand out in these two chapters.

---

13. Unknown. *Christian Writing Decoded: The Didache*. Wyatt North. 2012

NOTES

An Introduction to Historic Heresies

Acts 20:28 *Be on guard for yourselves and for all the flock, among which the Holy Spirit has made you overseers, to shepherd the church of God which He purchased with His own blood. I know that after my departure savage wolves will come in among you, not sparing the flock; and from among our own selves men will arise, speaking perverse things, to draw away the disciples after them.*

1 Timothy 4:1 *But the Spirit explicitly says that in later times some will fall away from the faith, paying attention to deceitful spirits and doctrines of demons, by means of the hypocrisy of liars seared in their own conscience as with a branding iron,*

2 Timothy 4:3 *For the time will come when they will not endure sound doctrine; but wanting to have their ears tickled, they will accumulate for themselves teachers in accordance to their own desires, and will turn away their ears from the truth and will turn aside to myths.*

- It is interesting that you will find these same heresies still alive in cults and false religions today.
- We should keep in mind that God uses all things for his good. In this case for biblical doctrine to be very intentionally defined as these heresies were dealt with.
- This will be a brief introduction. We will get into these deeper as this study progresses.

FIRST CENTURY HERESIES

Any view of God other than the biblical view of God is idolatry!

Judaizers

- What did the Judaizers believe?
  - They taught that in addition to having a relationship with Jesus, you must keep the Mosaic Law.
  - They attempted to force the Mosaic Law on all believers. (Examples found in: Acts and Galatians)
- What groups today are like the Judaizers? Seventh Day Adventists, Roman Catholics, etc.

This heresy was dealt with within the pages of Scripture. (Galatians; Acts 15:1–21)

Ebionism

- Ebionism means "poor."
- Most of what we know about them comes from the Church Fathers who wrote polemics against them because they were considered to be heretics.
  i. Justin Martyr wrote about them, as did Ireneaus who was the first to call them Ebionite.
  - What did Ebionism teach?
    - They were the theological descendants of the Judaizers.
    - In addition to what the Judaizers believe, the Ebionites denied the deity of Jesus, the Trinity, the virgin birth, and the death of Jesus as an atonement for original sin.
  - What is original sin?
    - The first sin ever committed by a man . . . Adam.
- They believed Jesus was adopted as the son of God when he was anointed with the Holy Spirit at his baptism, therefore he became the messianic king-priest of Israel.
  i. We will deal with "adoptionism" later in this chapter when we get to Monarchianism.

When we get to the 1900s, we will learn about the "Restorationist Movement." Many of these heresies resurface during this time through The Church of Christ, The Church of Jesus Christ of Latter-day Saints, The Jehovah's Witnesses, Pentecostal, and others who all claim that they are getting back to a primitive form of Christianity.

Docetism

- Docetism means to appear.

What is Docetism?

- They believe that Jesus did not take on a literal physical body, only the appearance of one.
  i. This idea came from the teachings of **Plato** who taught that this world is an inferior reflection of the true, pure spiritual world that stood outside of physical reality.
  ii. Docetism took Plato's teaching further by believing that matter is inferior and evil. They believe that the only thing that is good is that which is spiritual.
      a. Therefore, Jesus would be contaminated or evil if he had a physical body.

- We see in **1st John** that this teaching was already a problem. *1:1 What was from the beginning, what we have heard, what we have seen with our eyes, what we have looked at and touched with our hands, concerning the Word of Life and the life was manifested, and we have seen and testify and proclaim to you . . . 4:2 By this you know the Spirit of God: every spirit that confesses that Jesus Christ has come in the flesh is from God.*

It is interesting that the first heresies were concerning the gospel of grace vs. works and concerning the humanity of Jesus.

SECOND CENTURY HERESIES

"There is only one safeguard against error, and that is to be established in the faith; and for that, there has to be prayerful and diligent study, and a receiving with meekness the engrafted Word of God. Only then are we fortified against the attacks of those who assail us."[1] Arthur Pink

Gnosticism

- What is Gnosticism?
    - Gnosticism was born from Docetism in the second century.
    - In addition to Docetism, Gnostics teach that they have a secret knowledge of salvation and the things of God.
    - Salvation is not that you are being saved from God because of sin, but saved from this evil, physical world, not by redemption but by knowledge.
    - It is an escape from this physical world into a higher form of existence much like the New Age today or Mormonism.

Joseph Smith (founder of Mormonism) said on April 7, 1844 in what is now known as the King Follett Discourse:

> "There are but very few beings in the world who understand rightly the character of God. If men do not comprehend the character of God, they do not comprehend their own character. Within humankind there is an immortal spark of intelligence, taught the Prophet, a seed of divine intellect or light which is as immortal as and coequal with God Himself. God is not, however, to be understood as one and singular. There are a multitude of Gods emanated from the First God, existing one above the other without end. He who humankind calls God was Himself once a man; and man, by advancing in intelligence, knowledge, consciousness—may be exalted with God, become as God."

---

1. Pink. *The Attributes of God*

An Introduction to Historic Heresies

- There are a number of Gnostic-like cults still today, other than Mormonism, such as Freemasonry. Many of the ideas of a secret knowledge or a new knowledge have crept into the visible church.

    - What does Gnosticism mean? Knowledge

- Christianity is the opposite of being secretive. Our greatest desire should be to teach anyone who will listen all that we have learned about the Bible and our God.

    i. Though the Gospel is a mystery to the lost, it is no secret. It is very clearly explained within the pages of Scripture and is our ultimate source of truth. The truth is our greatest treasure and ought to be sought with every ounce of energy in our being. Likewise, we are to share that treasure with anyone who will listen.

Marcionism

- What is Marcionism?

    - It was born from Gnosticism in AD 144 by Marcion of Sinope.
    - Marcion believed that the teachings of Christ were incompatible with the God of the Old Testament.

- He held to a canon, that is now known as the Gospel of Marcion, which included ten books from Paul and the Gospel of Luke. He rejected the Hebrew Old Testament and the other books of the New Testament.
- He believed the God of the Old Testament was righteous and wrathful and the God of the New Testament was love and mercy.

    - Would you serve an unrighteous or non-wrathful God and what would the implications be if God were so?
    - What president of the United States was essentially Marcion? Thomas Jefferson

i. Thomas Jefferson was a student of the Bible, but only liked the moral teachings of Jesus. He cut out of his Bible all of the miraculous events and hard teachings of Jesus with a sharp instrument.

ii. He also cut pages out of the Bible that had to do with anything moralistic and glued them into a book that he called "*The Life and Morals of Jesus of Nazareth.*"

iii. He became very similar to Marcion because of the effect of The Enlightenment that we will study about later.

Monarchianism

- What is Monarchianism?
    - It teaches that God exists as a single ruler. This came in two forms:

1. **Modalism**
    i. Considers God to be one person who works through the different "modes" of Father, Son, and Holy Spirit.
        a. In the Old Testament God was in the mode of Father. In the New Testament God was in the mode of the Son. And in the Church age God was in the mode of the Spirit.
    ii. Modalism is still held by Oneness Pentecostals and other various groups.

2. **Adoptionism**
    i. Teaches that the Son was not co-eternal with the Father, and that Jesus Christ was essentially granted godhood (adopted) for the plans of God and for his own perfect life and works.
        a. Adoptionism is still held by Unitarianism and the Unitarian Church.

- What is Unitarianism? God is one person, as opposed to the Trinity.

Montanism

- What is Montanism?
  - Montanism was founded by Montanus. It was known at the time as "New Prophecy."
  - They believed their prophecies were a new revelation that fulfilled the teachings of the apostles.
  - Montanus traveled with two prophetesses claiming that their new prophecies were binding on the church.
  - They were very strict on their followers' morals and lifestyles. This led to legalism.

"The Montanists condemned other Christians as "unspiritual" if they would not embrace the New Prophecy, calling Catholics "prophet-killers" for their refusal to accept Montanist prophets as genuine."[2]

- Does this sound familiar? Some Charismatic churches do the same today.

- This is one of the heresies that motivated the church to put together a canon of Scripture.

THIRD CENTURY HERESIES

Manichaeism

- What is Manichaeism?
  - It was founded by Mani (216–74).
  - There is no omnipotent good power, instead there is only a dualistic struggle between good and evil.
  - In each person, the good part (the soul of light) wars against the evil part (the body of darkness). Salvation comes from identifying oneself with light (or soul).
  - He mixed three different religions together: Gnosticism, Christianity, and Zoroastrianism.

2. Needham. 2000 years of Christ's Power

- What is Zoroastrianism? Yin and Yang, good and evil... good will one day win. It dates back to BC 6.
- Mani believed that you should suffer in order to be faithful.
  - Does the Bible teach that you ***should*** suffer or that you ***will*** suffer to be faithful?
  - What is the difference?
- Manichaeism has a god that is powerless to do anything. He sets back and hopes that someone will do the right thing so that he can save them.
  - Is that the God of the Bible?
  - What is meant by God being omnipotent? God has unlimited power.

Novatianism

Note—The word heresy today means to stray from orthodox Christian essential doctrine and teach something that is anathema or damnable. However, the word heresy originally meant to teach something that divides. This is the case we find here with the Novatians.

  - What is Novatianism?
    - It was founded by Novatian. (200–258)
    - Novatian taught that Christians who had been baptized but denied the faith during persecution could not be forgiven or restored to the church.
    - Novatians believed that if someone denied Christ their lives were saved but their souls were lost.
- Christian persecution rose to becoming empire wide during Decius's reign (249–51). If you were accused of being a Christian, you had the choice to deny Christ or die in a very painful and horrendous way.

- After Decius died in battle, persecution was minimized for a short while, and at this time people who had denied Christ wanted to be reinstated into the church.
    i. This caused major division. Similar things have happened recently with the fall of the Soviet Union. This has also happened in China
  - Is someone who denies Christ in the face of death to save their own life a Christian?
  - What apostle denied Christ to avoid persecution? Peter
    i. Christian martyrdom is a reality in many parts of the world.
    ii. Christian martyrdom and persecution have never ceased.
    iii. God has always used persecution to cleanse his church of false Christians. We haven't reached that point in America today, but we are not immune to it. The church in America is full of apostasy and heresy. God will not tolerate that for long.

FOURTH CENTURY HERESIES

Apollinarianism

  - What is Apollinarianism?
    - It was taught by Apollinaris the Younger, Bishop of Laodicea.
    - It denies that Jesus had a soul. Jesus had a human body with a divine mind. It is like a hand put inside of a glove. The hand was God and the glove was Jesus's human body.
    i. Jesus is a middle ground between God and man.
  - What heresy influenced Apollinaris? Gnosticism

We will cover Apollinarianism more when we get to page 119

Donatism

- What is Donatism?
  - It is similar to Novatianism, but under the persecution of Diocletian rather than Decius.
  - They required their members to be re-baptized as Donatists.
  - They taught that the clergy must be faultless to be effective.
- Does God use flawed people, or must we reach faultlessness in order to be effective?

- This is a flawed view of sanctification.
- To reach faultlessness by our own sheer determination will result in one of two things happening:

1. Being self-righteous and prideful.
2. Crashing and burning in a sea of pity and despair because you cannot.
   - What is the correct thing to do to grow in sanctification?
     - Pray and ask God to give you his grace and then lean fully on him to accomplish this as you actively pursue holiness.
   - Should churches ask members to be re-baptized?

Arianism

- What is Arianism?
  - It was taught by Arius.
  - It attacks the deity of Christ and denies the Trinity.

- Arianism caused a major division in the church. It is one of the heresies that resulted in an ecumenical council and a creed, both of which we will study when we get to the chapter on Controversies and Councils.

An Introduction to Historic Heresies

- What religious groups are Arian today? The Jehovah's Witnesses

• We will cover Arianism more when we get to page 80.

FIFTH CENTURY HERESIES

Pelagianism

- This was taught by Pelagius.
- What is Pelagianism?
  - Pelagianism teaches that everyone has the ability to freely choose to do good all of the time, whether in Christ or not.
  - It attacks the primacy and sufficiency of God's grace in salvation.
  - It denies the Federal imputation of sin from Adam to all of mankind. Federal imputation is also called the Doctrine of Federal Headship. (**Romans 5:18**)
    i. In other words, all people are born in the same state as Adam was created, without the curse of sin.
- What religious groups are Pelagian today? Recently, Charles Finney and all of his followers after his death.

• The majority of churches are now influenced by Pelagianism or Semi Pelagianism.

• Semi-Pelagianism is another word for Arminianism which teaches that you must choose Christ rather than being chosen by Christ. It is a misunderstanding of the sovereignty of God, even though the majority of Arminians wouldn't think of it that way. They redefine the sovereignty of God to suit their preconceived notions.

  i. This is understandable because the natural man is Pelagian.

• Many Pelagians and Semi-Pelagians see a God who chooses his family as a monster, so they try to defend him by claiming that it is man's choice rather than Gods.

- i. The problem with that is that it is not found anywhere in Scripture, and the verses they try to point to are taken out of context.
    - Who gets the glory if man chooses God? Who gets the glory if God chooses man?
        - i. You would have to be smarter, wiser, or possess some inherently greater quality than your neighbor who heard the same gospel as you but didn't choose God if Pelagianism or Semi-Pelagianism were true.
            - a. That would give you a reason to boast.
    - Does God need you to defend him or justify his actions?
- We will cover this more when we get to the Nicene Fathers and the five points of Arminianism.

Monophysitism

- Also known as Eutychianism.
    - What is Monophysitism?
        - The word mono means what? One.
        - The word physite (or physis) means what? It is the Greek word for nature.
        - They believe that the deity of Jesus absorbed into the humanity of Jesus forming one nature, which is something different.
        - i. An example would be that if you mix powder and water together you can get something entirely different . . . jello.
        - Jesus was neither truly God nor truly man.
        - Jesus had one will, that of the divine.
        - i. He was either divinely human or humanly divine.
- We will study more about the Monophysite heresy when we get to the Council of Chalcedon.

Nestorianism

- What is Nestorianism?
  - Two natures in one body that are separated, like oil and water.

- This is another heresy that resulted in an ecumenical church council and another creed being formed.
- We will study this more when we get to page 120.
  - What is the difference between a distinction and a separation?

RC Sproul: "The most important distinction you can learn is the difference between a distinction and a separation. If I distinguish your body from your soul, I haven't harmed you, but if I separate your body from your soul, I have killed you."[3]

---

3. Sproul. *The Christian and Science*

NOTES

The Apologists
The Apologetics and Polemics of the Church Fathers
Second Century

- What is the difference between apologetics and polemics?

We defined polemics at the beginning of this study. Do you remember what it is? Being inwardly focused on the church in a critical manner. Polemics is a sheepdog guarding the sheep from wolves.

- What is apologetics? It is the Greek word to speak in defense of something.
    - Christian apologetics is the defense of God's word from attack from outside sources.

The Bible is full of apologetics and polemics. In church history there were a certain group of men known as the Apologists that lived during the second century. Christians during this time had to meet secretly. This stirred up speculation on exactly what was happening in these secret meetings. These speculations, as often do, turned into accusations. The accusations led to persecution because of the seriousness of their nature. The apologists stood up in defense of Christ's church. They wanted not just the people, but the governing officials to understand what was happening in Christian meetings. They wanted people to understand why they would risk their very lives to assemble and worship the one true God.

- These are four of the accusations which led to the persecution in which the apologists responded to:

1. Being atheists
    i. Because they didn't believe in the polytheism of the pagans.
   - What is polytheism? Believing in or worshiping more than one god.
2. Being sexually immoral
    i. Because the Christians met in secret and little was known by the pagans about what took place at these meetings.
3. Being cannibals
    i. Because of a misunderstanding of the Lord's Supper, Christians were accused of drinking literal blood and eating literal flesh.
4. Being insurrectionists
    i. Because they refused to worship the emperor and openly gave their highest allegiance to Christ.
        a. Apologists responded by showing that Christians were submissive to the government and understood that God had appointed the emperor to power.
   - Who were the apologists?
     - Quadratus; Tatian AD 110–72; Aristides; Athenagoras AD 133–90; Justin Martyr AD 100–165; Theophilus AD 181; Hegesippus AD 180; Melito AD 190; Some scholars include Clement of Alexandria, Tertullian, and Cyprian.
     i. These men not only defended the faith against false teachers, but specifically against the Roman government because of Roman persecution.

JUSTIN MARTYR AD 100–165

- Justin studied philosophy in his quest for wisdom and truth. He eventually discovered the Bible and converted to Christianity.
    i. Of all of the quests ever undertaken by man, there is none greater than the quest for truth.

The Apologists

ii. A diligent quest for truth will always lead to Scripture... the source of absolute truth in which true wisdom is only found.

- Justin attempted to build a bridge between Christianity and philosophy, calling the Bible "the true philosophy" arguing that Christianity is the fulfillment of all true philosophical knowledge.

    i. This sets the foundation for men like Clement of Alexandria who tries to Christianize Platonism.

    - What is Platonism? Basically, the philosophical ideas that came from Plato.

- Justin's *1st and 2nd Apologies* or defenses of the faith were written to demonstrate to the emperor and the Roman senate, "given their reputation as fair-minded and educated men," the injustice of persecuting the Christians, since Christianity is "the true philosophy."
- In his *Dialogue with Trypho* (who was a Jewish man), he argues from Scripture that Jesus is the Messiah[1] and that Christians are the true people of God.[2]
- Fragments of his work "*On the Resurrection*" remain. In this writing he argues for the bodily resurrection of Jesus Christ.
- He was martyred in Rome around AD 165 during the reign of Marcus Aurelius.

    i. Just before his execution he was commanded to recant being a Christian. Justin reportedly replied, "No one who is rightly minded turns from true belief to false."

Excerpts from Justin Martyr

- This quote is in regard to Christian worship. This was in reference to the "secret meetings" accusations. This is the earliest record of what worship was like in the church.

---

1. Jesus the Messiah: **Isaiah 9:6–7; John 1:1–2 and 14; Matthew 1:23**
2. Christians are the people of God: **Romans 9:6–8; Galatians 3:28–29**

"On the day called Sunday there is a gathering together in the same place of all who live in a given city or rural district. The memoirs of the apostles or the writings of the prophets are read, as long as time permits. Then when the reader ceases, the president (pastor) in a discourse admonishes and urges the imitation of these good things. Next, we all rise together and send up prayers. When we cease from our prayer, bread is presented and wine and water. The president in the same manner sends up prayers and thanksgivings, according to his ability, and the people sing out their assent, saying the 'Amen.' A distribution and participation of the elements for which thanks have been given is made to each person, and to those who are not present they are sent by the deacons. Those who have means and are willing, each according to his own choice, gives what he wills, and what is collected is deposited with the president. He provides for the orphans and widows, those who are in need on account of sickness or some other cause, those who are in bonds, strangers who are sojourning, and in a word, he becomes the protector of all who are in need. But Sunday is the day on which we all hold our common assembly, because it is the first day on which God, having wrought a change in the darkness and matter, made the world; and Jesus Christ our Savior on the same day rose from the dead. For He was crucified on the day before that of Saturn (Saturday); and on the day after that of Saturn, which is the day of the Sun, having appeared to His apostles and disciples, He taught them these things, which we have submitted to you also for your consideration. "(*The First Apology*)[3]

- Does this first quote sound anything like our church services today?
- If not, what are the differences?

This next quote is regarding the distinction between God the Father and God the Son.

"Then I replied, 'Reverting to the Scriptures, I shall endeavor to persuade you, that He who is said to have appeared to Abraham, and to Jacob, and to Moses, and who is called God, is distinct from him who made all things,—numerically, I mean, not (distinct) in will. For I affirm that He has never at any time done anything which He who made

---

3. Needham. *2000 Years of Christ's Power*

The Apologists

the world—above whom there is no other God... has not wished him both to do and to engage Himself with.[4] (*Dialogue with Trypho*)

- Is it clear that Justin didn't believe that God was a single person?
    i. This is before the Trinity was clearly defined by the Council of Nicaea.

TATIAN AD 110-72

- He was a student of Justin Martyr.
- Tatian's writings reflect a great degree of dislike for Greek philosophy and Hellenistic (Greek) culture. He didn't agree with his teacher, Justin, when it came to philosophy.
    i. He believed that the church did not go far enough in rejecting the influence of society (Greek philosophy).
- He began his own Christian Gnostic sect that was rejected by orthodox Christianity as heretical.
- His followers rejected marriage as adulterous, condemned eating meat in any form, and forbade drinking wine—even during the Lord's Supper (an example of overcorrection).
    - Here is a good question to start a church split (just kidding). Is it wrong to drink wine?
- His "*Address to the Greeks*" attempts to show that paganism is worthless, and that Christianity by contrast is the only reasonable faith.
- He wrote "*The Diatessaron*" which is a major work of harmonizing the four New Testament Gospels (Into one Gospel book) which became the standard for Syrian Churches until the fifth century.

> Chapter 4 of *Tatian the Assyrian's Address to the Greeks* "For what reason, men of Greece, do you wish to bring the civil powers, as in a pugilistic encounter, into collision with us? And, if I am not disposed to comply with the usages of some of them, why am I to be abhorred as a vile miscreant? [3] Does the sovereign order

---

4. Justin. *Dialogue with Trypho* P. 56

the payment of tribute, I am ready to render it. Does my master command me to act as a bondsman and to serve, I acknowledge the serfdom [like a peasant slave]? Man is to be honored as a fellowman; [4] God alone is to be feared . . . He who is not visible to human eyes, nor comes within the compass of human art. Only when I am commanded to deny Him, will I not obey, but will rather die than show myself false and ungrateful. Our God did not begin to be in time: [5] He alone is without beginning, and He Himself is the beginning of all things. God is a Spirit, [6] not pervading matter, but the Maker of material spirits, [7] and of the forms that are in matter; He is invisible, impalpable [unable to be felt or touched], being Himself the Father of both sensible and invisible things. Him we know from His creation and apprehend His invisible power by His works. [8] I refuse to adore that workmanship which He has made for our sakes. The sun and moon were made for us: how, then, can I adore my own servants? How can I speak of stocks and stones as gods? For the Spirit that pervades matter [7] is inferior to the more divine spirit; and this, even when assimilated to the soul, is not to be honored equally with the perfect God. Nor even ought the ineffable God to be presented with gifts; for He who is in want of nothing is not to be misrepresented by us as though He were indigent [poor]. But I will set forth our views more distinctly."[5]

- What are some of the theological concepts that we see in this quote?

ATHENAGORAS OF ATHENS AD 133–90

- Athenagoras was a Platonist before becoming a Christian.
- He became a Christian after reading Scripture to refute it.
    i. He was a pagan whose quest for truth led him to the absolute truth of Scripture, like many others throughout church history.
    - Should you ever take something taught to you by someone you deeply admire as absolute truth without comparing it to Scripture?

---

5. Titian. *Address to The Greeks*

The Apologists

- He pleaded with the emperor for justice for the mistreated Christians and refuted the idea that they were cannibals or atheists.
- Two of his writings survived: *An Apology or Embassy for the Christian* and *A Treatise on the Resurrection*.

> Chapter 3 of *Embassy for the Christian* "Three things are alleged against us: atheism, Thyestean feasts, Œdipodean intercourse. But if these charges are true, spare no class: proceed at once against our crimes; destroy us root and branch, with our wives and children, if any Christian[4] is found to live like the brutes. And yet even the brutes do not touch the flesh of their own kind; and they pair by a law of nature, and only at the regular season, not from simple wantonness; they also recognize those from whom they receive benefits. If anyone, therefore, is more savage than the brutes, what punishment that he can endure shall be deemed adequate to such offences? But, if these things are only idle tales and empty slanders, originating in the fact that virtue is opposed by its very nature to vice, and that contraries war against one another by a divine law (and you are yourselves witnesses that no such iniquities are committed by us, for you forbid information›s to be laid against us), it remains for you to make inquiry concerning our life, our opinions, our loyalty and obedience to you and your house and government, and thus at length to grant to us the same rights (we ask nothing more) as to those who persecute us. For we shall then conquer them, unhesitatingly surrendering, as we now do, our very lives for the truth›s sake."[6]

- Chapter 10 of *Embassy for the Christian* is interesting as well because it is dealing with the Trinity. Jehovah's Witnesses and others accuse us of inventing the Trinity at the Council of Nicaea, which is around one hundred years after this writing.

    i. Keep in mind that the word "Trinity" had not been coined at this time.

> 'That we are not atheists, therefore, seeing that we acknowledge one God, uncreated, eternal, invisible, impassible [incapable of suffering], incomprehensible, illimitable [without limits], who is apprehended by the understanding only and the reason, who is encompassed by light, and beauty, and spirit, and power

---

6. Athenagoras. *Embassy for the Christian*

ineffable [too great to be expressed in words], by whom the universe has been created through His Logos, and set in order, and is kept in being—I have sufficiently demonstrated. [I say "His Logos"], for we acknowledge also a Son of God. Nor let anyone think it ridiculous that God should have a Son. For though the poets, in their fictions, represent the gods as no better than men, our mode of thinking is not the same as theirs, concerning either God the Father or the Son. But the Son of God is the Logos of the Father, in idea and in operation; for after the pattern of Him and by Him were all things made, the Father and the Son being one. And, the Son being in the Father and the Father in the Son, in oneness and power of spirit, the understanding and reason (νοῦς καὶ λόγος) of the Father is the Son of God. But if, in your surpassing intelligence, it occurs to you to inquire what is meant by the Son, I will state briefly that He is the first product of the Father, not as having been brought into existence (for from the beginning, God, who is the eternal mind [νοῦς], had the Logos in Himself, being from eternity instinct with Logos [λογικός]); but inasmuch as He came forth to be the idea and energizing power of all material things, which lay like a nature without attributes, and an inactive earth, the grosser particles being mixed up with the lighter. The prophetic Spirit also agrees with our statements. "The Lord," it says, "made me, the beginning of His ways to His works."[20] The Holy Spirit Himself also, which operates in the prophets, we assert to be an effluence of God, flowing from Him, and returning back again like a beam of the sun. Who, then, would not be astonished to hear men who speak of God the Father, and of God the Son, and of the Holy Spirit, and who declare both their power in union and their distinction in order, called atheists? Nor is our teaching in what relates to the divine nature confined to these points; but we recognize also a multitude of angels and ministers, whom God the Maker and Framer of the world distributed and appointed to their several posts by His Logos, to occupy themselves about the elements, and the heavens, and the world, and the things in it, and the goodly ordering of them all."[7]

- What are some of the theological concepts we see in this chapter from Athenagoras?

---

7. Athenagoras. *A plea for the Christians*

CLEMENT OF ALEXANDRIA AD 150-215 (EGYPT)

- Clement was the teacher of Origen who we will study later.
- He made use of Greek philosophy in an effort to defend Christianity. He believed philosophy was complementary to Christianity.
    - Is philosophy something a Christian should avoid?
- He held to a form of Christian Platonism.
    i. He believed that all truth is God's truth. There is truth found in the teachings of Plato which can be used to teach the church.
- He wrote three well known works: *Exhortation to the Greeks*, *The Instructor*, and *The Miscellanies*.
- Let's look at chapter 1 of *The Instructor*. Clement of Alexandria's writing is hard to digest, so we will break it down into a few sections in order to take pause and think about what he is saying.

> Chapter 1 of *The Instructor* "As there are these three things in the case of man, habits, actions, and passions; habits are the department appropriated by hortatory [to exhort] discourse the guide to piety, which, like the ship's keel, is laid beneath for the building up of faith; in which, rejoicing exceedingly, and abjuring our old opinions, through salvation we renew our youth, singing with the hymning prophecy, "How good is God to Israel, too such as are upright in heart!" All actions, again, are the province of preceptive discourse; while persuasive discourse applies itself to heal the passions. It is, however, one and the self-same word which rescues man from the custom of this world in which he has been reared, and trains him up in the one salvation of faith in God."[8]

- What does the word piety mean? It is the reverent quality of being devoted to what you believe.
- What is the main point of the above excerpt?
    - This is mainly dealing with godly habits.

---

8. Clement (of Alexandria). *The Instructor: Book 1*

- Have you developed any godly habits?
- What are some of the godly habits a believer should develop?

• Some of the things we see concerning godly habits from the above excerpt are:

  i. Godly habits are for "the building up of" the believers "faith."
  ii. Godly habits replace your "old opinions" and are the evidence of true belief.
  iii. Godly habits lead to "actions" and are of the "providence" of God. So He gets all of the glory rather than you believing you have accomplished something on your own.
  iv. Godly habits replace earthly passions with godly passions, which grow you in the process of sanctification.

"When, then, the heavenly guide, the Word, was inviting men to salvation, the appellation [identifying name] of hortatory was properly applied to Him: his same word was called rousing (the whole from a part). For the whole of piety is hortatory, engendering [to cause to develop] in the kindred faculty of reason a yearning after true life now and to come. But now, being at once curative and preceptive, following in His own steps, He makes what had been prescribed the subject of persuasion, promising the cure of the passions within us. Let us then designate this Word appropriately by the one name Tutor (or Paedagogue, or instructor)." (pahee-dag-o-gue)[9]

- What New Testament writer uses the word *Tutor* in his Epistles? Paul.

  i. The tutor, or Paedagogos, was a strict disciplinarian in a child's life. In the book of Galatians, it is referring to the Mosaic Law of God.

"The Instructor being practical, not theoretical, His aim is thus to improve the soul, not to teach, and to train it up to a virtuous, not to an intellectual life. Although this same word is didactic [moral instruction], but not in the present instance. For the

---

9. Clement (of Alexandria). *The Instructor*

The Apologists

word which, in matters of doctrine, explains and reveals, is that whose province it is to teach. But our Educators being practical, first exhorts to the attainment of right dispositions and character, and then persuades us to the energetic practice of our duties, enjoining on us pure commandments, and exhibiting to such as come after representations of those who formerly wandered in error. Both are of the highest utility,—that which assumes the form of counselling to obedience, and that which is presented in the form of example; which latter is of two kinds, corresponding to the former duality,—the one having for its purpose that we should choose and imitate the good, and the other that we should reject and turn away from the opposite."[10]

- What biblical concepts do we see in this excerpt?
- The Law of God has two purposes for an individual. What are they?

1. "first exhorts to the attainment of right dispositions." The Law shows the impossibility to keep it and it shows our need for a savior who kept it for us. The Law shows that the right disposition before God is only found through faith.
2. "then persuades us to the energetic practice of our duties" Once we are in right disposition before God (justified) the Law shows us how to grow in holiness (sanctification.)

"Hence accordingly ensues the healing of our passions, in consequence of the assuagements [to make something burdensome less painful] of those examples; the Paedagogue strengthening our souls, and by His benign [general] commands, as by gentle medicines, guiding the sick to the perfect knowledge of the truth."

- What is the main idea of this excerpt?

"There is a wide difference between health and knowledge; for the latter is produced by learning, the former by healing. One, who is ill, will not therefore learn any branch of instruction till he is quite well. For neither to learners nor to the sick is each injunction invariably expressed similarly; but to the former in such a way as to lead to knowledge, and to the latter to health. As, then, for those of us who are diseased in body a physician

10. Clement (of Alexandria). *The Instructor*

is required, so also those who are diseased in soul require a paedagogue to cure our maladies; and then a teacher, to train and guide the soul to all requisite knowledge when it is made able to admit the revelation of the Word. Eagerly desiring, then, to perfect us by a gradation [a series of successive changes] conducive to salvation, suited for efficacious discipline, a beautiful arrangement is observed by the all-benignant [favorable] Word, who first exhorts, then trains, and finally teaches."[11]

- Discuss the biblical concepts that you see in this excerpt.

TERTULLIAN AD 155–240 (NORTH AFRICA)

- Tertullian was teaching at the same time as Clement of Alexandria but took the opposite position . . . all lies are Satan's lies . . . rejecting anything that had error in it. Therefore, he rejected philosophy.
    i. He coined the saying "What has Athens to do with Jerusalem?"

- He once enjoyed the games in the arena in which he was profoundly affected by the testimonies of Christians who were martyred there. This could have led to his conversion.
    i. Christian martyrdom has played a huge role in the conversion of God's elect throughout history.
        - What do you think of God using the martyrdom of godly men to drive others to himself?

- He wrote in Latin in which he expanded the language because he couldn't find words or terms to express what he wanted to convey.
    i. One of the helpful terms he came up with was "trinitas" or Trinity.

- This division of teaching between Clement of Alexandria and Tertullian led to the question; Should the church assimilate with culture or reject culture? This is still a major area of division today.

11. Clement (of Alexandria). *The Instructor:*

The Apologists

   i. Scripture tells us to be in the world but not part of the world. Tertullian believed that Clement wanted to be in the world and part of the world. Clement believed Tertullian wanted to not be in the world at all.

  - How has the assimilation of culture into Christianity affected the church?

- Clement thought using Greek philosophy would make Christianity appealing to those who liked Greek philosophy.

  - Should Christianity be appealing to the world?

- Tertullian was more fundamental which led him to eventually turn to Montanism (page 39). Not because he agreed with their doctrine, but because they were strict in lifestyle.

- In a way liberalism is represented by Clement of Alexandria and legalism is represented by Tertullian.

   i. This division still goes on today. The broader evangelical church would represent Clement and would try to incorporate or assimilate anything in culture to try to make Christianity relevant to society. The fundamental church would represent Tertullian in which you would want to separate as much as possible from society in order to stand apart. Conservative Christians would stand somewhere in the middle.

Chapter 1 of *The Prescription Against Heretics* "The character of the times in which we live is such as to call forth from us even this admonition, that we ought not to be astonished at the heresies (which abound) neither ought their existence to surprise us, for it was foretold that they should come to pass; nor the fact that they subvert the faith of some, for their final cause is, by affording a trial to faith, to give it also the opportunity of being "approved." Groundless, therefore, and inconsiderate is the offence of the many who are scandalized by the very fact that heresies prevail to such a degree. How great (might their offence have been) if they had not existed. When it has been determined that a thing must by all means be, it receives the (final) cause for which it has its being. This secures the power through which it exists, in such a way that it is impossible for it not to have existence."[12]

- Does God use heresies to strengthen the true church and if so who does this apply to today?

---

12. Tertullian. *The Sacred Writings of Tertullian Volume 1: The Prescription Against Heretics.*

NOTES

The Ante-Nicene Fathers
Third Century

- The first five hundred years after the death of the last apostle (John) is the period in which we consider the church leaders to be "church fathers."
- The church fathers are divided in time by the Council of Nicaea in AD 325. The following are the third century church fathers prior to the Council of Nicaea.

IRENAEUS AD 130–202 (GREECE-FRANCE)

- Irenaeus was discipled by Polycarp who was discipled by John.
- He was known as a polemicist rather than an apologist.
- He wrote a book called "*Against Heresies*" which was a polemic against Gnosticism.

> "***But it is not possible that the Gospels can be either more or fewer in number than they are.*** For since there are four zones of the world in which we live, and four principal winds, while the church has been scattered throughout the world, and since the pillar and ground of the Church is the Gospel and the spirit of life, it is fitting that she should have four pillars, breathing incorruption on every side, and vivifying human afresh. From this fact, it is evident that the Logos, the fashioner of all, he that sits on the cherubim and holds all things together, when he was

manifested to humanity, gave us the gospel under four forms but bound together by one spirit."[1]

"We have received the disposition of our salvation **by no others**, but those by whom the Gospel came to us (namely, the apostles) which they then preached, and afterwards by God's will delivered to us in the Scriptures, to be the pillar and ground of our faith."[2]

- We see an interesting perspective on the four Gospels in the first quote.
    - What biblical doctrines can we see in the above two excerpts?
        - The apostleship did not continue after the death of the last one . . . John.
        - We also can see an early version of Sola Scriptura. Scripture alone is our authority.

"The ancient tradition of the apostles is **believing in one God, the Creator of heaven and earth, and all things therein, by means of Christ Jesus, the Son of God**; who, because of His **surpassing love** towards His creation, condescended to be **born of the virgin**, He **Himself uniting man through Himself to God**, and having **suffered** under Pontius Pilate, and rising again, and having been **received up in splendor**, shall **come in glory, the Savior of those who are saved**, and **the Judge of those who are judged**, and **sending into eternal fire those who transform the truth**, and despise His Father and His advent."[3]

- There was an oral tradition and the written tradition (Bible). The oral tradition was a summary of Scripture.
    - Why was there an oral tradition? Lack of copies of Scripture and illiteracy.
    - What biblical doctrines can we see in the above quote?
        - Jesus is the creator of heaven and earth.
        - Jesus is the Son of God.

1. Irenaeus. *The Early Church at Work and Worship Vol. 1*
2. Irenaeus. *An Exposition of the Thirty-nine Articles* P. 140
3. Irenaeus. *Ante-Nicene Fathers:Against Heresies*. P. 417

- Jesus loves his creation.
- Jesus was born of a virgin.
- Jesus is truly God and truly man.
- Jesus suffered.
- Jesus's sacrifice, substitution, and propitiation was accepted by God being "received up in splendor."
- Jesus is coming back in "glory."
- Jesus is "Savior" of only those "who are saved" and he is the "Judge" of everyone else.
- It is Jesus who sends people to hell, not "people's actions" like many claim today.
- We can also see two members of the Trinity.
- He taught "***eternal fire***" rather than annihilationism.

- What is annihilationism? Those who do not make it into the eternal kingdom of God are annihilated. Their souls are not tormented in hell but cease to be.
  i. Many people believe this because they cannot reconcile the eternal agony of hell.
  ii. Others believe annihilationism because they cannot understand how God can be both love and just. They believe that the punishment does not fit the crime because they do not understand God's holiness.

ORIGEN AD 184-253

- Origen was discipled by Clement of Alexandria.
- He is known for his brilliance, which turns into a double-edged sword.
  i. When he was correct, he was brilliantly correct and when he was wrong, he was brilliantly wrong.
- He is also known as the father of systematic theology.

- He popularized the allegorical hermeneutic (The allegorical school of Alexandria was born out of Origen's ideas.)

  - What is an allegory? A story in which the true meaning is not found in the story. There is a secret meaning that would be revealed by the storyteller. This has had a tremendous, negative impact throughout church history.

- He taught Universalism. Universalism influenced guys all the way through church history.

  - What is Universalism? It is the belief that all people will eventually be redeemed.

    i. Origen even taught that Satan would eventually be redeemed.

- In 545 AD he was deemed a heretic at the Council of Constantinople.
- We will look at Chapter 5 of *Book 8* of *Contra Celsum* in which he is writing apologetics to a man named Celsus who has written books against Christianity.

    i. Celsus was a pagan and believed in all of the polytheistic Greek gods. Keep that in mind as we read Origen's response.

"Whilst there are thus many gods and lords, whereof some are such in reality, and others are such only in name, we strive to rise not only above those whom the nations of the earth worship as gods, but also beyond those spoken of as gods in Scripture, of whom they are wholly ignorant who are strangers to the covenants of God given by Moses and by our Saviour Jesus, and who have no part in the promises which He has made to us through them. That man rises above all demon-worship who does nothing that is pleasing to demons; and he rises to a blessedness beyond that of those whom Paul calls gods, if he is enabled, like them, or in any way he may, to look not at the things which are seen, but at the things which are unseen. And he who considers that the earnest expectation of the creature waits for the manifestation of the sons of God, not willingly, but by reason of him who subjected the same in hope, while he praises the creature, and sees how it shall be freed altogether from the bondage of corruption, and restored to the glorious liberty of the children of God,—such a one cannot be induced to combine with the service of God the service of any other, or to serve two masters. There is therefore nothing seditious or factious in the language of those who hold these views, and who refuse to serve more masters than one. To them Jesus Christ is an all-sufficient Lord, who Himself instructs them, in order that when fully instructed He may form them into a kingdom worthy of God, and present them to God the Father. But indeed they do in a sense separate themselves and stand aloof from those who are aliens from the commonwealth of God and strangers to His covenants, in order that they may live as citizens of heaven, coming to the *living God, and to the city of God, the heavenly Jerusalem, and to an innumerable company of angels, to the general assembly and Church of the first-born, which are written in heaven.*"[4]

- Discuss some of the biblical doctrines found in this excerpt.
- Many of Origen's teachings led to the growth of **Asceticism**, which is a lifestyle characterized by the abstinence of sensual pleasures for the pursuit of spiritual growth.
    - Is asceticism an overreaction to hedonism?
    - How can both be dangerous of Christians?

CYPRIAN OF CARTHAGE AD 200–258

- Cyprian is known for trying to bring unity to the church while holding to doctrinal purity.
    i. People who had denied Christ over persecution wanted back into the church. This wound up splitting the church. Cyprian wanted to bring unity back. He accepted them as long as they were repentant.
        a. Because of the split in the church, Cyprian wrote letters attempting to unify the church.
- Unity, like most doctrines in Scripture, has a certain amount of tension to it:

4. Origen. *The Ante-Nicene Fathers: Translations of the Writings Vol. 4*. P. 641

      i. Christians are commanded to seek unity within the body.

      ii. Christians are commanded to maintain doctrinal purity and reject false teaching.

      iii. Cyprian did a good job teaching both.

- There cannot be true unity without correct doctrine, or it becomes superficial.

"He can no longer have God for his Father who has not the Church for his mother . . . he who gathers elsewhere than in the Church scatters the Church of Christ: not is there any other home to believers but the one Church"[5] Cyprian

> From Cyprian's *Treatise 1*: "But, beloved brethren, not only must we beware of what is open and manifest, but also of what deceives by the craft of subtle fraud. And what can be more crafty, or what more subtle, than for this enemy, detected and cast down by the advent of Christ, after light has come to the nations, and saving rays have shone for the preservation of men, that the deaf might receive the hearing of spiritual grace, the blind might open their eyes to God, the weak might grow strong again with eternal health, the lame might run to the church, the dumb might pray with clear voices and prayers—seeing his idols forsaken, and his lanes and his temples deserted by the numerous concourse of believers—to devise a new fraud, and under the very title of the Christian name to deceive the incautious? He has invented heresies and schisms, whereby he might subvert the faith, might corrupt the truth, might divide the unity. Those whom he cannot keep in the darkness of the old way, he circumvents and deceives by the error of a new way. He snatches men from the Church itself; and while they seem to themselves to have already approached to the light, and to have escaped the night of the world, he pours over them again, in their unconsciousness, new darkness; so that, although they do not stand firm with the Gospel of Christ, and with the observation and law of Christ, they still call themselves Christians, and, walking in darkness, they think that they have the light, while the adversary is flattering and deceiving, who, according to the apostle's word, transforms himself into an angel of light, and equips his ministers as if they were the ministers of righteousness, who

---

5. Cyprian. *Invitation to Church History World*. P. 88

maintain night instead of day, death for salvation, despair under the offer of hope, perfidy under the pretext of faith, antichrist under the name of Christ; so that, while they feign things like the truth, they make void the truth by their subtlety. This happens, beloved brethren, so long as we do not return to the source of truth, as we do not seek the head nor keep the teaching of the heavenly Master."[6] Cyprian

- Discuss some of the biblical doctrines in the above quote.

---

6. Cyprian. *The Ante-Nicene Fathers: Volume 5: Treatise 1.* P. 422

NOTES

Are the Solas Something New?

- What does the term "evangelical" mean? It is German for gospel.
    i. It was coined by Martin Luther during the Reformation.
- Martin Luther considered those who held to sola fide and sola Scriptura as evangelical. The other three solas flow from these two:
    i. Sola Scriptura, the Word of God alone is our authority for
    ii. Sola Fide (Faith alone) by the means of
    iii. Sola Gratia, Grace alone on the basis of
    iv. Sola Christus, the work of Christ alone for
    v. Soli Deo Gloria, the Glory of God alone
- Roman Catholics have argued that the five Solas of the Reformation were invented by Martin Luther and there is no history of this belief prior to the Reformation.
    i. Roman Catholics believe in synergism rather than monergism.
      - What is synergism?
        - Synergism teaches that man must cooperate with God in order to be justified. 1-part God and 1-part man = salvation or faith + works = salvation.
      - What is monergism?
        - Monergism teaches God alone does everything for the salvation of his elect.

Are the Solas Something New?

- Below is a list of Roman Catholic doctrines concerning justification.

The Catholic Catechism "all men may attain salvation through faith, baptism, and observance of the Commandments" (P2068; ellipsis in original; emphasis mine)

   i. This is what the Judaizers were teaching in Acts 15 and to the churches of Galatia.

The Catholic Encyclopedia: "The sinner is formally justified and made holy by his own personal justice and holiness such that over and above faith other acts are necessary for justification including acts of charity, penance with contrition, and almsgiving."

Catholic Answers Website: "Even though only God's grace enables us to love others, these acts of love please him, and he promises to reward them with eternal life (Rom. 2:6–7, Gal. 6:6–10). Thus good works are meritorious . . . Our faith in Christ puts us in a special grace filled relationship with God so that our obedience and love, combined with our faith, will be rewarded with eternal life."

Romans 11:6 *If it is by grace, it is no longer on the basis of works, otherwise grace is no longer grace.*

- The root of Justification is grace alone through faith alone based on the work of Christ alone.

   i. Good works are ***the fruit*** or evidence of our salvation, not the basis of our right standing before God.

- What does the word "Reformation" mean?

   - The word Reformation means to (re)-form something that has been changed or deformed.

   i. The reformers were not coming up with something new but concerned with reforming something deformed by the Roman Catholic system.

Below is a portion of the verses concerning Sola Scriptura

2 Timothy 3:16 *All Scripture is inspired by God and profitable for teaching, for reproof, for correction, for training in righteousness.*

Acts 17:11 *Now these were more noble-minded than those in Thessalonica, for they received the word with great eagerness, examining the Scriptures daily to see whether these things were so.*

1 Corinthians 4:6 *Now these things, brethren, I have figuratively applied to myself and Apollos for your sakes, so that in us you may learn not to exceed what is written, so that no one of you will become arrogant in behalf of one against the other.*

Mark 7:6–9 *And He said to them, "Rightly did Isaiah prophesy of you hypocrites, as it is written: 'THIS PEOPLE HONORS ME WITH THEIR LIPS, BUT THEIR HEART IS FAR AWAY FROM ME. 7 'BUT IN VAIN DO THEY WORSHIP ME, TEACHING AS DOCTRINES THE PRECEPTS OF MEN.' 8 "Neglecting the commandment of God, you hold to the tradition of men." 9 He was also saying to them, "You are experts at setting aside the commandment of God in order to keep your tradition.*

Below is a portion of the verses concerning Sola Fide

The entire book of **Galatians**. We will look at one verse : **2:16** *nevertheless knowing that a man is not justified by the works of the Law but through faith in Christ Jesus, even we have believed in Christ Jesus, so that we may be justified by faith in Christ and not by the works of the Law; since by the works of the Law no flesh will be justified.*

Ephesians 2:8–9 *8 For by grace you have been saved through faith; and that not of yourselves, it is the gift of God; 9 not as a result of works, so that no one may boast.*

Quotes from Church Fathers on Sola Fide

Clement of Rome (30–100) "And we Christians, too, being called by his will in Christ Jesus, are **not justified by ourselves, nor by our own wisdom, or understanding, or godliness, or works** which we have wrought in holiness of heart; **but by that faith** through which, from the beginning, Almighty God has justified all men; to whom be glory forever and ever. Amen."[1]

Polycarp (69–160) "I rejoice that the secure **root of your faith**, proclaimed from ancient times, even now continues to abide and **bear fruit** in our Lord Jesus Christ. he persevered to the point of death on behalf of our sins; and God raised him up after loosing the labor pains of Hades. Even without seeing him, you believe in him with an

---

1. *First Epistle to the Corinthians*, 32.4

inexpressible and glorious joy that many long to experience. For you know that ***you have been saved by a gracious gift—not from works but by the will of God through Jesus Christ.***"[2]

> Augustine (354–430) "If Abraham was not justified by works, how was he justified? The apostle goes on to tell us how: What does scripture say? Abraham believed God, and it was reckoned to him as righteousness. Abraham, then, was justified by faith. Paul and James do not contradict each other: good works follow justification. James dwells on an action performed by Abraham that we all know about: he offered his son to God as a sacrifice. That is a great work, but it proceeded from faith. I have nothing but praise for the superstructure of action, but I see the foundation of faith; I admire the good work as a fruit, but I recognize that it springs from the root of faith."[3]

Augustine "When someone believes in him who justifies the impious, that faith is reckoned as justice to the believer, as David too declares that person Blessed whom ***God has accepted and endowed with righteousness, independently of any righteous actions*** (Rom 4:5–6) What righteousness is this? ***The righteousness of faith, preceded by no good works, but with good works as its consequence.***"[4]

> Epistle to Diognetus (First or early Second century) (This also points out the doctrine of substitutionary atonement) "He gave his own Son as a ransom for us, the holy One for transgressors, the blameless One for the wicked, the righteous One for the unrighteous, the incorruptible One for the corruptible, the immortal One for them that are mortal. For what other thing was capable of covering our sins than his righteousness? By what other one was it possible that we, the wicked and ungodly, could be justified, than by the only Son of God? O sweet exchange! O unsearchable operation! O benefits surpassing all expectation! That the wickedness of many should be hid in a single righteous One, and that the righteousness of One should justify many transgressors!"[5]

---

2. Polycarp. *Epistle to the Philippians*, 1.2–3
3. Augustine. *Exposition 2 of Psalm* 31, 2–4
4. Augustine. *Justification Volume 1*. Michael Horton
5. Unknown. *The Justification Reader: Epistle to Diognetus*

Prosper of Aquitaine (390–455) "Just as there are no crimes so detestable that they can prevent the gift of grace, so too there can be no works so eminent that they are owed in deserved judgment that which is given freely. ***Would it not be a debasement of redemption in Christ's blood, and would not God's mercy be made secondary to human works, if justification, which is through grace, were owed in view of preceding merits, so that it were not a gift of a Donor, but the wages of a laborer?***"[6]

- When did the Roman Catholic Church lose sight of the true gospel?

  Geisler & Betancourt write: "Roman Catholicism as it is known today is not the same as the Catholic Church before 1215. Even though the split between East and West occurred in 1054, most non-Catholics today would have been able to belong to the Catholic Church before the thirteenth century. Regardless of certain things the church permitted, none of its official doctrinal proclamations regarding essential salvation doctrines were contrary to orthodoxy. While the development of Roman Catholicism from the original church was gradual, beginning in early centuries, one of the most significant turning points came in 1215, when one can see the beginning of Roman Catholicism as it is subsequently known. It is here that the seeds of what distinguishes Roman Catholicism were first pronounced as dogma. It is here that they pronounced the doctrine of transubstantiation, the primacy of the bishop of Rome, and seven sacraments. Many consider this a key turning point in the development of Roman Catholicism in distinction from non-Catholic forms of Christianity."[7]

- It is important to note that the reformers were reacting to this apostasy that began to dominate in the thirteenth century. We will learn more about this when we get to chapter 14.

  John Calvin "Moreover, (the Roman Church) unjustly set the ancient fathers against us (I mean the ancient writers of a better age of the church) as if in them they had supporters of their own impiety. If the contest were to be determined by patristic

---

6. Prosper as quoted by MacArthur. *The Shepherd As Theologian*
7. Geisler & Betancourt. *Is Rome the True Church?*

authority, the tide of victory—to put it very modestly—would turn to our side. Now, these fathers have written many wise and excellent things. Yet the good things that these fathers have written they (the Roman Catholics) either do not notice or misrepresent or pervert. But we do not despise them (the church fathers); in fact, if it were to our present purpose, I could with no trouble at all prove that the greater part of what we are saying today meets their approval." *The Institutes of the Christian Religion* ("patristic" refers to early Christian theologians)[8]

---

8. Calvin. *Institutes of the Christian Religion.*

NOTES

Nicene Christianity

- This is a time of major transition within the Roman Empire.
- Persecution of Christians has been increasingly intense up to this point. It is now, in what seems to be the nick of time, that Constantine comes to power.
- Constantine was convinced that he was converted when he was marching with his armies against Maxentius in 312 AD according to Lactantius, a great cross in the sky appears and underneath was written, "In this sign, conquer." **Eusebius** (page 83) says that Constantine doesn't know which god has given him this sign in the sky, but that he was so moved by his vision of the cross that he vowed to worship no other God than the one represented to him. So, he begins to seek out others who might help him to learn more about what he saw. It is known that Bishops regularly traveled with Constantine; Maternus from Cologne, Recticius from Autun, Marinus from Arles, and Ossius from Cordoba. It is likely that these Bishops affirmed to him that Jesus was the only begotten son of God and that the cross he had seen in his vision was a symbol of Jesus's triumph over death.
- Constantine issued the **Edict of Milan** in 313 AD which protects Christians.
    i. Theodosius, sixty-seven years later, makes Christianity the official religion of Rome with the **Edict of Thessalonica**.
- In 324 he became the emperor of both the eastern and western halves of Rome.

- In 325 he held the first general church council in Nicaea which is the second church council in history. Remember the first was The Council of Jerusalem in **Acts** around 50 AD.
- He didn't want to be baptized until just before he died. It is speculated that he wanted to live the way he wanted until the end and then hope that baptism would wash away his sins.

> **Robert Godfrey:** "Many more modern historians have said in a lot of ways the conversion of Constantine was disastrous, or at least very difficult for the church, because from this moment on in all of Western history the life of the church and the life of the state are intertwined. And from this point on for much of Western history, the state becomes to some extent a supporter of the church, becomes part of the way in which the church operates. And it's very interesting Constantine establishes himself as emperor in 312 and in the very next year, 313. In the very next year, 313, the church appeals to him to render a theological judgment. There's a split in the church in North Africa, and the church tries to settle the split, they can't, and they appeal to the emperor to make a decision, a theological decision on who's right in the church and who's wrong, and when Constantine makes his decision, of course the losers won't listen, and Constantine sends troops into North Africa to suppress what he regards as the false church.
>
> So, almost in one year the Roman Empire goes from being a persecutor of the church to being a military defender of the true church according to its wisdom. And from that moment on in Western history over and over and over, the power of the government will be used, the claim will be made, in the interest of true religion.[1]

> John Calvin writes in "*A Treatise on Relics*": I have described, in the preceding chapter, the causes which made Christian worship gradually to deviate from its primitive purity, and to assume a character more adapted to the ideas of the heathen population,—numbers of whom were continually joining the church. It was, particularly since the time of Constantine, because its festivals, becoming every day more numerous, and its sanctuaries more solemn, spacious, and adorned with greater splendor,—its ceremonies more complicated,—its emblems more diversified,—offered to the Pagans an ample compensation for

---

1. Godfrey. *The Church and the State After Constantine*

the artistic pomp of their ancient worship . . . Paganism tried to borrow from Christianity its dogmas and its morals; Christianity took from Paganism its ornaments." 13 [015] Christianity would have become triumphant without these transformations. It would have done it later than it did, but its triumph would have been of a different kind from that which it has obtained by the assistance of these auxiliaries. "Christianity," says the author quoted above, "retrograded [moving backward]; but it was this which made its force." It would be more correct to say, that it advanced its external progress at the expense of its purity; it gained thus the favor of the crowd, but it was by other means that it obtained the approbation [praise or commendation] of the cultivated minds . . . The church made a compromise with Paganism in order to convert more easily its adherents [people that support it],—forgetting the precepts of the apostle, to beware of philosophy and vain traditions, (Col. ii. 8,) as well as to refuse profane and old wives' fables, (1 Tim. iv. 7.) And it cannot be doubted that St Paul knew well that a toleration of these things would have rapidly extended the new churches, had the quantity of the converts been more important than the quality of their belief and morals . . . . Hero-worship is innate to human nature, and it is founded on some of our noblest feelings,—gratitude, love, and admiration.—but which, like all other feelings, when uncontrolled by principle and reason, may easily degenerate into the wildest exaggerations, and lead to most dangerous consequences. It was by such an exaggeration of these noble feelings that Paganism filled the Olympus with gods and demigods,—elevating to this rank men who have often deserved the gratitude of their fellow-creatures, by some signal services rendered to the community, or their admiration, by having performed some deeds which required a more than usual degree of mental and physical powers. The same cause obtained for the Christian martyrs the gratitude and admiration of their fellow-Christians, and finally converted them into a kind of demigods. This was more particularly the case when the church began to be corrupted by her compromise with Paganism, which having been baptized without being converted, rapidly introduced into the Christian church, not only many of its rites and ceremonies, but even its polytheism [more than one god], with this difference, that the divinities of Greece and Rome were replaced by Christian saints, many of whom received the offices of their Pagan predecessors.[2]

2. Calvin. *A Treatise on Relics*

- Because Christianity was now controlled by the state . . . to go against the state was considered treason. Just like today, treason was punishable by death.
- Theodosius came to power fifty years later and ended the controversy in 380 when he established Nicene (Trinitarian) Christianity as the official religion of Rome.
    i. Unfortunately, this led to persecution of any person who was not a Christian.
- In 438 Theodosius II issued the Theodosian Code, which inflicted the penalty of death on those who denied the Trinity and on those who repeated baptism. (The Donatists)

THE COUNCIL OF NICAEA

- This is the second ecumenical (or worldwide) church council since Jerusalem in **Acts 15**.
- Three hundred eighteen bishops met in AD 325 for this council.
- The controversy was over the nature of Christ which was stirred by a man named Arias.

Arianism (Arias from Egypt)

- What does Arianism believe?
    - Arianism denies the Trinity.
    - They believe that Jesus was a creature made by the Father to do his creative work. He was then elevated to the Son of God because of his great virtue.
    - They believe Jesus was created alongside Lucifer and the angels.
- **Arias** (AD 256–336) questioned Alexander of Alexandria's teaching that Jesus was co-existent, co-eternal, and co-equal with God the Father.

Nicene Christianity

    i. This was a logical view. Logic was more important to Arias than the understanding of truth. We cannot dismiss logic, however, when it comes to God who is beyond our grasp of full comprehension. We must be careful in how logic is applied.

- Arias was condemned as a heretic, but Arianism had become such a problem that Constantine had to hold a council.
- Arias and his followers put his teaching to songs and music that became very popular, which led to this becoming a whole movement in Rome.
- Fights erupted in the streets and people were killed over this dispute.
    - i. Constantine didn't care what decision was made by the council, he just wanted to put an end to the dispute.
- The council body questioned how such a subordinated Christ—who was more than human, yet less than fully God—could impart salvation to humanity.
    - If Jesus wasn't truly God would his sacrifice be sufficient?
- Three positions on the deity of Christ were presented:

1. Hetero-ousious, (of a different substance) which was Arius's view.

    Logos is not co-eternal, co-essential with, or co-equal with the Father. He was a son born, such that there was a moment before the creation of the world when the Son was begotten or created. "If the Father begat the Son, he that was begotten had a beginning and there was a time when the Son was not."

    - What does "Logos" mean? (**John 1:1**) It means Word and refers to Jesus.

2. Homo-ousios, (of the same substance) which was Alexander's and Athanasius's view, along with all of church history.

    Logos is co-eternal with the Father, never to change.

3. Homoi-ousios (Of a similar substance)

An attempt to mediate between the other two views. Jesus was divine but not deity in the sense of being of the same nature as the Father.

Arias eventually adopted this view.

- Hetero-ousious was immediately rejected by the council whose job was to affirm what the church historically had always believed.
- Homoi-ousios was presented by Eusebius and quickly rejected as well.
- Three hundred sixteen of the three hundred eighteen bishops who were there affirmed what is called the Nicene Creed.

The Nicene Creed

> We believe in one God, the Father almighty, maker of heaven and earth, of all things visible and invisible. And in one Lord Jesus Christ, the only Son of God, begotten from the Father before all ages, God from God, Light from Light, true God from true God, begotten, not made; of the same essence as the Father. Through him all things were made. For us and for our salvation he came down from heaven; he became incarnate by the Holy Spirit and the virgin Mary, and was made human. He was crucified for us under Pontius Pilate; he suffered and was buried. The third day he rose again, according to the Scriptures. He ascended to heaven and is seated at the right hand of the Father. He will come again with glory to judge the living and the dead. His kingdom will never end. And we believe in the Holy Spirit, the Lord, the giver of life. He proceeds from the Father and the Son, and with the Father and the Son is worshiped and glorified. He spoke through the prophets. We believe in one holy catholic and apostolic church. We affirm one baptism for the forgiveness of sins. We look forward to the resurrection of the dead, and to life in the world to come. Amen.

- What modern day cult would be considered Arian? The Jehovah's Witnesses.

- Modern day Arians or Jehovah's Witnesses would take a Scripture like **Romans 8:2;** "*that He might be the first-born among many brethren*" and try to prove that Jesus is a creature.
- They also have their own bible called the New World Translation.
    - i. This translation has morphed with every new version to change its message in order to promote the Witnesses heretical doctrine.

> John MacArthur: "In Jewish culture the term first-born always referred to a son, unless a daughter was specifically stated. Because the first-born male child in a Jewish family had a privileged status, the term was often used figuratively to represent preeminence. In the present context that is clearly the meaning. As it is in almost every instance in the New Testament, the term brethren is a synonym for believers. God's primary purpose in His plan of redemption was to make His beloved Son the first-born among many brethren in the sense of Christ's being uniquely preeminent among the children of God. Those who trust in him become God's adopted children, and Jesus, the true Son of God, graciously deigns to call them his brothers and sisters in God's divine family (Matt. 12:50; cf. John 15:15). God's purpose is to make us like Christ in order to create a great redeemed and glorified humanity over which he will reign and be forever preeminent."[3]

- The secondary issue addressed at the Council of Nicaea was the date of Easter which also was controversial and needed to be resolved. They messed it up and now the date changes every year. It should have been at Passover.
    - i. Anti-Semitism had crept into the church and they wanted to distance themselves from the Jews.

Eusebius of Caesarea (275–339)

- Eusebius was a polemicist and an historian, known as the father of church history because of his extensive work.

---

3. MacArthur. *Jesus, the Firstborn Among Many Brethren*

- He was present at the Council of Nicaea.
- He contributed much in the way of church history, but I want to point out one of his writings on Penal Substitutionary Atonement. Penal Substitutionary Atonement has been attacked in recent years, being called a new doctrine that was born out of the Reformation.

> 19. "And the Lord hath laid on him our iniquities, and He bears our sins. Thus the Lamb of God, that taketh away the sins of the world, became a curse on our behalf: Whom, though he knew no sin, God made sin for our sake, giving Him as redemption for all, that we might become the righteousness of God in Him.
>
> 24. And the Lamb of God not only did this, but was chastised on our behalf, and suffered a penalty He did not owe, but which we owed because of the multitude of our sins; and so He became the cause of the forgiveness of our sins, because He received death for us, and transferred to Himself the scourging, the insults, and the dishonor, which were due to us, and drew down on Himself the apportioned curse, being made a curse for us."[4]

Also see the Epistle to Diognetus on page 73.

---

4. Eusebius. *The Book of Eusebius* #3

NOTES

The Nicene Fathers
Fourth Century

ATHANASIUS (296-373)

- Athanasius became the bishop shortly after the Council of Nicaea.
- He gets exiled several times (during changes of power) because of his immovable stance on the Trinity and earns the phrase "Athanasius against the world."
- He wrote a book in response to Arius called *On the Incarnation of the Word of God*.
- God sovereignly used this man to uphold the truth of the Trinity during this time.

The Athanasian Creed

> Now this is the catholic faith: We worship one God in trinity and the Trinity in unity, neither confusing the persons nor dividing the divine being.
> For the Father is one person, the Son is another, and the Spirit is still another.
> But the deity of the Father, Son, and Holy Spirit is one, equal in glory, coeternal in majesty.
> What the Father is, the Son is, and so is the Holy Spirit.
> Uncreated is the Father; uncreated is the Son; uncreated is the Spirit.
> The Father is infinite; the Son is infinite; the Holy Spirit is infinite.

Eternal is the Father; eternal is the Son; eternal is the Spirit: And yet there are not three eternal beings, but one who is eternal; as there are not three uncreated and unlimited beings, but one who is uncreated and unlimited.

Almighty is the Father; almighty is the Son; almighty is the Spirit: And yet there are not three almighty beings, but one who is almighty.

Thus the Father is God; the Son is God; the Holy Spirit is God: And yet there are not three gods, but one God.

Thus the Father is Lord; the Son is Lord; the Holy Spirit is Lord: And yet there are not three lords, but one Lord.

As Christian truth compels us to acknowledge each distinct person as God and Lord, so catholic religion forbids us to say that there are three gods or lords.

The Father was neither made nor created nor begotten; the Son was neither made nor created, but was alone begotten of the Father; the Spirit was neither made nor created, but is proceeding from the Father and the Son.

Thus there is one Father, not three fathers; one Son, not three sons; one Holy Spirit, not three spirits.

And in this Trinity, no one is before or after, greater or less than the other; but all three persons are in themselves, coeternal and coequal; and so we must worship the Trinity in unity and the one God in three persons.

Whoever wants to be saved should think thus about the Trinity.

It is necessary for eternal salvation that one also faithfully believe that our Lord Jesus Christ became flesh.

For this is the true faith that we believe and confess: That our Lord Jesus Christ, God's Son, is both God and man.

He is God, begotten before all worlds from the being of the Father, and he is man, born in the world from the being of his mother—existing fully as God, and fully as man with a rational soul and a human body; equal to the Father in divinity, subordinate to the Father in humanity.

Although he is God and man, he is not divided, but is one Christ.

He is united because God has taken humanity into himself; he does not transform deity into humanity.

He is completely one in the unity of his person, without confusing his natures.

For as the rational soul and body are one person, so the one Christ is God and man.

He suffered death for our salvation. He descended into hell and rose again from the dead.

He ascended into heaven and is seated at the right hand of the Father.

He will come again to judge the living and the dead.

At his coming all people shall rise bodily to give an account of their own deeds.

Those who have done good will enter eternal life, those who have done evil will enter eternal fire.

This is the catholic faith.

One cannot be saved without believing this firmly and faithfully.

- While we are on the subject of the Trinity, let's look at two more ... slightly more recent confessions of faith concerning this subject. These should be looked at closely by today's church who has largely turned away from creeds and confessions of faith, tragically so I must add.

1689 Baptist Confession: Of God and of the Holy Trinity

1. The Lord our God is but one only living and true God; whose subsistence is in and of himself, infinite in being and perfection; whose essence cannot be comprehended by any but himself; a most pure spirit, invisible, without body, parts, or passions, who only hath immortality, dwelling in the light which no man can approach unto; who is immutable, immense, eternal, incomprehensible, almighty, every way infinite, most holy, most wise, most free, most absolute; working all things according to the counsel of his own immutable and most righteous will for his own glory; most loving, gracious, merciful, long-suffering, abundant in goodness and truth, forgiving iniquity, transgression, and sin; the rewarder of them that diligently seek him, and withal most just and terrible in his judgments, hating all sin, and who will by no means clear the guilty.

2. God, having all life, glory, goodness, blessedness, in and of himself, is alone in and unto himself all-sufficient, not standing in need of any creature which he hath made, nor deriving any glory from them, but only manifesting his own glory in, by, unto, and upon them; he is the alone fountain of all being, of whom, through whom, and to whom are all things, and he hath

most sovereign dominion over all creatures, to do by them, for them, or upon them, whatsoever himself pleaseth; in his sight all things are open and manifest, his knowledge is infinite, infallible, and independent upon the creature, so as nothing is to him contingent or uncertain; he is most holy in all his counsels, in all his works, and in all his commands; to him is due from angels and men, whatsoever worship, service, or obedience, as creatures they owe unto the Creator, and whatever he is further pleased to require of them.

3. In this divine and infinite Being there are three subsistence's, the Father, the Word or Son, and Holy Spirit, of one substance, power, and eternity, each having the whole divine essence, yet the essence undivided: the Father is of none, neither begotten nor proceeding; the Son is eternally begotten of the Father; the Holy Spirit proceeding from the Father and the Son; all infinite, without beginning, therefore but one God, who is not to be divided in nature and being, but distinguished by several peculiar relative properties and personal relations; which doctrine of the Trinity is the foundation of all our communion with God, and comfortable dependence on him.

Westminster Confession of 1646: Of God, and Of the Holy Trinity

1. There is but one only, living, and true God, who is infinite in being and perfection, a most pure spirit, invisible, without body, parts, or passions; immutable, immense, eternal, incomprehensible, almighty, most wise, most holy, most free, most absolute; working all things according to the counsel of his own immutable and most righteous will, for his own glory; most loving, gracious, merciful, long-suffering, abundant in goodness and truth, forgiving iniquity, transgression, and sin; the rewarder of them that diligently seek him; and withal, most just, and terrible in his judgments, hating all sin, and who will by no means clear the guilty.

2. God hath all life, glory, goodness, blessedness, in and of himself; and is alone in and unto himself all-sufficient, not standing in need of any creatures which he hath made, nor deriving any glory from them, but only manifesting his own glory in, by, unto, and upon them. He is the alone fountain of all being, of whom, through whom, and to whom are all things; and hath most sovereign dominion over them, to do by them, for them, or upon them whatsoever himself pleaseth. In his sight

all things are open and manifest, his knowledge is infinite, infallible, and independent upon the creature, so as nothing is to him contingent, or uncertain. He is most holy in all his counsels, in all his works, and in all his commands. To him is due from angels and men, and every other creature, whatsoever worship, service, or obedience he is pleased to require of them.

3. In the unity of the Godhead there be three persons, of one substance, power, and eternity: God the Father, God the Son, and God the Holy Ghost: the Father is of none, neither begotten, nor proceeding; the Son is eternally begotten of the Father; the Holy Ghost eternally proceeding from the Father and the Son.

The Death of Arius as recorded by Athanasius

You have asked me to tell you about the death of Arius.

I debated with myself for a long time about whether or not to give you an answer, afraid that someone might assume I was taking pleasure in his death. But, since there has been a debate among your colleagues concerning the Arian heresy—in which the question was raised as to whether or not Arius was restored to the church before he died—I think it is necessary to give an account of his death. That way your question will be put to rest, and, at the same time, it will silence those who are contentious. My guess is that, when the incredible circumstances surrounding his death become known, even those who raise such questions will no longer doubt that the Arian heresy is hateful in the sight of God.

I was not in Constantinople when he died, but Macarius the presbyter was there, and I heard about what happened from him.

Arius, on account of his politically-powerful friends, had been invited to appear before the emperor Constantine. When he arrived, the emperor asked him whether or not he held to the orthodox beliefs of the universal church. Arius declared with an oath that he did, and gave an account of his beliefs in writing. But, in reality, he was twisting the Scriptures and not being honest about the points of doctrine for which he had been excommunicated.

Nonetheless, when Arius swore that he did not hold the heretical views for which he had been excommunicated, Constantine dismissed him, saying, "If your faith is orthodox, you have done well to swear; but if your beliefs are heretical, and you have sworn falsely, may God judge you according to your oath."

When Arius left the emperor, his friends wanted to immediately restore him to the church. But the bishop of Constantinople (a man named Alexander), resisted them, explaining that the inventor of such heresies should not be allowed to partake in communion. But Arius's friends threatened the bishop, saying, "In the same way that we brought him to the emperor, against your wishes, so tomorrow—though it be contrary to your wishes—Arius will have communion with us in this church." They said this on a Saturday.

When Alexander heard this, he was greatly distressed. He went into the church and stretched out his hands before God, and wept. Falling on his face, he prayed, "If Arius is allowed to take communion tomorrow, let me Your servant depart, and do not destroy that which is holy with that which is unholy. But if You will spare Your church (and I know that You will spare it), take note of the words of Arius's friends, and do not give Your inheritance to destruction and reproach. Please remove Arius from this world, lest he should enter the church and bring his heresy with him, and error would be treated as if it were truth." After the bishop finished praying, he retired to his room deeply concerned.

Then an incredible and extraordinary thing happened. While Arius's friends made threats, the bishop prayed. But Arius, who himself was making wild claims, unexpectedly became very ill. Urged by the necessities of nature he withdrew, and suddenly, in the language of Scripture, "falling headlong, he burst open in the middle," and immediately died where he lay. In an instant, he was deprived not only of communion, but of his very life.

That was the end of Arius.

His friends, overwhelmed with shame, went out and buried him. Meanwhile, the blessed bishop Alexander, amidst the rejoicing of the church, celebrated communion on Sunday with holiness and orthodoxy, praying with all the brethren. They greatly glorified God, not because they were taking joy in a man's death (God forbid!), for "it is appointed for men once to die," but because this matter had been resolved in a way that transcended human judgments.

For the Lord Himself had judged between the threats of Arius's friends and the prayers of the bishop Alexander. He condemned the Arian heresy, showing it to be unworthy of communion with the church. God made it clear to everyone, that although Arianism might receive the support of the emperor and even all mankind, yet it ought to be condemned by the church.

THE CAPPADOCIAN FATHERS (335-95)

- Who were the Cappadocian Fathers? Basil the Great, Gregory of Nyssa, and Gregory of Nazianzus.
- Where was Cappadocia? Modern day Turkey.

- The Cappadocian Fathers are best known for uniting in order to stand against Arianism.
    i. After the Council of Nicaea there were a number of bishops who sided with Arias and fought against the Nicene Creed. The Cappadocian Fathers fought against these bishops and helped firmly establish the teaching of the Trinity in the church.

- They are the ones responsible for adding "Holy Spirit" to the Nicene Creed forty-five or so years later at the Council of Constantinople.

"Let us then examine the points one by one. He (the Holy Spirit) is good by nature, in the same way as the Father is good, and the Son is good; the creature on the other hand shares in goodness by choosing the good. He knows "The deep things of God" (2 Cor. 3:17) the creature (by contrast) receives the manifestation of ineffable things through the Spirit. He quickens together with God, who produces and preserves all things alive, and together with the Son who gives life. "He that raised up Christ from the dead," it is said, "shall also quicken your mortal bodies by the spirit that dwells in you." (1 Cor 2:10–11) and again "my sheep hear my voice, and I give unto them eternal life," but Spirit "also, it is said, "gives life," (Rom 8:11) and again "the Spirit," it is said, "is life, because of righteousness." (John 10:27–28) And the Lord bears witness that "it is the Spirit that quickens; the flesh profits nothing." (2 Cor 3:6) How then shall we alienate the Spirit from His quickening power, and make Him belong to lifeless nature? Who is so contentious, who is so utterly without the heavenly gift, and unfed by God's good words, who is so devoid of part and lot in eternal hopes, as to serve the Spirit from the Godhead and rank him with the creature? Basil[1]

- Have you ever thought of the Holy Spirit as a force rather than a person? Discuss some of the work that the Holy Spirit does.

AMBROSE OF MILAN (339–97)

- Ambrose was the governor of Liguria and Emilia in Milan.
- He became Bishop of Milan while trying to find a replacement after the death of Bishop Auxentius. Auxentius was an Arian and his death caused division between Trinitarians and Arians as to who would replace him.
    i. Ambrose went to bring peace among the uproar. Even though he was a Trinitarian, both sides highly respected him. They began to chant "Ambrose, bishop!" He refused the office at first, yet finally accepted the position.
- He was an outstanding preacher and upholder of orthodoxy.
    i. Augustine was converted while in Milan while listening to the great orator Ambrose.
- His writing consists of ethics and morality against Paganism and Arianism. He also advocated the separation of church and state.
- Some scholars believe he wrote the Athanasian Creed.
- Below is an excerpt from one of Ambrose's sermons. Discuss some of what stands out in this message:

> 7. **Without doubt if the Lord hath appointed me to this combat, it is in vain that you have kept sleepless watch and ward through so many nights and days; the will of Christ will be performed.** For our Lord Jesus Christ is Almighty, this is our faith; and therefore, what he bids to be done will be fulfilled, nor does it become us to run counter to the divine will.
>
> 8. Ye have heard what has been read today: The Savior commanded an ass's colt to be brought to him by the apostles and

---

1. Basil. *Nicene and Post-Nicene Fathers*

commanded that if anyone sought to hinder them, they should say, (**S. Luke xix. 35**) *The Lord hath need of him.* What if now also he hath commanded this ass's colt, that is the colt of that animal **which is wont to bear a heavy burthen, such as is the condition of man**, to whom it is said, (**Matt. xi. 28. etc.**) *Come unto Me all ye that labour and are heavy laden, and I will give you rest: take My yoke upon you, for My yoke is easy*: what, I say, if he hath now commanded this colt to be brought to him, sending forth those apostles who now having put off the body, wear, invisibly to our eyes, the guise of angels? Will they not say, should any one seek to hinder them, *The Lord hath need of him*, **if either the desire of this life, or flesh and blood, or the conversation of the world, for perhaps we are acceptable to some persons, should seek to hinder them? But he who loves me here, cannot give a better testimony of his affection than by suffering me to become a sacrifice for Christ**; because (**Phil. i. 23**) *to be dissolved and to be with Christ is much better; howbeit,* **to remain in the flesh is more needful for your sakes.** Ye have therefore, my beloved brethren, no cause for fear, *for I know that whatever I shall suffer, I shall suffer for Christ*. And I have read that **I ought not to fear those who can kill the flesh**, and I have heard One say, (**Matt. x. 39**) *He who loses his life for My sake, shall find it.*

15. And did I not go out daily to make visits, or go to the tomb of the Martyrs? Did I not in going and returning pass close by the Royal palace? And yet no man arrested me, though they wished to drive me from the city, as they shewed afterwards by saying, 'Leave this city, and go where thou wilt.' **I expected, I confess, something great, to be burned or slain with the sword for the name of Christ, but they offered me delights in the place of sufferings; and yet the soldiers of Christ seeks not for delights but for sufferings**. Wherefore let no man trouble you by the intelligence that they have prepared a carriage, or that Auxentius, who calls himself Bishop, has uttered what he thinks terrible words.

34. Moreover they assert that the people have been beguiled by the strains of my hymns. I deny not this either. It is a lofty strain, than which nothing is more powerful. For **what can be more powerful than the confession of the Trinity, which is daily celebrated by the mouth of the whole people**? All zealously desire to make profession of their faith; they know how to confess in verse the Father and the Son and the Holy Spirit. Thus, all are become teachers who were scarcely able to be disciples.

35. But what can be more lowly than for us to follow the example of Christ, Who (Phil. iii. 7) *being found in fashion as*

a man humbled himself being made obedient unto death. And again, by obedience he delivered all: (Rom. v. 19) For as by the disobedience of one man many were made sinners, so by the obedience of one Man shall many be made righteous. If then he was obedient let them learn from him the lesson of obedience, to which we adhere, saying to them who raise odium against us, on the Emperor's account, We render to Cæsar the things that are Cæsar's, and to God the things that are God's. To Cæsar tribute is due, we deny it not; the church is God's, and must not be given up to Cæsar, because the Temple of God cannot by right be Cæsar's.[2]

JEROME (347–420)

- Jerome is best known as a scholar.
- He translated the Scriptures into Latin, known as *The Latin Vulgate*.
    i. The canon had already been established.
    ii. Jerome and Augustine disagreed on whether it was necessary to know Hebrew to translate the Old Testament. Augustine believed it was enough to know Greek because of the Septuagint.
- Jerome wanted to put the Scriptures into the language of the people. Roman Catholics, a thousand years later, refuse to let them be translated into any other language, though Latin was no longer the common language.
- He translated the Greek word "metanoia" which means repentance, into the word penance which causes confusion later in Roman Catholicism.
    i. Roman Catholics started teaching that penance must be performed for reconciliation after one had been baptized.
- He also included the apocrypha in his Vulgate which again causes problems later. However, he was very clear in his introduction that the apocrypha was neither inspired nor canonical. He thought

---

2. Ambrose. *The Letters of S. Ambrose.*

they were helpful for edification. Eleven-hundred years later at the Council of Trent the Roman Catholic Church embraces the apocrypha as canonical.

"As then the Church reads Judith, Tobit and the books of Maccabees, but does not admit them among the canonical Scriptures, so let it read these two volumes (Wisdom of Solomon and Ecclesiasticus) for the edification of the people, not to give authority to doctrines of the Church"[3]

- He preferred to be left to himself to study his books which consisted largely of the church fathers and Scripture.
- He wrote many biblical commentaries and wrote polemics against Arius and Pelagianism.
- He emphasized the exegetical study of Scripture and the importance of Christ-centered preaching.
    i. This is the correct way to preach . . . exegetically and Christ-centered.
    ii. Today many pastors focus on man-centered topical sermons.
        a. A term has been applied to this type of preaching called Moralistic Therapeutic Deism.
        b. Application is often the replacement of exegesis which confuses the job of The Holy Spirit with the pastor.
- He overemphasized the merits of celibacy including the perpetual virginity of Mary.
    i. Prior to Constantine, to be a Christian was a radical thing. After Constantine everyone was professing to be a Christian because it was the state religion, and some of the ideas of being radical gave people the idea to move into the desert or wilderness to be alone, practicing asceticism and morality. This led to the idea that suffering and celibacy was holy which led to the idea that Mary must have been a perpetual virgin. Many of the bishops fled to the desert during exile and spent time with these hermits or radicalized Christians.

---

3. Jerome. *Preface to Jerome's Works*. P. 492.

a. If you remember, suffering in order to be faithful is known as Monasticism which got suffering and faithfulness backwards.

- Is it biblical for us to remove ourselves entirely from the world and become hermits or start Christian societies? Why is this a bad idea?

Letter LIII To Paulinus "*A mind willing to learn deserves commendation even when it has no teacher*. What is of importance to me is not what you find but what you seek to find. Wax is soft and easy to mold even where the hands of craftsman and modeler are wanting to work it. It is already potentially all that it can be made. The apostle Paul learned the Law of Moses and the prophets at the feet of Gamaliel and was glad that he had done so, for armed with this spiritual armor, he was able to say boldly "the weapons of our warfare are not carnal, but mighty through God to the pulling down of strongholds;" armed with these we war "casting down imaginations and every high thing that exalteth itself against the knowledge of God, and bringing into captivity every thought to the obedience of Christ; and being in a readiness to revenge all disobedience." He writes to Timothy who had been trained in the holy writings from a child *exhorting him to study them diligently and not to neglect the gift which was given him with the laying on of the hands of the presbytery*. To Titus he gives commandment that among a bishop's other virtues (which he briefly describes) *he should be careful to seek a knowledge of the Scriptures*: A bishop, he says, must hold fast "the faithful word as he hath been taught *that he may be able by sound doctrine both to exhort and to convince the gainsayers.*" Jerome[4]

- What is Jerome's main point in this excerpt?

JOHN CHRYSOSTOM (347–407)
THE BISHOP OF CONSTANTINOPLE

- John is best known as a preacher.
- He stressed a grammatical-historical context for the interpretation of Scripture. Allegorizing Scripture had become popular after Origen.

---

4. Jerome. *The Letters: To Paulinus.*

- He desired a monastic life and became a hermit. Like many hermits, his health was damaged as a result of self-inflicted suffering.
- After becoming a bishop, he became known as "Golden Mouthed" due to both his ability to preach and his great oratory skills.
- He was a great expositor of Scripture including the books of Genesis, Matthew, John, Romans, Galatians, Corinthians, Ephesians, 1 Timothy, and Titus. He wrote commentaries on these books that are known as his Homilies.

"For we ought to unlock the passage by first giving a clear interpretation of the words. What then does the saying mean? We must not attend to the words merely, but turn our attention to the sense, and learn the aim of the speaker, and the cause and the occasion, and by putting all these things together turn out the hidden meaning."[5] John Chrysostom

  i. These are all the building blocks of a literal, grammatical, historical hermeneutic. When a Bible teacher strays from this, his aim will be at the wrong thing.
    - What are hermeneutics?
      - Hermeneutics refers to the way that you interpret the Bible as a whole book. The key to good hermeneutics or Bible interpretation is **context, context, context.** The best way to interpret Scripture is by other Scriptures.

- His Homilies are very clear that salvation is by faith through grace. He is very heavy on Lordship salvation because, much like today, everyone was claiming to be Christians but without showing any fruit.

> Homilies on Hebrews "O! the wisdom of the apostle! or rather, not the wisdom of Paul, but the grace of the Spirit is the thing to wonder at. For surely he uttered not these things of his own mind, nor in that way did he find his wisdom. (For whence could it be? From the knife, and the skins, or the workshop?) But it was from the working of God. For his own understanding did not give birth to these thoughts, which was then so mean and slender as in nowise to surpass the baser sort; (for how could it, seeing it spent itself wholly on bargains and skins?) but the grace of the Spirit shows forth its strength by whomsoever it will."[6]

---

5. Chrysostom. *Selected Homilies.* P. 157
6. Chrysostom. *Nicene and Post-Nicene Fathers: Homilies on Hebrews.* P. 367

- What does Chrysostom do at the beginning of this excerpt? Points our attention to Paul and then skillfully pulls our eyes toward God . . . showing what?

AUGUSTINE (354-430) THE BISHOP OF HIPPO

- Augustine is best known for systematic theology.
- He stands as the most influential person in church history prior to Martin Luther.
- His mother was a Christian named Monica; Santa Monica is named after her. She is an example of living out the Christian life to win her family, which almost all became Christians because of her witness and faithfulness to the gospel.
- Augustine turned his back on the gospel in his youth. He lived with a woman out of wedlock for fourteen years. They had a son who died at the age of thirteen.
- He referred to God as "the Hound of Heaven" who was busy tracking him down because he always seemed to be fleeing God.
  - What attribute of God reflects him being the Hound of Heaven, and is this comforting?
- His most famous books are *City of God* and *Confessions of St. Augustine*.
- All the Doctrines of Grace (five points of Calvinism) are found in his writings.
- Augustine responded polemically to Pelagian who denied the consequences of the fall and taught that good works can lead to redemption, among other heresies.
- Augustine taught that we have free will but free will is limited to only being able to sin.
  - i. Men's free will always chooses to do that which is sinful and cannot choose that which is righteous because our will has been enslaved by sin after the fall of Adam. They are dead in their trespasses and sins as Scripture puts it.

- He emphasized the depravity of human nature due to the sin of Adam (original sin) and the necessity of divine predestination and the priority of faith over reason.
    i. Pelagianism emphasizes human ability and free will rather than depravity and sinfulness . . . even the possibility of living without sin. Adam's sin applied only to Adam and there was no result or fall of mankind into the curse of sin.
    ii. A middle ground was developed (like all controversies) later called Semi-Pelagianism. It emphasized that faith begins independently of God's grace, although such grace is subsequently necessary for salvation. Roman Catholics and Arminianism will take this position. See page 228 for more on Arminianism.

On Nature and Grace, against Pelagius "Man's nature, indeed, was created at first faultless and without any sin; but that nature of man in which everyone is born from Adam, now wants [needs] the Physician, because it is not sound. All good qualities, no doubt, which it still possesses in its make, life, senses, intellect, it has of the Most High God, its Creator and Maker. But the flaw, which darkens and wakens all those natural goods, so that it has need of illumination and healing, it has not contracted from its blameless Creator-but from that original sin, which it committed by free will. Accordingly, criminal nature has its part in most righteous punishment. For, if we are now newly created in Christ, we were, for all that, children of wrath, even as others, "But God, who is rich in mercy, for His great love wherewith He loved us, even when we were dead in sins, hath quickened us together with Christ, by whose grace we were saved."[7] Augustine

Confessions "Great are You, O Lord, and greatly to be praised: great is Your power, and of Your wisdom there is no end. And man, being a part of Your creation, desires to praise You, man, who bears about with him his mortality, the witness of his sin, even the witness that You 'resist the proud,'—yet man, this part of Your creation, desires to praise You. You move us to delight in praising You; for You have formed us for Yourself, and our hearts are restless till they find rest in You Lord . . . And those who seek the Lord shall praise Him. Let me seek You, Lord, in calling on You, and call on You in believing in You; for You have

---

7. Augustine. *On Nature and Grace*. Ramsey. P. 321

been preached unto us, O Lord, my faith calls on You,—that faith which You have imparted to me, which You have breathed into me through the incarnation of Your son, through the ministry of Your preacher."[8] Augustine

- Discuss some of the doctrines found in the above excerpt.
    - How important is it for us to understand imputation?

PELAGIUS (360-420)

- Pelagius was Augustine's opposition, probably the most influential heretic after Arius.
- He taught that good works can eventually lead to redemption.
- He believed humans are basically good and have the free will to choose what is right.
- He denied the consequences of Adam's fall.
- These heresies are known as **Pelagianism**.
- Let's take a very quick look at **The Doctrine of Federal Headship** in order to see what Scripture teaches.

Genesis 3:4-5 *4 The serpent said to the woman, "You surely will not die! 5 "For God knows that in the day you eat from it your eyes will be opened, and* <u>you will be like God</u> . . .

- The Doctrine of Federal Headship is taken from Romans chapter 5. It shows that Adam was the representative of the entire world . . . all of his descendants. We are all born into sin. This is one of the many reasons Pelagius was deemed a heretic.
    i. Many Bible teachers have said that if there is one spot that your Bible should always open to, it is Romans chapter 5.

Romans 5:12-14 *12 Therefore, just as **through one man sin entered into the world**, and death through sin, **and so death spread to all men**, because all sinned—13 for until the Law sin was in the world, but sin is not **imputed** when there is no law. 14 Nevertheless **death reigned from***

---

8. Augustine. *The Life and Writings of St. Augustine. The Confessions*

Adam until Moses, even over those who had not sinned in the likeness of the offense of Adam, *who is a type of Him who was to come.*

Sin entered into the world. It is important to understand that sin has no physical or spiritual substance, it is an action against God's command. A command that reflects his nature. *Death spread to all men* because all men were in Adam's loins. *because all sinned,* is a Greek aorist tense (past tense without duration or completion of action) indicating that at one specific point in time all men sinned . . . pointing to Adam. Death was in the world before God gave the Law. There would be no death if there were no sin.

Paul brilliantly uses contrasts in many of his writings. It is important to understand this in order to see the overall context of what he is teaching. Here we see that he uses the contrast of the first Adam who imputed sin to everyone in contrast to the last Adam (Jesus). Jesus imputed righteousness to all who will believe. Just as we all were not physically present when Adam sinned, we were not physically present when Jesus was crucified. This is the tragedy and beauty of imputation.

- Sin was imputed from our "federal head" Adam to all people ever born. That is the first part of Federal Headship. The second part is concerning the last Adam, Jesus (**1 Corinthians 15:40**) who imputed righteousness to all who would believe.

Romans 5:15–17 *15 But the free gift is not like the transgression. For if by the transgression of the one the many died, much more did the grace of God and the gift by the grace of the one Man, Jesus Christ, abound to the many. 16 The gift is not like that which came through the one who sinned; for on the one hand the judgment arose from one transgression resulting in condemnation, but on the other hand the free gift arose from many transgressions resulting in justification. 17 For if by the transgression of the one, death reigned through the one, much more those who receive the abundance of grace and of the gift of righteousness will reign in life through the One, Jesus Christ.*

Semi-Pelagianism (enter the middle ground)

- It agrees with the curse on mankind after Adam's fall and that man is depraved.

- It still agrees with the free will choice of man when it comes to justification. In other words, man can still do one thing right.
    i. This leads to a synergistic view of salvation that man is involved in the process of justification. This will become the Arminian view.

If man has even the smallest part in choosing salvation, even by the wiggling of a finger to get God's attention, wouldn't that give a degree of glory to that person? If the wiggling of a finger came from that person, where did this thought, or response come from? Was there some integral quality that this person possesses that their neighbor does not . . . and if so where did that come from?

NOTES

The History of Eschatology

Before we get into this topic, I understand that for many people this is a hot button issue. And it is for that reason that I will give you my stance at the start of this chapter. I will be critical of all the major views of eschatology and do not consider myself to hold fully to any of them. I must say that I have embraced three of the views we are about to review, at one time or the other, and I carefully studied each from its source of greatest scholarship. However, I stand with the church fathers and take a literal view of Scripture attempting to keep the same hermeneutic from beginning to end and would call myself a premillennialist. If you are teaching a class and hold to a different eschatology, I suggest you look critically at my work and help your students to research and study for themselves. We must be careful not to pick our favorite ball team, to always root for them leaving out careful scholarship. A word of advice is this: never study anything whether it be eschatology or soteriology from the view of its critics. Go to the ones that embrace your topic first. If you are studying Calvinism don't study it from an Arminian whose goal is to refute it. Find its greatest scholars. And if you are studying amillennialism, postmillennialism, or premillennialism, do the same. A study of premillennialism from an amillennialist perspective will not help you decide for yourself.

- Eschatology is not something we should divide over; it is not essential to salvation. However, it is nevertheless, very important. Prophecy takes up as much as one-fourth of the Scriptures, so we should not take it lightly.
- There are four major views concerning the millennium.

1. **Amillennialism** (no-millennium) teaches that Jesus does not set up a physical kingdom on earth in the future, rather he set up a spiritual kingdom at his resurrection. They believe this is fulfilled by the church which includes both Jew and Gentile.
2. **Premillennialism** (chiliasm [kil-ee-az-uhm]) teaches that there is a literal, physical, future one-thousand-year millennium after the second coming of Christ.
    i. Within premillennialism there are two major camps: Dispensationalism and Historic Premillennialism. (there are additional nuances as well)
        a. **Dispensationalism** places Israel at the center of the one-thousand-year millennium in order to fulfill prophecies of the Old Testament that have not been fulfilled yet.
        b. **Historic Premillennialism** believes the millennium is for the church.
3. **Postmillennialism** teaches that through the gospel the world is getting better. After the world is Christianized it will usher in the return of Christ. We are currently in the millennial kingdom.
    i. This was popular among the Puritans because of the surge in Christianity and return to orthodoxy during that time.
    ii. **Dominionism** (also known as "Kingdom Now Theology") has a similar view and is popular today by **the 7-mountain mandate** of the New Apostolic Reformation. They believe that Christ will return after seven things have been conquered by Christians including: government, religion, art/entertainment, family, education, business and media. (See page 308)
4. **Preterism** teaches that <u>all</u> of bible prophecy was fulfilled in 70 AD with the destruction of Jerusalem.

- Hermeneutics is at the heart of this debate.
    - Do we keep to a literal, grammatical, historical hermeneutic for all of Scripture or do we change our hermeneutic to a spiritual allegory when it comes to prophecy and certain books of the Bible?

- Some amillennial scholars imply that if you apply a literal hermeneutic to Scripture you will come out a premillennialist:

Herman Bavinck: "All the prophets, with equal vigor and force, announce not only the conversion of Israel and the nations but also the return to Palestine, the rebuilding of Jerusalem, the restoration of the temple, the priesthood, and sacrificial worship, and so on. Prophecy pictures for us but one single image of the future. And this image is either to be taken literally as it presents itself (and premillennialists take it) or this image calls for a very different interpretation that is attempted by chiliasm [Premillennialism]."[1]

William Masselink: "If all prophecy must be interpreted in a literal way, the chiliastic (premillennial) views are correct; but if it can be proved that these prophecies have a spiritual meaning, then chiliasm must be rejected"[2]

Anthony Hoekema: "Amillennialists, on the other hand, believe that though many Old Testament prophecies are indeed to be interpreted literally, many others are to be interpreted in a nonliteral way."[3]

Graeme Goldsworthy: "It could be argued that, though the details may be hard to pin down because of the prophetic preference for poetic imagery and metaphor, the big picture is abundantly clear. On this basis, the literalist asserts that God reveals through the prophets that his kingdom came with the return of the Jews to Palestine, the rebuilding of Jerusalem, and the restoration of the temple . . . The literalist must become a futurist, since a literalistic fulfillment of all Old Testament prophecy has not yet taken place."[4]

- What is a strawman argument? It is an intentional misrepresentation of your opponent's stance in order to easily refute it.
    i. Strawman arguments or improper understanding of premillennialism is mostly what you will hear because there is no argument against premillennialism found in Scripture without reading into Scripture simply what it does not say. These will mostly be things learned from the leaders of the ball team they are rooting for.

1. Bavinck. *The Last Things*
2. Masselink. *Why Thousand Years?* P. 31
3. Hoekema. *The Meaning of the Millennium*. P. 172
4. Goldsworthy. *Gospel-Centered Hermeneutics*. P. 170

- Why would Scripture be interpreted in any other way than literal and where in church history does amillennialism arise?

• In John McArthur's sermon called "Why every Calvinist should be a Premillennialist" he asks four questions:

1. Does the Old Testament support Amillennialism?
2. Were the intertestamental Jews Amillennialist?
3. Does the New Testament support Amillennialism?

(Does it refute a literal millennium?)

4. Was Christ an Amillennialist?

The answer to all of these questions is no.

- We could also ask, were the early church fathers amillennial?

• The early church fathers were not amillennialist, but premillennialist. There is no record for the first two and a half centuries that would point at all to amillennialism.

Philp Schaff (A nineteenth century historian) wrote: "The most striking point in the eschatology of the ante-Nicene age is the prominent chiliasm, or millenarianism, that is the belief of a visible reign of Christ in glory on earth with the risen saints for a thousand years, before the general resurrection and judgment. It was indeed not the doctrine of the church embodied in any creed or form of devotion, but a widely current opinion of distinguished teachers, such as Barnabas, Papias, Justin Martyr, Irenaeus, Tertullian, Methodius, and Lactantius.[5]

Roger E. Olson (A recent Professor of Theology at Truett Theological Seminary) writes: Augustine (in the fourth century) developed what has come to be known as amillennialism, where most of the earliest church fathers were premillennialists.[6]

> Leon J. Wood (a twentieth century theologian) writes: "There is a general agreement among scholars that the view of the early church was premillennial. That is, Christians held that Christ

---

5. Schaff. *History of the Christian Church*. P. 614
6. McArthur. *Christ's Prophetic Plans*

would rule over a literal, earthly kingdom for one thousand years, assisted by raptured saints. No church fathers of the first two centuries are known to have disagreed with this view. The following may be listed as those who favored it: from the first century, Aristio, John the Presbyter, Clement of Rome, Barnabas, Hermas, Ignatius, Polycarp, and Papias. From the second, Pothinus, Justin Martyr, Melito, Hegisippus, Tatian, Irenaeus, Tertullian, and Hippolytus."[7]

Ephraim of Nisibis (306–73) (Pseudo-Ephraim) " For all the saints and elect of God are **gathered, prior to the tribulation** that is to come, and are taken to the Lord lest they see the confusion that is to overwhelm the world because of our sins."[8]

- As we see from Ephraim, dispensationalism did not start with John Nelson Darby as others like to claim.

  Papias (as quoted by Irenaeus) "The blessing that is foretold belongs without question to the times of the kingdom, when the righteous will rise from the dead and rule, and the creation that is renewed and set free will bring forth the dew of heaven and the fertility of the soil and abundance of food of all kinds. Thus the elders who saw John, the disciple of the Lord, remembered hearing him say how the Lord used to teach about those times, saying. "The days are coming when vines will come forth, each with ten thousand boughs and on a single bough will be ten thousand branches. So too the remaining fruits and seeds and vegetation will produce in similar proportions. And all the animals who eat this food drawn from the earth will come to be at peace and harmony with one another, yielding in complete submission to humans. Papias as well, and ancient man- the one who heard John and was a companion of Polycarp—gives a written account of these things in the fourth of his books."[9]

  Justin Martyr: (*Dialogue with Trypho the Jew*)" I and others, who are right-minded Christians on all points, are assured that there will be a resurrection of the dead, and a thousand years in Jerusalem, which will then be built, adorned, and enlarge, [as] the prophets Ezekiel and Isaiah and others declare. We have perceived, moreover, that the expression, "The day of the Lord is

---

7. Wood. *The Bible & Future Events*. P. 35
8. Ephraim. *The Bride Redeemed*
9. Papias. *The Apostolic Fathers*. P. 93

as a thousand years," is connected with this subject. And further, there was a certain man with us, whose name was John, one of the apostles of Christ, who prophesied, by a revelation that was made to him, that those who believed in our Christ would dwell a thousand years in Jerusalem; and that thereafter the general, and, in short, the eternal resurrection and judgement of all men would likewise take place."[10]

Irenaeus "But when this Antichrist shall have devastated all things in this world, he will reign for three years and six months, and sit in the temple at Jerusalem; and then the Lord will come from heaven in the clouds, in the glory of the Father, sending this man and those who follow him into the lake of fire; but bringing in for the righteous the times of the kingdom, that is, the rest, the hallowed seventh day; and restoring to Abraham the promised inheritance, in which kingdom of the Lord declared, that 'many coming from the east and from the west should sit down with Abraham, Isaac, and Jacob.'"[11]

Note: The Alexandrian school of hermeneutics started the amillennial view with Clement of Alexandria around 250 AD. This school took an allegorical hermeneutic of Scripture. Amillennialism grows with Origen and is eventually popularized by Augustine, who changes his eschatology from historic premillennial.

Four factors that contribute to amillennialism

1. Replacement Theology

- Replacement theology, or "supersessionism" teaches that the church has replaced or superseded the Jews as the true people of God.

    i. Proponents of this view will argue that the church simply continued from the Jews rather than replacing them.

- In the early church, replacement theology began to develop as animosity between Jews and Christians grew more intense.

    i. Much like Martin Luther's frustration with the Jews because they would not accept Christ; the early church began to view Jews as the enemy.

10. Justin. *Dialogue with Trypho*
11. Irenaeus. *The Ante-Nicene Fathers*. P. 560

The History of Eschatology 111

- Is it easy to make someone or a people group your enemy because they are different from you or will not cooperate with you?

- *The Epistle of Barnabas* was a premillennial book. It treats the prophecies of Daniel as premillennial yet uses allegorical hermeneutics and replacement theology which lays the groundwork for amillennialism.

- The nation of Israel was destroyed in 70 AD and the early church believed it was living in the first part of the Tribulation prior to the final three and a half years ruled by the Antichrist as we saw mentioned by Irenaeus. With a destroyed Israel, the early church saw no room for it to ever be reestablished as a nation as it will be in 1948. How can God's promises be fulfilled to a nation that does not exist?

- Constantine seemingly established what would be viewed as a Christian kingdom on earth or millennial kingdom.

- After the western half of Rome falls, the Roman Catholic Church sees itself as the millennial kingdom.

2. Allegorical Hermeneutics

- We already noted that *The Epistle of Barnabas* adopted the allegorical hermeneutic.
- Origen comes up with the three-fold meaning of Scripture:
    i. The literal meaning
    ii. The spiritual meaning
    iii. The ethical meaning
    iv. Augustine adds a fourth, eschatological.
        a. Paganism used allegorical meanings to teach moralistic virtues to people because their gods had become so bad in *The Iliad and Odyssey*, their stories couldn't be taken literally.

Fred Tatford (A modern writer) "The first prominent opponent (of a literal millennium) was Clement of Alexandria, who had been influenced by Platonic idealistic philosophy and had adopted the Greek allegorical method of interpretation of the Scriptures. Clement's teaching was carried much further by his pupil Origen (who had also been affected by the system of allegorization originally formulated by Aristobulus in 160 BC)"[12]

- Remember that Gnostics teach that the material is inferior to the spiritual.

Paul Benware (A modern writer) "Origen and other scholars in Alexandria were greatly influenced by Greek philosophy and attempted to integrate that philosophy with Christian theology. Included in Greek philosophy was the idea that those things that were material and physical were inherently evil. Influenced by this thinking, these Alexandrian Scholars concluded that an earthly kingdom of Christ with its many physical blessings would be something evil."[13]

3. An aversion to supposed sensuality

- This is a result of the influence of Gnosticism and Monasticism as well.
- Opponents of the millennial view, especially by the fourth century, came to view premillennialism as the system that motivated Christians with the promise of future carnal enjoyments. They rejected premillennialism out of an aversion to such sensual pleasures.
    i. We still see this today, especially with regards to the rapture of the church in which some claim is escapism.

Keith Mathison (A modern Theologian) "Early in his Christian life, Augustine had been attracted to millennialism, but he later rejected it. His rejection of it, it seems, was largely due to some of the excessively carnal versions of millennialism that were current in his day."[14]

Augustine "This opinion (a future literal millennium after the resurrection) might be allowed, if it purposed only spiritual delight unto the saints during this space (and we were one of the same opinion ourselves); but seeing that avouchers hereof affirm that the saints after this resurrection shall do nothing but revel in fleshly banquets, where the cheer shall exceed both modesty and measure, this is gross and fit

---

12. Nathan Busenitz: *Lecture 14: Historical Theology 1*. 2012
13. Benware. *Understanding End Times Prophecy*
14. MaArthur. *Christ's Prophetic Plans*

for none but carnal men to believe. But they that are really and truly spiritual do call those of this opinion Chiliasts."[15]

- John Piper refutes these ideas of sensuality with what he calls "Christian Hedonism" in his book *Desiring God*. Our ultimate and total joy is found only in God himself.

4. Medieval Confirmation

- Augustine's eschatology became the eschatology of the Middle Ages. He is referred to as the "father of amillennialism."

Millard J. Erickson (A Modern Theologian) "The first three centuries of the church were probably dominated by what we would today call premillennialism, but in the fourth century an African Donatist named Tyconius propounded a competitive view. Although Augustine was an arch opponent of the Donatists, he adopted Tyconius's view of the millennium. This interpretation was to dominate eschatological thinking throughout the Middle ages."[16]

- Fast forward to the Reformation and eschatology was not their focus. They accepted the amillennialism that they had been taught.

To give an analogy; if the world were at war and you had to choose between stopping a nuclear holocaust or stopping a soldier charging at your army with nothing more than a bugle, what would be your focus? The reformers spent their time and energy on understanding and teaching more pressing issues.

   i. It is strange that John Calvin fought for a grammatical, historical hermeneutic yet when it came to prophecy, he was inconsistent by using an allegorical approach.

- What are grammatical, historical hermeneutics? The way to interpret Scripture by looking at the context, the historic setting, and the original language. It also looks at all passages of Scripture and how they all tie together perfectly. Think of it as harmony within an orchestra. They are all playing the same song. If one wrong note is played it stands out.

15. Augustine. *The City of God*
16. Erickson. *Christian Theology*

John Calvin: "The error of allegory has been the source of many evils. Not only did it open the way for the adulteration of the natural meaning of Scripture but also set up boldness in allegorizing as the chief exegetical virtue. We must . . . entirely reject the allegories of Origen, and of others like him, which Satan, with the deepest subtlety, has endeavored to introduce into the church, for the purpose of rendering the doctrine of Scripture ambiguous and destitute of all certainty and firmness. Let us know that the true meaning of Scripture is the genuine and simple one and let us embrace and hold it tightly. Let us . . . boldly set aside as deadly corruptions, those fictitious expositions which lead us away from the literal sense."[17]

- An example of Calvin's inconsistent hermeneutic related to prophecy:

Amos 9: 11 *"In that day I will raise up the fallen booth of David, And wall up its breaches; I will also raise up its ruins And rebuild it as in the days of old; 12 That they may possess the remnant of Edom And all the nations who are called by My name," Declares the Lord who does this. 13 "Behold, days are coming," declares the Lord, "When the plowman will overtake the reaper And the treader of grapes him who sows seed; When the mountains will drip sweet wine And all the hills will be dissolved. 14 "Also I will restore the captivity of My people Israel, And they will rebuild the ruined cities and live in them; They will also plant vineyards and drink their wine, And make gardens and eat their fruit. 15 "I will also plant them on their land, And they will not again be rooted out from their land Which I have given them," Says the Lord your God.*

John Calvin on Amos 9: "Here the Prophet describes the felicity which shall be under the reign of Christ: and we know that whenever the Prophets set forth promises of a happy and prosperous state to God's people, they adopt metaphorical expressions, and say, that abundance of all good things shall flow, that there shall be the most fruitful produce, that provisions shall be bountifully supplied; for they accommodated their mode of speaking to the notions of that ancient people; it is therefore no wonders if they sometimes speak to them as to children. At the same time, the Spirit under these figurative expressions declares, that the kingdom of Christ shall in every way

---

17. Calvin. *John Calvin's Exegesis of the Old Testament*. P. 107

be happy and blessed, or that the Church of God, which means the same thing, shall be blessed, when Christ shall begin to reign ... Further, what is here said of the abundance of corn and wine, must be explained with reference to the nature of Christ's kingdom. As then the kingdom of Christ is spiritual, it is enough for us, that it abounds in spiritual blessings; and the Jews, whom God reserved for himself as a remnant, were satisfied with this spiritual abundance. If anyone objects and says, that the Prophet does not speak here allegorically; the answer is ready at hand, even this,—that it is a manner of speaking everywhere found in Scripture, that a happy state is painted as it were before our eyes, by setting before us the conveniences of the present life and earthly blessings: this may especially be observed in the Prophets, for they accommodated their style, as we have already stated, to the capacities of a rude and weak people."[18]

---

18. Calvin, John. *Commentary on the Minor Prophets. Amos 9:11 and 15*

NOTES

Controversies and Councils

- An ecumenical council refers to both eastern and western churches of Rome coming together for the sake of resolving controversy.

    i. The first three councils involved more than Roman church leaders, such as the Assyrians, Persians, and others.

- How many ecumenical councils were there, and can you name them? There were seven ecumenical councils:

1. Nicaea
2. Constantinople
3. Ephesus
4. Chalcedon
5. The Second Council of Constantinople
6. The Third Council of Constantinople
7. The Second Council of Nicaea

- We stand on what Scripture says and not what councils say. The councils were to back, defend, and clarify what is taught in Scripture. However, as we have seen previously, they sometimes got a little sidetracked and the seventh council particularly got way off track.
- Central to these controversies is the nature of Christ . . . who is he?

    i. They fought for three centuries over this. Even though it was settled at these councils, the controversy still rages on today, partly because of our ignorance of church history and Christology.

- They fought over every detail of the nature of Christ. This shows how important that every detail is!
    i. This should be encouraging to us because they actually cared about getting every detail as accurate as possible.
    - How important is it to get Jesus's nature correct?

- Unfortunately, today most evangelicals probably believe some type of heresy concerning the nature of Christ. This is due in part to a lack of teaching Christology from church pastors and leaders.

JESUS OF THE SCRIPTURES IS TRULY GOD AND TRULY MAN

Note: "100 percent" or "fully" are not good terms to describe Jesus. It paints the misunderstanding that his incarnation is full yet divided rather than inseparable.

Pick your Heresy	100 Percent God	100 Percent man
Ebionism	**Denied** page 34	**Affirmed**
Docetism/Gnosticism	**Affirmed** page 35-36	**Denied**
Arianism	**Denied** page 42	**Affirmed** (a creature)
Monarchianism	**Denied** page 38	**Affirmed**
Apollinarianism	**Affirmed** (hand in glove or God inhabits the shell of the person Jesus) page 41	**Denied** (no soul)
Nestorianism	**Affirmed** (two separate persons in one body) page 45	**Affirmed** (water and oil in one container)

Pick your Heresy	100 **Percent God**	100 **Percent man**
Eutychianism (Monophysitism) [One nature]	**Affirmed** (human nature absorbed into God creating a third nature) page 44	**Affirmed** (a hybrid isn't really fully anything, Jell-O)
Monothelitism	**Affirmed** (both natures had one will) page 124	**Affirmed** (no temptation)
New Apostolic Reformation	**Denied** (emptied himself or Kenosis) page 307	**Affirmed** (miracles by the power of the Spirit)

- The Chalcedonian creed uses very intentional words. They chose the word "truly" to describe the nature of Jesus to avoid confusion.
    - What is the theological term for Jesus being truly God and truly man (Vere Deus/Vere homos)? The hypostatic union

THE COUNCIL OF NICAEA IN AD 325 (THE FIRST COUNCIL)

- We learned about this council starting on page 80, please refer back for review.

THE COUNCIL OF CONSTANTINOPLE IN AD 381 (THE SECOND COUNCIL)

- It was called by Emperor Theodosius.
- Once again this is dealing with Arianism.
- They dealt with the question: Is the Holy Spirit deity?
    i. This council added the Holy Spirit to the Nicene Creed.
- They dealt with **Apollinarianism** which taught that the two natures of Jesus could not co-exist in the same person. Jesus was human so he sinned and sinful nature could not share the same body with

divine nature. God takes on the shell of the human body of Jesus and makes him divine at some given point. (Like a hand in a glove)

- **Apollinaris of Laodicea** denied that Jesus had a soul. Jesus only had the flesh of a human body with a divine mind.

  - In Apollinaris's view could Jesus atone for the sins of mankind?

- Gregory of Nazianzus stated at this council: "Whatever is not assumed is not healed." Meaning that if Jesus did not have a soul or mind, he wouldn't be fully human, therefore he could not atone for humanity.

Hebrews 2:17 *Therefore, He had to be made like His brethren in all things, so that He might become a merciful and faithful high priest in things pertaining to God, to make propitiation for the sins of the people.*

- The Council deemed Apollinarianism to be an inadequate view of Christ.
- Apollinaris was so obsessed with the nature of the Incarnation that he forgot the reason for the Incarnation.

THE COUNCIL OF EPHESUS IN AD 431 (THE THIRD COUNCIL)

- It was called by Emperor Theodosius II by request of Nestorius.
- They dealt with **Nestorianism** by asking the question; Was Mary (Christokos) the birth giver of Christ or (Theotokos) the birth giver of God?

  i. Nestorius preferred Christokos because he wanted to separate the two natures of Jesus (two personalities).

- It is true that Mary is the birth giver of Christ and it is true that she is the birth giver of God. However, Nestorian was emphasizing the human nature as if separate from his God nature.

- Nestorianism basically teaches that Jesus was fully God and fully human in one person but turned on and off his divinity like a light switch.
    - In Nestorius's view, could Jesus atone for the sins of mankind?
        i. This view of the atonement is inadequate. Who died on the cross?
- Cyril opposed Nestorius and there was a bitter public conflict that led Nestorius to request a council.
    i. Ironically the council deemed Nestorius a heretic.
- The council took the Theotokos position emphasizing that even at the point of birth Jesus was truly God as well as truly man.
- The intent of the council calling Mary the "Mother of God" really had nothing to do with Mary, but the divinity of Christ.
    i. This would be later distorted by the Roman Catholic Church who essentially elevates Mary to the point of worshiping her.
- Some historians don't believe that Nestorius went so far as to teach that Jesus has two natures in one person that are separated like he was accused of. They argue that his followers twisted into that position later.

THE COUNCIL OF CHALCEDON IN AD 451 (THE FOURTH COUNCIL)

- It was called by Emperor Marcian.
- More heresies arose concerning the nature of Christ.

Eutychianism (Monophysitism)

- Eutyches was at the Council of Ephesus and had an over-reaction to the Nestorian heresy. He said that Jesus's humanity was essentially dissolved or obliterated by his divine nature, describing it as being "dissolved like a drop of honey in the sea."

- In Eutyches's view, could Jesus atone for the sins of mankind? No
    i. Though Eutyches confirmed both natures of Christ, in reality, he denied both because the blending of them created something entirely different, like powder and water = jello.

- Leo, the Bishop of Rome, offers the solution to most Christological errors and heresies in response to Eutyches, and probably thinking of the abundance of others:
    i. He stated that we must recognize both the **true** humanity and **true** deity of Christ.
    ii. He stated that Jesus has two distinct natures yet one personality and is perfect in both. **The hypostatic union** refers to having both divine and human natures in one person. Hypostatic means nature or essence.
    iii. He stated that Jesus was born of the Virgin Mary.
    iv. He stated that Jesus had two natures without confusion, change, division or separation.

The Chalcedonian Creed is an excellent explanation of the hypostatic union. Any view outside of what is laid out by this creed will more than likely be heretical.

Chalcedonian Creed (AD 451)

We, then, following the holy Fathers, all with one consent, teach men to confess one and the same Son, our Lord Jesus Christ, the same perfect in Godhead and also perfect in manhood; truly God and truly man, of a reasonable [rational] soul and body; consubstantial [co-essential] with the Father according to the Godhead, and consubstantial with us according to the manhood; in all things like unto us, without sin; begotten before all ages of the Father according to the Godhead, and in these latter days, for us and for our salvation, born of the virgin Mary, the mother of God, according to the manhood; one and the same

Christ, Son, Lord, only begotten, to be acknowledged in two natures, inconfusedly, unchangeably, indivisibly, inseparably; the distinction of nature's being by no means taken away by the union, but rather the property of each nature being preserved, and concurring in one Person and one Subsistence, not parted or divided into two persons, but one and the same Son, and only begotten, God the Word, the Lord Jesus Christ; as the prophets from the beginning [have declared] concerning him, and the Lord Jesus Christ himself has taught us, and the Creed of the holy Fathers has handed down to us.

- What is known as: **The four negatives of the creed**:

1. Mixture
2. Confusion (or changeable)
3. Division
4. Separation
    i. The Monophysite heresy confused the natures of Christ and mixed them together to form something else. Nestorianism both divided and separated the natures of Christ.

THE SECOND COUNCIL OF CONSTANTINOPLE IN AD 553 (THE FIFTH COUNCIL)

- We are concerned with the theological issues and not the other issues when studying these councils.
- Basically, this council presented reiterations of the Council of Chalcedon for the eastern churches.
    i. The hypostatic union had been settled at Chalcedon in the west. However, in the east the controversy continued.
    ii. The west had a large majority of **Monophysites** who fought against the orthodox view of the hypostatic union that had become known as **Dyophysite**.
        a. "Mono" meaning one nature.
        b. "Dyo" meaning two natures.

THE THIRD COUNCIL OF CONSTANTINOPLE IN AD 680 (THE SIXTH COUNCIL)

- Now that Jesus's natures are clear, what about his will?
- This council dealt with **Monothelitism** that teaches that Jesus has two natures, but one will.
    - Does Jesus have two natures and two wills, or two natures and one will?
        i. Monothelitism was deemed to be a heresy.

An excerpt from The Exposition of Faith from this council.

> We also proclaim two natural willings or wills in him and two natural operations, without separation, without change, without partition, without confusion, according to the teaching of the holy Fathers—and two natural wills not contrary to each other, God forbid, as the impious heretics have said they would be, but his human will following, and not resisting or opposing, but rather subject to his divine and all-powerful will. For it was proper for the will of the flesh to be moved naturally, yet to be subject to the divine will, according to the all-wise Athanasius. For as his flesh is called and is the flesh of God the Word, so also the natural will of his flesh is called and is God the Word's own will, as he himself says: "I came down from heaven, not to do my own will, but the will of the Father who sent me," calling the will of the flesh his own, as also the flesh had become his own. For in the same manner that his all-holy and spotless ensouled flesh, though divinized, was not destroyed, but remained in its own law and principle also his human will, divinized, was not destroyed, but rather preserved, as Gregory the divine says: "His will, as conceived of in his character as the Saviour, is not contrary to God, being wholly divinized." We also glorify two natural operations in the same our Lord Jesus Christ, our true God, without separa- tion, without change, without partition, without confusion, that is, a divine operation and a human operation, as the divine preacher Leo most clearly says: "For each form does what is proper to it, in communion with the other; the Word, that is, performing what belongs to the Word, and the flesh carrying out what belongs to the flesh." We will not therefore grant the existence of one natural operation of God and the creature, lest we should either raise up into the divine

nature what is created, or bring down the preeminence of the divine nature into the place suitable for things that are made. For we recognize the wonders and the sufferings as of one and the same person], according to the difference of the natures of which he is and in which he has his being, as the eloquent Cyril said. Preserving therefore in every way the unconfused and undivided, we set forth the whole confession in brief; believing our Lord Jesus Christ, our true God, to be one of the holy Trinity even after the taking of flesh, we declare that his two natures shine forth in his one hypostasis, in which he displayed both the wonders and the sufferings through the whole course of his dispensation, not in phantasm but truly, the difference of nature being recognized in the same one hypostasis by the fact that each nature wills and works what is proper to it, in communion with the other. On this principle we glorify two natural wills and operations combining with each other for the salvation of the human race.

- In the Monothelite view, could Jesus atone for the sins of mankind? Why?
    - If Jesus did not have a human will separate from his God nature, he would not be tempted as man.

THE SECOND COUNCIL OF NICAEA IN AD 787 (THE SEVENTH COUNCIL)

- Orthodoxy jumps ship at this council.
- The implementation of icons was established which is a violation of the second commandment.

Exodus 20: 4 *You shall not make for yourself an idol, or any likeness of what is in heaven above or on the earth beneath or in the water under the earth.*

- We will talk more about this when we get to the iconoclast controversy.

NOTES

The Fall of Western Rome
Middle Ages

- **Theodosius the Great** (379–95): After his death Rome split into east and west under two emperors.
    i. The eastern half of Rome remained intact until the 1400s.
- What was once a great kingdom is now looked at as weak and vulnerable. Various tribes and groups begin to attack Rome.
- By 476 western Rome was under the control of barbarians and this is the beginning of the Middle Ages.
- These barbarian tribes become the nations of Europe that remain today.
    i. They shared certain Roman customs, including Latin as a written language and Christianity.
    ii. Christianity was really the only unifying factor between these kingdoms.
- The emperor was previously considered the head of the church, now that there was no Emperor of Rome, the pope is considered its head.
- In 800, the Franks took control of a significant amount of Europe.
    i. The pope crowned Charlemagne the Emperor. He was the first to unite western Europe since the Roman Empire. He was the king of the franks and Lombards and emperor of Rome.

- The Franks stop the spread of Islam that was coming in from North Africa into Spain and spreading across Europe at the Battle of Tours in 732.

THE RISE OF ISLAM

- Why look at the rise of Islam?
    - It is birthed out of a major distortion of the Bible.
    - Understanding the rise of Islam will help us understand our study on the Crusades. Islam was and still is the largest threat to Christianity.

Mohammed (570–632)

- He was a shepherd-boy who became wealthy later as a merchant.
- He had epileptic attacks in which he thought was the devil's work, but later at age forty he said it was god communicating to him.
- He said god, through an angel, was transmitting visions to him through his wife Khadija. In these visions was the message that he was the prophet of the Arabian god Allah.
    i. When Khadija died, Mohammed married many wives.
- The Koran is what Islam looks to as their holy book.
    i. It was written down by Mohammed's followers as he preached publicly.
    ii. The Koran rewrites history to include Allah as the god of national Israel.
    iii. Within the Koran it states that the writings of Moses, David, and the gospel of Jesus are all true, yet it both defies and defiles them.
- Mohammed's preaching was not well received at first, so he started using propaganda to become credible.

-
  - i. He launched a military campaign to subdue the world with three-hundred five followers.
  - ii. His army captures the black stone in Mecca.
- Mohammed fell ill and died in the year 632.
- It is interesting that both Islam and Mormonism begin when a self-proclaimed prophet claims divine revelation from an angel. Mohammed claims the angel Gabriel and Joseph Smith claims the angel Moroni.
  - i. They are very similar in many ways.
    - a. They both practiced polygamy.
    - b. They both were very violent. Mormons, not so much today, but their history was.
    - c. They are both legalistic.
    - d. They both deny the deity of Jesus.
    - e. They both appeal to the Bible to gain traction, credibility, and an audience.
    - f. They both view their founder as the prophet.
- Islam spreads within a hundred years from Spain to India in what is known today as the Muslim world.
- Below are their six articles of faith:

1. God: There is only one God who is Allah. He is all powerful but not personal and cannot be known.
2. Angels: Existence of angels is fundamental. The angel Gabriel appeared to Mohammed.
3. Scripture: There are four inspired books: Torah of Moses, Psalms of David, Gospel of Jesus Christ, and the Koran. Only the last was not corrupted by Jews and Christians and thus stands.
4. Prophets: God has spoken through six great prophets: Adam, Noah, Abraham, Moses, Jesus, and Mohammed. Mohammed is last and greatest.
5. The Last Days: There will be days of resurrection and judgement. Those who obey receive Paradise and pleasure, those who do not will be tormented in hell.

6. Fate: All is predestinated, and life is mere fatalism as one lives out his fate. The decrees of God (Kismet) are a central teaching of Islam.

- Below are their five pillars of faith that they claim are essential for salvation.

1. Profession of faith or creed (Kalima): "There is no god but Allah, and Mohammed is his prophet."
2. Worship (Namaz): Ritual prayer five times per day facing Mecca.
3. Almsgiving (Zakat): An obligatory payment for charitable and religious purposes.
4. Fasting (Ramadan): During the month of Ramadan they must fast during the day and eat at night.
5. Pilgrimage (Hajj): Make a pilgrimage to Mecca once in a lifetime. Activities include visiting the Sacred Mosque and kissing the Black Stone. (Ka'aba)

- There is also a sixth duty, Jihad, the Holy War. This duty requires one to go to war to spread Islam or defend it against infidels. Those who die in Jihad are guaranteed eternal life in Paradise.
- It is interesting that their eschatology is essentially premillennialism turned backwards (some amill's believe in a literal Tribulation as well). The rest of this outline will show their eschatology as compared to premillennialism.
- They believe that Jesus was a man and a prophet. He is not the son of god because god has no son. He ascended to heaven like Elijah.

    i. He is in heaven now standing next to Allah waiting for Allah to send him back. When Allah sends him back, he will correct all the Christians, who have misunderstood who he is.
    ii. He will get married, have children, die and be buried next to Mohammed.

THREE GREAT SIGNS

The first sign

- The first man to come to earth at the end is Mahdi or the Twelfth Imam.
    i. He will slaughter all who will not worship Allah in order to establish the everlasting world-dominating kingdom of Islam.
    ii. He is their long-awaited savior.
    iii. His army will carry black flags with the word "Punishment" written on it.
    iv. He will establish his rule in Jerusalem on the temple mount.

    John MacArthur "When the Mahdi arrives, he will discover hidden scriptures—he will discover them, interestingly enough, somewhere near the Sea of Galilee—and there will be there hidden scriptures, hidden gospels, and a hidden Torah, and they will be the true scriptures, which will be used by the Mahdi to show the Jews and the Christians they were wrong—that their scriptures were the false scriptures. Let me summarize: the Mahdi will be a messianic figure. He will be a descendant of Mohammed. He will be an unparalleled, unequaled leader. He will come out of a crisis of turmoil. He will take control of the world. He will establish a new world order. He will destroy all who resist him. He will invade many nations. He will make a seven-year peace treaty with the Jews. He will conquer Israel and massacre the Jews. He will establish Islamic world headquarters at Jerusalem. He will rule for seven years, establish Islam as the only religion. He will come on a white horse with supernatural power. He will be loved by all people on earth. If that sounds familiar, that is a precise description of the biblical Antichrist "[1]

- The Bible's Antichrist is Islam's Savior.

---

1. MacArthur. *The Grim Reality of the Last Days.* March 20, 2011

The second sign

- The second man to come or second sign is Jesus.
    i. Mahdi is greater than Jesus, so Jesus comes to assist Mahdi.

John MacArthur "He will worship Allah, and thus he will lead all Christians who will follow him to reject their notion of Jesus and accept the real Jesus, who is nothing but a prophet and a man. He will establish worldwide Sharia law. He will become the greatest Muslim evangelist, and he will be the final witness on the day of judgment against non-Muslims. Christians everywhere will affirm that they were wrong—that the gospel is wrong, the New Testament is wrong, He didn't die, He didn't rise, He isn't God, He isn't the Son of God—he himself will come back and point out how wrong we've been.

He will correct all misinterpretations and all misrepresentations. Let me quote what their literature says: "He will shatter crosses"—that's metaphoric for the destruction of the church, a symbol of Christianity, being placed in the church. "He will kill pigs. He will abolish the tax on non-Muslims because there won't be any living non-Muslims—can't tax dead people—and then he will do one more thing: he will kill the Islamic Antichrist; he will kill the Islamic Antichrist.

Then he will die and be buried by Mohammed, but not until he has destroyed Christianity by revealing who he really is." Who is this? You compare what he does to the false prophet in the book of Revelation—chapter 13, 16, 19, 20 refer to the beast's coming out of the earth, the false prophet—who aids and abets the Antichrist. He is—as the Mahdi is the exact replica of the Antichrist, the Jesus prophet in Islam is the exact parallel to the false prophet, who aids and abets the Antichrist."[2]

The third sign

- The third man to come or the third sign is the Antichrist or Dajjal.
    i. He comes to earth riding a mule, is blind in one eye and is an infidel.

---

2. MacArthur. *The Grim Reality of the Last Days*. March 20, 2011

ii. He claims to be Jesus, the son of God.
  iii. He attempts to stop Mahdi but the true Jesus will slaughter him.

John MacArthur "This is their view of the true Christ; our Jesus is their Antichrist; our Antichrist is their redeemer. It is a satanic counterfeit that is in complete reverse."[3]

- Does it seem like Mohammed either read the book of Revelation or was taught it by someone?

---

3. MacArthur. The Grim Reality of the Last Days. March 20, 2011

NOTES

The Canon

- How do you know the right books made it into the canon of Scripture?
  - Jesus affirmed the Old Testament and authorized the New Testament.

- Here are a few verses from Matthew where Jesus affirms the Old Testament: Matthew 5:17–18; 10:15; 12:40; 19:3–5; 21:5, 13, 16, and 42; 24:38–39
- Below are two places in one book where Jesus authorized the New Testament:

John 14:23-26 *Jesus answered and said to him, "If anyone loves Me, he will keep My word; and My Father will love him, and We will come to him and make Our abode with him. He who does not love Me does not keep My words; and the word which you hear is not Mine, but the Father's who sent Me. These things I have spoken to you while abiding with you. "But the Helper, the Holy Spirit, whom the Father will send in My name, He will teach you all things,* **and bring to your remembrance all that I said to you.**

John 16:12-15 *"I have many more things to say to you, but you cannot bear them now. But when He, the Spirit of truth, comes, He will guide you into all the truth; for He will not speak on His own initiative, but whatever He hears, He will speak; and He will* **disclose to you** *what is to come. He will glorify Me, for He will take of Mine and will* **disclose it to you.** *All things that the Father has are Mine; therefore I said that He takes of Mine and will* **disclose it to you.**

- What was the criteria for the books selected that went into the canon?
    - The books that bear the mark of apostolic authority are recognized for the New Testament. The books that have been recognized by the Jews for the Old Testament.
- What does the word canon mean? Measuring rod

- The written Word of God consists of that which God has revealed through the inspiration of the Holy Spirit.

2 Peter 1:20-21 *But know this first of all, that no prophecy of Scripture is a matter of one's own interpretation, for no prophecy was ever made by an act of human will, but men moved by the holy Spirit spoke from God.*

- How many books are in the canon? Sixty-six
- How many authors? Forty human and one divine
- How long did the canon take to write? Approximately fifteen-hundred years.
- Did the Holy Spirit possess the prophets and apostles, causing them to uncontrollably write Scripture like a robot? No, we can clearly see their personalities in each book.

- The church did not establish the canon. Rather, the church recognized and affirmed the canon. For the New Testament, this was based on whether or not a book was written under the authority of an apostle. The Old Testament canon had already been used for hundreds of years by the Jews.
    - What was the criteria to be an apostle?
        - They must be an eyewitness of the resurrected Christ.

Acts 1:21-22 21"*Therefore it is necessary that of the men who have accompanied us all the time that the Lord Jesus went in and out among us—22 beginning with the baptism of John until the day that He was taken up from us—one of* **these must become a witness with us of His resurrection.**

- They must be directly appointed by Jesus Christ.

Mark 3:13-14 *13 And He went up on the mountain and summoned those whom He Himself wanted, and they came to Him. 14 And He appointed twelve, so that they would be with Him and that He could send them out to preach,*

- They must be able to confirm his mission and message with miraculous signs.

Matthew 10:1 *Jesus summoned His twelve disciples and gave them authority over unclean spirits, to cast them out, and to heal every kind of disease and every kind of sickness.*

- Paul and James were both recognized as apostles in Scripture.
  - What about Mark?
    - Mark wrote the memoirs of Peter, under the supervision of Peter. (see page 26)
  - What about Luke?
    - He investigated eyewitness accounts of Jesus and his ministry. He also had apostolic oversight by Paul. Paul affirms **Luke** as part of Scripture in **1 Timothy 5:18** where he quotes Luke.
  - What about Hebrews?
    - This one is tough because the author is unknown. It has been critically and closely examined for over two thousand years and is hermeneutically perfect.
    - The early church considered Hebrews as Scripture and a number of Christian leaders attributed it to Paul. It certainly appears that it was at least written under his authority.
  - What about Jude?
    - Jude was the half-brother of Jesus. It was written under the oversight of his brother James.
  - What about the Apocrypha?
    - The Jews as well as Jesus and the early church never considered it as Scripture.

- Marcion tore pages out of his Bible because he believed the God of the Old Testament was not the same as the God of the New Testament. This forces the church to start assembling the books that had always been known to be Scripture. They made sure that all the books met the criteria mentioned above. They did not choose the books, they only reaffirmed what was already known to be Scripture and put those books together.
    - What is the difference between inerrancy and infallibility?
        - The doctrine of inerrancy: In the original autographs is without error.
        - The doctrine of infallibility: Incapable of error in any way and at any time.

Put simply, I can be inerrant for a little while, but I can never be infallible.

NOTES

The Middle Ages

- What are some of the other names for what is known as "The Middle Ages?"
    - "The Dark Ages" or "The Mid-Evil Times"
- What is the time period of The Middle Ages?
    - They begin in 476 with the fall of Rome and they end in 1453 with the fall of Constantinople.
- Historians divide this one thousand-year period into two halves: 476–1054 and 1055–1453.

1. The first half is known as the "early" or "low middle ages."
2. The second half is known as the "late" or "high middle ages."

- This period of time isn't as foundational in terms of theology as the first five-hundred years were. However, more heresies were introduced as the Roman Catholic Church (RCC) began to develop further.
- During this time, the church in the west is developing into the RCC. The church in the east is developing into the Eastern Orthodox Church. When the western half of the Roman Empire falls, the city of Rome is all that is left that has any power. They are no longer accountable to the eastern cities of the Roman Empire. At the start of this period of time, we would be able to agree with most of what the RCC was teaching. Of course, this becomes a progressive downhill slide as we shall see.

LEO THE GREAT (400–461)

- He was involved in the Nestorian and Eutyches disputes and was significant in the adoption of the Chalcedonian Creed.
- In 445 he told Dioscorus, the bishop of Alexandria, that the Alexandrian church should submit to Rome just as Mark (who established the church in Alexandria) would have submitted to Peter (who established the church in Rome).
    i. In other words, because Peter founded the church at Rome and was the head of the apostles likewise Rome was the head of the church.

Note: In reality, Peter may not have founded the church at Rome. Paul wrote the book of Romans and never addresses Peter or mentions him. Peter becomes the pastor in Rome, but probably after the book of Romans was written.

- He obtained a decree from Valentinian III (The Western Roman Emperor) which declared the primacy of Rome and threatened objectors with legal repercussions. This forces the other churches in the west to submit. The Second Council of Ephesus was called over the dispute between Antioch and Alexandria in the east. Leo attempted to assert himself into this by sending some of his representatives. They were rejected by Dioscorus because he didn't trust them. When Leo heard of this, he deemed the council to be void. Because of this it is not recognized as an ecumenical church council.
    i. Later, at the Council of Chalcedon, they upheld Leo's assertion that the council was void and favored Leo's orthodox position on the matter (Eutychianism/Monophysitism), which greatly enhanced Rome's influence on the eastern churches as well.

- Leo was a great leader.
    i. When Attila the Hun came to the gates of the city to conquer Rome. Leo was sent out as the delegate by the Emperor. Leo convinced Attila to not attack Rome. This took the respect of the Roman people to all new heights for Leo.

- Leo believed that Peter was the Rock (**Matthew 16:18**) and he was Peter's successor.

  - Who is the Rock?

- Early Church Fathers did not interpret **Matthew 16:18** the way Leo did. Here are a few of many references:

    Tertullian "If, because the Lord has said to Peter, 'Upon this rock I will build My church,' 'to thee have I given the keys of the heavenly kingdom;' or, 'Whatsoever thou shalt have bound or loosed in earth, shall be bound or loosed in the heavens,' you therefore presume that the power of binding and loosing has derived to you, that is, to every church akin to Peter, what sort of man are you, subverting and wholly changing the manifest intention of the Lord, conferring (as that intention did) this (gift) personally upon Peter? 'On thee,' he says, 'will I build my church;' and, 'I will give thee the keys' . . . and, 'Whatsoever thou shalt have loosed or bound' . . . In (Peter) himself the church was reared; that is, through (Peter) himself; (Peter) himself essayed the key; you see what key: 'Men of Israel, let what I say sink into your ears: Jesus the Nazarene, a man destined by God for you, and so forth. (Peter) himself, therefore, was the first to unbar, in Christ's baptism, the entrance to the heavenly kingdom, in which kingdom are 'loosed' the sins that were beforetime 'bound;' and those which have not been 'loosed' are 'bound,' in accordance with true salvation."[1]

    Origen "And if we too have said like Peter, 'Thou art the Christ, the Son of the living God,' not as if flesh and blood had revealed it unto us, but by the light from the Father in heaven having shone in our heart, we become a Peter, and to us there might be said by the Word, 'Thou art Peter,' etc. For a rock is every disciple of Christ of whom those drank who drank of the spiritual rock which followed them, and upon every such rock is built every word of the church, and the polity in accordance with it; for in each of the perfect, who have the combination of words and deeds and thoughts which fill up the blessedness, is the church built by God.
    But if you suppose that upon the one Peter only the whole church is built by God, what would you say about John the son

---

1. Tertullian, *On Modesty* P. 99

of thunder or each one of the apostles? Shall we otherwise dare to say, that against Peter in particular the gates of Hades shall not prevail, but that they shall prevail against the other apostles and the perfect? Does not the saying previously made, 'The gates of Hades shall not prevail against it,' hold in regard to all and in the case of each of them? And also, the saying, 'Upon this rock I will build my church?' Are the keys of the kingdom of heaven given by the Lord to Peter only, and will no other of the blessed receive them? But if this promise, 'I will give unto thee the keys of the kingdom of heaven,' be common to others, how shall not all things previously spoken of, and the things which are subjoined as having been addressed to Peter, be common to them?

'Thou art the Christ, the Son of the living God.' If anyone says this to him . . . he will obtain the things that were spoken according to the letter of the gospel to Peter, but, as the spirit of the gospel teaches to everyone who becomes such as that Peter was. For all bear the surname 'rock' who are the imitators of Christ, that is, of the spiritual rock which followed those who are being saved, that they may drink from it the spiritual draught. But these bear the surname of rock just as Christ does. But also as members of Christ deriving their surname from Him they are called Christians, and from the rock, Peters . . . And to all such the saying of the Savior might be spoken, 'Thou art Peter' etc., down to the words, 'prevail against it.' But what is the it? Is it the rock upon which Christ builds the church, or is it the church? For the phrase is ambiguous. Or is it as if the rock and the church were one and the same? This I think to be true; for neither against the rock on which Christ builds his church, nor against the church will the gates of Hades prevail. Now, if the gates of Hades prevail against any one, such an one cannot be a rock upon which the Christ builds the church, nor the church built by Jesus upon the rock." (Allan Menzies, *Ante-Nicene Fathers* (Grand Rapids: Eerdmans, 1951), Origen, *Commentary on Matthew*, Chapters 10–11).[2]

Eusebius "'And he sent out arrows, and scattered them; he flashed forth lightnings, and routed them. Then the channels of the sea were seen, and the foundations of the world were laid bear, at thy rebuke, O Lord, at the blast of thy nostrils' (Ps. 18.14) . . . By 'the foundations of the world,' we shall understand the strength of God's wisdom, by which, first, the order of the universe was established, and then, the world itself was founded—a

2. Origen. *Ante-Nicene Fathers: Commentary on Matthew*

world which will not be shaken. Yet you will not in any way err from the scope of the truth if you suppose that 'the world' is actually the church of God, and that its 'foundation' is in the first place, that unspeakably solid rock on which it is founded, as Scripture says: 'Upon this rock I will build my church, and the gates of hell shall not prevail against it'; and elsewhere: 'The rock, moreover, was Christ.' For, as the apostle indicates with these words: 'No other foundation can anyone lay than that which is laid, which is Christ Jesus.' Then, too, after the Savior himself, you may rightly judge the foundations of the church to be the words of the prophets and apostles, in accordance with the statement of the apostle: 'Built upon the foundation of the apostles and the prophets, Christ Jesus himself being the cornerstone.' These foundations of the world have been laid bare because the enemies of God, who once darkened the eyes of our mind, lest we gaze upon divine things, have been routed and put to flight—scattered by the arrows sent from God and put to flight by the rebuke of the Lord and by the blast from his nostrils. As a result, having been saved from these enemies and having received the use of our eyes, we have seen the channels of the sea and have looked upon the foundations of the world. This has happened in our lifetime in many parts of the world."[3]

Augustine "In a passage in this book, I said about the apostle Peter: 'On him as on a rock the church was built' . . . But I know that very frequently at a later time, I so explained what the Lord said: 'Thou art Peter, and upon this rock I will build my church,' that it be understood as built upon Him whom Peter confessed saying: 'Thou art the Christ, the Son of the living God,' and so Peter, called after this rock, represented the person of the church which is built upon this rock, and has received 'the keys of the kingdom of heaven.' For, 'Thou art Peter' and not 'Thou art the rock' was said to him. But 'the rock was Christ,' in confessing whom, as also the whole church confesses, Simon was called Peter. But let the reader decide which of these two opinions is the more probable."[4]

Augustine "And I tell you . . . *'You are Peter, Rocky, and on this rock I shall build my church, and the gates of the underworld will not conquer her. To you shall I give the keys of the kingdom. Whatever you bind on earth shall also be bound in heaven; whatever you loose on earth shall also be loosed in heaven'* (Mt. 16:15–19).

3. Eusebius. *Commentary on the Psalms*, M.P.G., Vol. 23, Col. 173, 176
4. Augustine. *The Fathers of the Church: St. Augustine: The Retractions*. P. 90–91

> In Peter, Rocky, we see our attention drawn to the rock. Now the apostle Paul says about the former people, '*They drank from the spiritual rock that was following them; but the rock was Christ*' (1 Cor 10:4). So this disciple is called Rocky from the rock, like Christian from Christ . . . Why have I wanted to make this little introduction? In order to suggest to you that in Peter the church is to be recognized. Christ, you see, built his church not on a man but on Peter's confession. What is Peter's confession? '*You are the Christ, the Son of the living God.*' There's the rock for you, there's the foundation, there's where the church has been built, which the gates of the underworld cannot conquer."[5]

- Peter's confession is the rock on which Christ built his church.
- Rome wasn't the only city that Peter established a church in. The idea that Rome should continue in Peter's succession with an apostolic leader called Pope is ridiculous to say the least. In fact, Peter appointed pastors in many cities who could claim the same thing.
    i. The church fathers that Rome tries to claim as Pope in the line of Peter, did not consider themselves to be apostolic in any way when you read their writings.

JUSTINIAN THE GREAT (EASTERN ROME 527-65)

- He established law which we still refer to today as Judeo-Christian law or values.
- He believed it was his divine mission to take back the entire Roman empire and restore it to its former glory.
    i. He was able to take back much of it at a very high cost of gold and resources. He ran out of money, which contributed to Islam being able to conquer all of the western regions that he had won and even some of Justinian's own eastern regions. Islam was able to conquer because the west had fallen, and the east was almost bankrupt trying to win the west back.

---

5. Augustine. *The Works of Saint Augustine A Translation for the 21st Century: Sermons.* P. 327

- He called the Second Council of Constantinople in 553 because of Nestorianism and Eutychianism still being a problem in the East. This council reiterates the Council of Chalcedon.

GREGORY THE GREAT (WESTERN ROME 540–604)

- He was known as a missionary pope.
    i. Until this time, no one that we are aware of since Paul attempted to spread Christianity to the world. As a result, a large percentage of the British Isles was converted. This was done through another man named Augustine of Canterbury (not to be confused with Augustine of Hippo.) Missionary work was focused primarily on kings and rulers. When they were converted, they would declare their people converted as well.
- Gregory was a great civil leader; he organized the distribution of food to the needy and rebuilt the aqueducts and defenses of Rome.
- He began to develop the practice of private penance.
- John Calvin in his *Institutes* (chapter 7) talks about Gregory and some of the Popes of this time period in good regard. He points back to these men to show how Rome progressively falls into apostasy.
- It is during this time that Islam becomes a major threat.

THE ICONOCLAST CONTROVERSY (730–842)

- Debate broke out in the Eastern Church over the use of icons (images that depicted Christ and biblical saints). Those who endorsed the use of icons were known as iconodules and those who did not were known as iconoclasts.
- In 695 the Byzantine Emperor Justinian II minted gold coins with the face of Christ on them which sparked a lot of the controversy.
- The Islamic army was winning city after city. This caused Christians, who were losing territory, to question if they were under the wrath

of God. They began to examine what they were doing in order to find anything that could be displeasing to him. **Breaking the second commandment was one of the things that was apparent to some** (Dyophysites).

    i. Going back to the Monophysite / Dyophysite controversy. The Dyophysites (Iconoclast) feared that an image of Christ would showcase His humanity and separate the full deity of Christ's nature. An image would swing people to focus on His humanity making the inseparable two natures of Christ separated.

    ii. The Iconodules argue that God himself made an image of God by Jesus becoming a man and walking on the earth. Jesus himself was an image, therefore an image of the man Jesus was not a violation of the second commandment. They also argued that they were not worshiping the icons but were venerating them.

- This line between worship and veneration becomes very blurry and even subjective. This becomes very clear when icons of Mary begin to essentially be worshiped; (praying too, lighting candles, kneeling down before, and crossing oneself before her and other icons.)

Note: This issue will surface again during the Reformation. John Calvin, Ulrich Zwingli, and others were strong Iconoclasts. Martin Luther was more of an Iconodule.

- Around 730, **Emperor Leo III** ordered that an icon of Christ that was at the palace of Constantinople, be replaced with a cross. He thought his military setbacks came from an overemphasis on the veneration of icons throughout the empire. A ban was placed on icons. **Pope Gregory II** condemned Leo's actions.

- Leo died in 740. His son **Constantine V** (741–75) worked to rid the empire of icons and many were destroyed.

    i. An underground movement of iconodules began to grow. **John of Damascus** was at the forefront of this movement, who is still influential in Eastern Orthodox churches.

- Constantine V died and his son **Leo IV** (775–80) continued his father's iconoclastic policies. However, his wife **Irene** was secretly an iconodule.
    i. When Leo died, Irene organized the Second Council of Nicaea (the seventh and final ecumenical council) in 787 which overruled Iconoclastic policies.

Note: Paganism worshiped icons of the Greek gods. Paganism begins to intertwine slowly with Christianity starting with Constantine. The worship of Greek icons is replaced with the veneration of the icons of Christ, Peter, Mary, Saints, etc.

- **Emperor Leo V** in 814 again reinstated a ban on icons in the east.
- Leo died and his son **Michael II**, and grandson, **Theophilus** came to power. Theophilus died in 842, his wife **Theodora** became co-regent with Michael III. In 843 Theodora (an in the closet iconodule) had icons restored in the empire and placed icons permanently into the Roman Catholic and Eastern Orthodox churches.

> **Eric Russell Chamberlin** in his book *The Bad Popes*: "There was no major clash between emperor and bishop on a purely religious matter until about 726. The reigning emperor was Leo III, by birth a hillman and by training a soldier, a simple, direct man who brought to the complexities of religious disputations a simple, direct approach. It was disastrous. His Christian subjects had nothing but praise for his edict that commanded the forcible baptism of Jews. But when he issued the first of his iconoclastic edicts, he spelled the doom of his empire in the West. The peoples of Italy were touched, for the first time, on a universally personal matter.
>
> The primitive Christians [or early] had attacked image worship as the work of the devil and there had been wholesale destruction of every type of idol when Christianity had at last triumphed. But over the succeeding centuries, the images crept back, appearing under new names but, to the critical eye, with an identical role. It was the Christians of the East who first began to feel that much of the pagan religion that their forefathers had destroyed, at such cost in martyr's blood, was insensibly being restored. Disturbed by the mockery of the neighboring iconoclastic Muslims, their devotion to images was in addition subjected to a strain of which their Western brethren were free.

In a decade, the infidel Muslims had overcome city after Christian city, each of which had been under the protection of some holy image. In vain, monks made the standard defense of supernatural prophylactics—that it was the lack of faith of the possessor, not the lack of virtue in the image, which rendered it useless. The religious disputation inevitable became political, bringing with it riots and the ever-present threat of civil war. The forthright Leo solved the problem, as he thought, by coming down on the side of the iconoclasts. In 726 he issued his edict commanding the breaking of all images throughout the empire, in the West as well as the East.

Gregory [the Pope] returned again and again to the theme that he and his followers did not worship, but only reverenced, images. But in referring to a threat of direct attack upon the great statue of St. Peter in Rome, he slipped into a curious and ambiguous phraseology. He himself had no fear of the emperor's rage. "I have but to retire twenty-four miles into the Campanian and you might as well follow the winds. But for the statue of St. Peter himself, which all the kingdoms of the West esteem as a god on earth, the whole West would take a terrible revenge." Whether he intended it to be understood that it was the statue, or Peter himself, whom the West held as a god on earth, the statement could have helped little to repudiate the charge that Europe was fast falling into idolatry.

[As a result of the pope's defiance, a battle broke out between imperial forces from the east and papal forces from the west]"[6]

THE DONATION OF CONSTANTINE

- It was a false document written during this time period attempting to rewrite history. It claimed that Constantine gave power to rule Rome to the pope. This document was believed at the time to be genuine and was the motivation behind future popes to claim that they were the ultimate power in Rome. This document was later proven to be a forgery.
    i. To be pope was no longer only a spiritual office but a political office as well.

---

6. Chamberlin. *The Bad Popes*

- This forgery was another motivating force behind Rome asserting its power over all of the other churches in the region and demanding them to submit.
- There was a battle of power, as a result of this corruption, in which seven people who claimed the position of pope were killed within a few years.
    i. One pope, **Stephen VII**, dug up the corpse of a rival pope, dressed it in robes, placed it upon the throne and had a mock trial in which he cut off three of the fingers of the dead pope because of being politically at odds. Pope Stephen was accused of going beyond the bounds of tolerance and was captured and strangled to death.

The Papacy Grows More and More Corrupt from AD 800–1000

- We are leading into why there had to be Reformation.

Pope Adrian I (772–95) was the first to be called Holy Father. He practiced Nepotism and tried to put his own cousins into office.

- Nepotism was practiced because being pope was more about being king than being a pastor.
    - What is Nepotism? When people that are in power give powerful jobs only to family.

Pope Leo III (795–816) In December of AD 800, Leo crowned Charlemagne with the imperial crown, marking the unofficial beginning of the Holy Roman Empire as a "Divine Theocracy."

- What is a theocracy? It is a system of government by divine guidance in which officials rule in the name of God or a god.

Pope Pascale I (817–24) murdered two officers to get elected. No investigation was allowed because they believed that "the pope has power over the souls of men."

Pope Adrian II (867–72) had an illegitimate son from the wife of Legate Eleutherius.

- Legate murdered the pope's daughter and wife in response.

The Middle Ages

Pope Stephen VII (896–97) was murdered by Pope John IX.

Pope John IX (898–900) was murdered by **Pope Leo V.**

Pope Leo V (903) was murdered by Pope Christophorus.

Pope Christophorus (903–4) was deposed or removed and was murdered by **Pope Sergius III.**

- The papacy was totally degraded from 880–1000. There were thirty popes reigning less than two years each.
- There is a serious problem with the supremacy of papal succession.
    i. They believe Peter appointed his successor and so on. Here this is broken, so where does it pick up?
- Because now the church is government led, power hungry people seek to become pope, not for teaching the truth of Scripture but for political power. Popes see themselves as being above kings or any power in the world.
    - Is a government led church a good thing? Why or why not?
    - Some Christians believe the public schools should allow the Bible to be taught by teachers like it once was. Is that a good idea? Why or why not?

THE GREAT SCHISM (1054)

- This is the divide between the early and late middle ages. (see page 140)
- **Pope Leo IX** sends Michael Cerularius of Constantinople a letter of delegation (believing the Donation of Constantine to be genuine) demanding that he be recognized as the most important of all church leaders and was the head of all churches because he is the direct descendant of Peter's authority.
    i. Rome was the lone church in the West while in the East there were four churches. These four churches never recognized Rome to be superior . . . only equal.

- Michael refused to affirm the letter of delegation.
    i. Cardinal Humbert excommunicated Michael for his refusal.
    ii. Michael excommunicated the entire Roman Catholic delegation.
- The Roman Catholic Church excommunicated the Eastern Orthodox Church and the Eastern Orthodox Church excommunicated Rome. This would be a permanent split.

Eastern Orthodox is still prevalent today in Greek and Russian Orthodoxy.

- Much like Rome, they are governed by **tradition** which they regard equal to Scripture.
- They believe that at each ecumenical council, Pentecost was repeated. So, the creeds that came from these councils are inspired equal to Scripture.
    i. When "the Son" was added to the Nicene Creed after "the Holy Spirit proceeds from the Father **and the Son**" (called the Filioque Clause), the East did not accept it because it was like adding words to Scripture. They were very offended.
- They emphasize **mystery** in theology believing there is much we cannot understand and should not understand, emphasizing the shadow rather than the light. This is probably a reaction to all the divisions concerning Christology. Just embrace the mystery of Christ.
- There isn't much systematic theology within this church. They enjoy the mystery of Scriptural doctrines rather than trying to understand it.
- They teach Theosis "the state of deity".

> Matt Slick "Theosis is the belief, mostly found within the Eastern Orthodox Church, that Christians can experience a union with God and become like him so much that they participate in the divine nature. This concept is also known as deification. Theosis

does not mean that they become Gods or merge with God but that they are deified. They participate in the "energies" of God with which he reveals himself to us in creation. But, these Christians are said to not participate in God's essence. Furthermore, this deification does not mean that a person stops sinning or no longer struggles with sin. Instead, theosis is a mystical union with God that proceeds throughout the person's life and culminates in the resurrection of the body. Some have said that this is equivalent to sanctification as taught in the Western churches.

Protestants do not use this term because of the natural error associated with becoming gods. We are not God, and we will never be God. God alone possesses His divine nature. False religions sometimes teach that we can become godlike and even gods. For this reason, we must be very careful when describing the doctrine of theosis, and we must also be careful not to adopt anything that would support the heresy of becoming divine by nature. At best, we become more like Christ as we increase in our relationship with him, but we do not in any way become divine."[7]

- Much like Rome, they are Iconodules.
- They believe that justification comes through baptism and keeping the sacraments which are: The Eucharist (Lord's Supper), Chrismation (basically membership), holy orders, penance, anointing of the sick, and marriage.
- They do not believe in Sola Scriptura because of tradition.

THE CRUSADES

- The Crusades began in an attempt to reclaim Holy Land from the Muslims.
- The word "crusades" means what? Fighting in the name of the cross. Which was a name given to these military excursions later on.
  - Was Christianity responsible for the Crusades? No and yes, we have already established that these popes were power hungry politicians rather than true Christians.

---

7. charm.org What is theosis?

- i. The people, however, became motivated by the pope's propaganda, to take back their lands. Since Muslims were declaring a Holy War, they decided to fight fire with fire.
  - ii. The pope sent out preachers who pointed to passages of Scripture in which Israel fought its enemies. They believed they were the new Israel, so they could fight as well.

- Augustine came up with a four-fold requirement for Christians fighting wars.

1. Comparative Justice: A just cause
2. Proportionality: A defensive battle to regain what had been lost
3. Competent Authority: Sanctioned by a legitimate authority
4. Right Intention: Fought by those who have right motives
   - Should we agree with Augustine's four-fold requirement for war?
     - i. The Crusades met all conditions, so the people fought.
     - ii. They didn't see themselves as taking what wasn't theirs but taking back what was lost. However, their good intentions got out of hand.

- Muslims had taken the city of Jerusalem in the year 636, yet allowed, at first, Christians to come visit holy sites until the year 1076 when new leaders took over. As a result, Christians trying to visit Jerusalem were often robbed, stoned, taken into slavery, and killed.
- The people were told that if they died in a holy war, they could bypass purgatory and go straight to heaven. As a result, we have our first warrior monks come on scene; **The Knights Templar** and **The Knights of Hospitaller**.
  - i. There was also an order called **Teutonic Knights** who led successful campaigns in the north that we don't often hear of.
- The Crusades had three stages: The first fifty years is a time of victory. The next fifty years is a time of defeat. The last one hundred years was a time of confusion and indifference and The Crusades collapsed.

- Both Muslims and Jews were targeted, not for conversion but annihilation. This was not about missions, but domination and territory.
    - i. The Jews were killed because they were viewed as the killers of Christ, and the rage of war spilled out on them.
- The Kingdom of Christ was confused with the kingdom of this world.

The First Crusade (1095)

- Muslim Seljuk Turks gained control of Palestine and started persecuting Jews and Christians. Europe started taking interest in a response.
- Muslims started threatening the security of Byzantium. Alexius, the emperor at Constantinople, called for aid from Pope Urban II. This was out of desperation, considering the East is calling on the West for support. Remember they had been at odds . . . splitting the church.
    - A great threat brought the churches together. What should unite the true church today?
- Pope Urban II urged Frankish nobles, in a sermon he preached, to recover Jerusalem from the Muslims. Godfrey and Bouillon took Jerusalem back in 1099.
    - i. Twenty-thousand untrained peasants got excited and marched to Byzantium to fight. They all got wiped out.
    - ii. The second wave consisted of princes, knights and trained soldiers who took back Nicaea, Antioch, and eventually Jerusalem.
- Superstition becomes strong during this time. Artifacts are discovered in recaptured territory from the time of Christ which are taken back to Rome. This turns into a frenzy to look for other artifacts from the time of Christ. Many things, whether or not from that time, were brought to Rome. This included the Holy Lance which pierced the side of Christ. Peter Bartholomew had a vision from St. Andrew of where to find it, which encouraged the soldiers to keep fighting.

-
  -
    - i. Superstition was a big factor in the morale of the fighting troops. This drove Roman Catholicism deeper into mysticism.
  - What is mysticism?
    - Mysticism is hard to define. It includes experiential knowledge of God as opposed to revealed revelation found only in Scripture. There is the idea of a next level, elitist experience with God or different classes of Christians. It often involves some type of secret knowledge much like Gnosticism. It includes the idea that God still speaks directly to people by dreams, vision, experiences or audibly.
    - i. Mysticism has heavily affected not only the RCC but also evangelical churches.

The Second Crusade (1147–1148)

- The Turks invaded the Christian outpost city of Edessa and either slaughtered or took as slaves, all of its people in 1146. This created fear that other areas were vulnerable as well. As a result, the formation of another crusade was brought about.
- Outside of Nicaea the German crusaders were slaughtered by the Turks.
- The second crusade was considered a failure after soldiers marched against Damascus and were defeated.
  - God is sovereign over all things, so why would he allow Christians to be slaughtered by evil people? What Old Testament Prophet is known for this question?

The Third Crusade (1189–1192)

- The Muslims retake Jerusalem again.
  - i. Muslims led by Saladin took Jerusalem back in 1187 and by 1190 they had also taken the majority of the crusaders' lands.

- Crusaders were successful at reclaiming the cities of Acre and Jaffa. However, they failed to reclaim Jerusalem.
  - The gospel had been put aside to focus on something deemed more pressing. What has been deemed more pressing than the gospel today?

The Fourth Crusade (1200–1204)

- Pope Innocent III still wanted to reclaim Jerusalem.
- In this crusade there were Christian against Christian fighting. Crusaders in the West did not have the money for the crusade, it was offered by the emperor in the East who was worried about being overthrown. The crusaders went to help but were never paid, so they attacked the city, raped the women, and ransacked much of the treasures and art.
- This further weakened both the East and the West.
- The union that had brought the East and West churches together was shattered.
  - This is an extreme example of church division, probably by people who only claimed to be Christians. What divides the church today and are there ever good reasons to divide?
    - Doctrine or lack of doctrine divides the visible church today. Theology or lack of theology divides the visible church today. Exegetical vs topical preaching, heresy, the social gospel, and many other things divide the visible church today. Are these divisions good? Yes.
- Unity is found in the invisible church no matter the building in which they meet.
  i. The reason there are so many denominations is because we are all sinners. Christ, however, unites us all. Secondary doctrinal issues are very important but are put aside across denominational barriers for the sake of the gospel in the invisible church.

ii. We can see examples of this at the Shepherds Conference that John MacArthur hosts at Grace Community Church. We can see unity at the Ligonier conferences that the late Dr. RC. Sproul was part of. Bible studies are hosted in people's homes that are interdenominational. The invisible church is unified, while the visible church is not.

The Children's Crusade (1212)

- This crusade was not ordered by the pope.
- A boy named Stephen of Cloyes supposedly had a dream, obviously caught up in all of the mysticism that was abundant. In his dream, himself and others went to the Holy Land and reclaimed it in the name of the pope. At the same time, a boy named Nicholas of Cologne gathered others from Germany to join this Crusade.
- The Children's Crusade resulted in thousands of children from France and Germany being sold into slavery or drowned at sea.
   i. These were teenage kids who felt compelled to fight for the Holy Land.
- They did not have any weapons but marched upon the Holy Land believing something miraculous would happen. They marched as far as the Mediterranean Sea and then waited. They expected God to part the Sea, like he did for Moses, so they could conquer the infidels. The story goes that seven ships came and offered to take the kids across the Sea. Many boarded these ships. The intention of the men aboard these ships was never to take the kids to the Holy Land. They met with Muslim ships and sold the kids into slavery. Some of the ships sank, drowning many of them.
- There are a number of stories and legends about the Children's Crusade. It is difficult to distinguish what really happened.
    - Does God speak to people today through dreams?
- Remember that they were caught up in mysticism. Looking for a mystical experience will lead to finding one in almost anything.

The Fifth Crusade (1219–1221)

- The Pope still wanted to re-occupy Jerusalem. In order to be successful at this they first had to re-occupy other cities.
- They launched an attack against Egypt. As a result, they recaptured Damietta.
- They were never successful in reclaiming Jerusalem.
- These crusades were marked by self-delusion in believing that God will always lead his people to victory. Though this is true, ultimately in death, God often purifies his church through its failures.
- Though the crusaders' leaders were self-deluded, a sense of hopelessness set in among the people.
    - True hope is only found in what?
        - God himself. If you are relying on your own strength and abilities in anything, your hope is in the wrong thing and you have made yourself an idol. When your hope is found in total dependence on God's goodness, no matter the outcome, you have true hope.

The Sixth Crusade (1229)

- In this crusade they were finally successful in reclaiming Jerusalem, not by war, but by diplomacy. Jerusalem would remain in Christian hands until 1244 at which time it once again came under the control of Muslims. It was words rather than blood that won this crusade.
    - What we see here isn't always possible, but what can we learn from this?
        - Action without wisdom can yield disastrous results. In this case wisdom was used prior to action.

- What is true wisdom and where does it begin?

Proverbs 9:10–12 10 *The fear of the Lord is the beginning of wisdom, And the knowledge of the Holy One is understanding. 11 For by me your days will be multiplied, And years of life will be added to you. 12 If you are wise, you are wise for yourself, And if you scoff, you alone will bear it.*

The Seventh Crusade (1248)

- Once again, they attempted to reclaim Jerusalem. They first invaded Egypt and were defeated. This launched an **Eighth Crusade** which rendered the same result.
- It would appear that Jerusalem would remain in Muslim hands, at least for now. One day Jesus will reclaim it. He always succeeds where men fail.
    - What are some of the lessons we can learn from The Crusades?

SCHOLARSHIP DURING THE CRUSADES (1095–1290)

Scholasticism began as an effort to explain how Christian theology and Greek philosophy could be reconciled. This effort attempted to answer questions and resolve supposed contradictions.

- The Greek language was no longer spoken in the West. Learning Greek became a part of scholastic training. As a result, the writings of the church fathers were discovered and translated which began to influence western thinking and theology.
- Remember that some early Christians were influenced by **Platonists**.
    i. **Plato** (429 BC—unknown) taught that this world is an imperfect reflection of a higher perfect spiritual realm. Everything in this world is inferior to the spiritual, including human attributes. Human attributes exist in a perfect form within a spiritual realm but here in the earthly realm we only have mere reflections of them.

- Because it somewhat seemed right, people began to try to fit it into Christian theology.

- One of the more helpful things Plato taught was the distinction between *"being"* and *"becoming."* In order for something to truly be a *being* it must have its existence fixed and unchangeable where humans are *becoming* because we are changing every second.

    i. Plato got some of this from Heraclitus (544 BC) who said, "The same man cannot step into the same river twice."
    - Why is Heraclitus correct?

- Only God is truly a Being. We know this as the Aseity of God.

    i. God depends on nothing for his existence. Men depend on God and God's provisions for our existence.

Aristotelianism came into Christian thinking through Muslim scholars during this time period.

- Aristotle (384-22 BC) was opposite of Plato by focusing on the material universe. The here and now.

    i. This was a good thing in one aspect because it contributed to the development of science from what Aristotle called the "empirical approach" or empirical method.

    a. The empirical method is based on collecting information by observation or experience and systematizing it.

    ii. Logic and reason are used in opposition to what Plato taught . . . spiritual faith and revelation. The seen vs the unseen.

- Aristotle believed the soul was mortal and would die.
- Prior to this point theologians believed faith precedes understanding, now they started believing reason precedes faith.

    - Which view is correct?

- Much of the subjects of study were not helpful such as "how many angels can dance on the head of a pin?" in which the Platonist would come up with a point and the Aristotelians would come up with a counterpoint. Then they would try to come to a conclusion.
- **Natural theology** was one of the developments that came from Aristotelianism. It is looking for the proof that God exists by the evidence found in nature or the creation. This is found in Scripture in the book of Romans chapter 1. This biblical teaching was simply given a name to define it.

DIVINE PROOFS

- **Divine proofs** were developed by **Anselm** and **Thomas Aquinas:**
  - What are divine proofs? Using natural observation or reason to prove the existence of God.

The Cosmological Argument

- This has to do with universal causation, first cause or metaphysical motion.
  - The creation is an <u>effect</u> which must have a what? A cause
- There cannot be an infinite number of causes that go back in time forever. There must be a first cause.

1. It is a fact that things exist.
2. Is it possible for things to not exist?
3. Whatever has the possibility of non-existence, yet exists, has been caused to exist by something or someone.
    i. Something cannot bring itself into existence since it must exist in order to do so.
4. There cannot be an infinite number of causes to bring something into existence.

    i. An infinite regression of causes ultimately would have no initial cause, which means there would be no cause of existence.

        a. The universe exists; therefore, it must have a cause.

5. There must be an uncaused cause of all things.
6. The uncaused cause must be God.

    i. If there isn't an uncaused cause, you cannot scientifically explain anything.

    - What are the strengths and what are the weaknesses of this argument?

The Teleological Argument

- What does teleology mean?
    - It is the combination of two Greek words: Telos, meaning end, goal or purpose. Logos, meaning reason or explanation.

- Design implies a designer.

1. We see that things that lack knowledge, such as natural bodies (trees, plants, etc.), act for an end. (Such as a flower growing toward the sunlight.)
2. They achieve their end not by chance, but by design.
3. Now whatever lacks knowledge cannot move towards an end unless it be directed toward that end by some being endowed with knowledge and intelligence, as the arrow is directed by the archer.
4. Therefore, some intelligent being exists by whom all natural things are ordered to their end.
5. This being we call God.

> "We see that things which lack knowledge, such as natural bodies, act for an end, and this is evident from their acting always, or nearly always, in the same way, so as to obtain the best result.

Hence it is plain that they achieve their end, not fortuitously, but designedly. Now whatever lacks knowledge cannot move towards an end, unless it be directed by some being endowed with knowledge and intelligence; as the arrow is directed by the archer. Therefore, some intelligent being exists by whom all natural things are directed to their end; and this being we call God."[8] Thomas Aquinas

- What are the strengths and what are the weaknesses of this argument?

The Moral Argument

- People have a conscience which must originate from a law giver.

1. There are different degrees to perfections among beings, for some are more nearly perfect than others.
2. But things cannot be more or less perfect unless there is a wholly perfect being.
3. Whatever is perfect is the cause of the less than perfect. The higher is the cause of the lower.
4. Therefore, there must be a perfect Being which is the cause of perfections of the less than perfect beings.
5. This we call God!

- What are the strengths and what are the weaknesses of this argument?

The Ontological Argument

- What does ontology mean?
  - "On" is the Greek word that means "being" and "logia" means "study."

---

8. Aquinas, Thomas. *The Philosophical Theology of St. Thomas Aquinas.* P. 120

- This is the conclusion of the other arguments mentioned. There must be a **Necessary Being.**
    i. This goes back to understanding the Aseity of God. A necessary being must have the power of "being" within himself and depends on nothing outside of himself.
- God cannot... not be. It is necessary that he exists, or nothing could exist.
    - What are the strengths and what are the weaknesses of this argument?

"If there is such a thing as a "now" there must be eternity. Because without eternity temporality is utterly impossible."[9] RC Sproul

There are more than these four proofs that I have mentioned. Over the years some of these have been expounded on by other Christian apologists.

Anselm's (1033–1109) view of the atonement.

- Different views of the atonement had begun to creep into theology including:
    i. Jesus paid a ransom to Satan for us.
    ii. Jesus's victory at the cross overpowered Satan and led a host of people to heaven.
    - Have you ever heard these taught by someone? Why are they wrong?
- Anselm believed that Jesus paid a ransom to God that pacifies his wrath and satisfies his justice. This is the platform that the reformers used in talking about penal substitution and substitutionary atonement. As we have already pointed out, penal substitutionary atonement wasn't a new doctrine birthed during the reformation or prior to it. Anselm brought a greater theological understanding of this doctrine, that still needed greater clarity which would come later.

9. Sproul. A sermon entitled *Eternity*

Ligonier: In penal substitution, the penalty that is due to us for our transgression is paid by a substitute, namely, Jesus Christ. The principle of penal substitution undergirds the old covenant sacrificial system. God told Adam that the penalty for sin was death (Gen. 2:16–17). In the old covenant sacrifices, the people placed their hands on the sacrificial animals, thereby identifying with them, and then the animals were put to death (see Lev. 4). This depicted the transfer of sin and guilt from the sinner to the substitute. The sinner could live because the animal died in the sinner's place, bearing the punishment the sinner deserved.[10]

- Man has all of the obligation but none of the ability, God has all of the ability but none of the obligation.

PETER ABELARD (1079–1142)

- Abelard believed that causing doubt would cause people to think, which would result in conclusions that would lead people to faith.
- He wrote a book called *Yes and No* in which he would present theological problems. He would argue both for and against these problems but would offer no conclusion. He wanted to create tension in order to make people think.
  - Is this a good practice for evangelism?
  - Does causing someone, who is outside of the invisible church, to doubt what they believe bring them to the knowledge of the truth?
  - What about someone who is inside of the invisible church when concerning doctrine and theology?

PETER LOMBARD (1096–1160)

- He wrote *Lombard's Sentences* which became the basis for theological learning in the universities. Universities were just coming into existence such as Bologna in 1088, Oxford in 1096, and Paris in 1150.

10. Article from Ligonier entitled *Penal Substitution*

- He helped the development of systematic theology. Most of his writings were good.
- Both John Calvin and Martin Luther quoted Lombard.
- *Lombard's Sentences* were also criticized by John Calvin, Martin Luther and other later scholars because of some of the Roman Catholic views that he held to. Calvin said that if Augustine said something slightly wrong, Lombard would completely corrupt it.
- This is a good example of how you can learn from someone that you do not always agree with.
  - What are some of the ways you can learn from people that you disagree with?

THOMAS AQUINAS (1225-1274)

- His family kidnapped him and held him for two years trying to convince him to become a Benedictine monk, because he wanted to become a Dominican monk. Dominican monks were influenced by Aristotelianism, where Benedictine were more Platonic.
- He wrote *Summa Theologica* which is a summary of theology. He also wrote *Summa contra Gentiles* which is an apologetic to unbelievers.
- He attempted to unite Aristotelianism with Augustinianism. He emphasized the importance of empirical thought and taught that truth comes to men through reason (general, natural revelation) and faith (special, supernatural revelation). Thus, faith and reason become the two primary ways through which theology is to be understood.
  - Is Aquinas correct on his view of theology?
- Today Christians are divided on whether or not he was good or bad for Christianity. He seems too Roman Catholic to most. He is looked at positively in the world of apologetics, however. Remember he came up with some of the **Divine Proofs**.

> "During the thirteenth century, the church faced a crisis of epistemology, the science of how we know what we know. At the time, Islam was a leading intellectual force in the Arab world

and in parts of Europe. Christian thinkers in Europe had to deal with Islamic philosophers who taught the "Double Truth Theory of Knowledge," which was a way that Islamic thinkers tried to reconcile the teachings of the ancient Greek philosophers with the teachings of the Qur'an, which Islam receives as divine revelation. The Double Truth Theory holds that something can be true according to divine revelation but false according to the natural knowledge we attain via philosophy and vice versa.

Thomas countered this theory by asserting that even natural knowledge, when it attains truth, is relying on divine revelation—the revelation that God gives in nature (see Ps. 19:1). Some things are known by natural revelation, such as chemistry and physics. Special revelation is the source of the knowledge of the mysteries of the faith, such as the doctrine of the Trinity. Finally, truths such as the existence of God are revealed in both Scripture and nature. Ultimately, Thomas said, none of these sources of truth contradict each other, even if we cannot always figure out how the truth of nature and Scripture fit together. All truth, Thomas said, is God's truth."[11]

Ligonier: "Thomas' epistemology can be said to hold in tension the biblical doctrines of creation and salvation. He believed that humans are created in the image of God (*imago Dei*) and therefore have within them the capacity for true and rational thinking. The fall, of course, has obscured this thinking and it leads us to error and sin, but the indelible image of our Creator has not, according to Aquinas, fallen out of our minds. Yet, as Thomas also taught, salvation comes by grace, through Christ, to this same sinful humanity. The doctrine of salvation teaches us that we are not perfect and that our sin can easily obscure the truth. Thomas thus lands on a proposed solution to the problem that he believes will hold both of these truths together: grace perfects nature; it does not destroy it. In other words, though our minds are fallen, they are not destroyed; also, though our natural minds are sinful, yet they receive grace to grasp the truth. This solution was ingenious in that it drew philosophy and science together rather than forcing them apart." Ryan Reeves[12]

---

11. Article from Ligonier entitled Thomas Aquinas and the Knowledge of God.
12. Ligonier Article: *The Significance of Thomas Aquinas*

The Middle Ages

CORRUPTION IN THE PAPACY CONTINUES

- On top of all the corruption we have already talked about, the Roman church mandated clergy to be celibate.
  - Why would they do that?
    - This was a strategic move to gain more land and power because men who owned land would no longer have an heir to pass that land on to and guess who would possess that land?
- Money from all European countries was sent to Rome, making Rome very wealthy. Rome was assuming government over all of these countries which eventually led to problems that we will see in the Babylonian Captivity.
- The Latin language is no longer spoken yet Rome continues to conduct Mass in Latin. Scripture was also read in Latin and was not available to the people.
- Rome had become so corrupt that when Martin Luther visited it, he was utterly appalled. He said people who lived in Rome have a saying; "If there is a hell surely Rome is built on top of it."

THE BABYLONIAN CAPTIVITY (1305-1377)

- The papacy was moved from Rome to France. This is called the Babylonian captivity because it lasted roughly seventy years.
  - Where did the idea to call it the Babylonian captivity come from? Israel's enslavement for seventy years to Babylon (**Jeremiah 25:11**).
- It seemed ridiculous to some of the European emperors, that the pope was governing the affairs of countries that he wasn't familiar with. They were tired of sending their money to him and being governed by him.

- **King Philip** of France was tired of Pope Boniface VIII meddling in the affairs of France. He refused to pay taxes to the pope. He decided to tax the clergy of France in defiance.
    i. **Pope Boniface VIII** Issued a papal bull forbidding the clergy to pay the king anything without papal approval.
    ii. King Philip reacted with an embargo which cut off the papacy from a significant source of revenue.
    iii. Pope Boniface VIII issued a papal bull declaring his supremacy as the "Roman Pontiff" and demanding "payment, benediction, and consecration of the tithes."
        a. It was a common belief that "If the king resisted the pope-he resisted God himself."
    iv. King Philip seized and confined the pope in prison where he was beaten and deprived of water and food. Pope Boniface was rescued by local citizens yet died three days later in 1303.
- **Pope Benedict XI** (1303–1304) was pope for only nine months and was believed to be poisoned.
- **Pope Clement V** (1305–1314) moved the papal city to Avignon because he was French. The papacy was now in control of the French once again. This is another example of papal succession being broken. For roughly seventy years, seven French popes refused to move the papacy back to Rome. This led to the Papal Schism.

THE PAPAL SCHISM (1378–1417)

- **Pope Urban V** (1362–1370) made an unsuccessful attempt to permanently move the papacy back to Rome.
- **Pope Gregory XI** (1370–1379) successfully moved to papacy back to Rome.
- **Pope Urban VI** (1378–1379) was elected on the grounds that he would move the papacy back to France. He agreed, however after his election he refused to follow through. This sparks the schism in

The Middle Ages

which there were many popes in Rome and France, each of which anathematized the other.

  - What does the word "anathema" mean? To condemn to hell.

- At one time there were three popes at the same time each anathematizing the other. (Gregory XII, Benedict XIII, and John XXIII)

THE COUNCIL OF CONSTANCE (1414-1418)

- All three popes were excommunicated by the Council of Constance and replaced by **Martin V** (1417–1431) ending the schism and moving the papacy to Rome. This was yet another breach in papal succession.
- Because of all of the corruption in the papacy, the balance of power is shifted to councils rather than popes.
- The Council of Constance burns Jan Hus at the stake for preaching that Jesus is the head of the church.

Jan Hus "This council is a scene of foulness, for it is a common saying among the Swiss that a generation will not suffice to cleanse Constance from the sin which the council has committed in this city."

During this time, the Roman Catholic Church falls deeper into mysticism

- They began to teach that every believer is supervised by an angel.

"We should invoke the help of our Guardian Angels daily. 'From infancy to death human life is surrounded by their watchful care and protection. Beside each believer stands an angel as protector and shepherd leading him to life.' (CCC #336)." (The diocese of Harrisburg Catholic Teaching on Angels)

- Relics begin to be worshiped including martyred saints and the bones of Polycarp.
- Mary began to be elevated even more than she had in the past . . . almost to the point of deity.

- Indulgences began to be sold to people.
    - What are indulgences?
        - A document the Roman Catholic Church began to sell to people in order to keep them or relatives out of, or shorten, their time in purgatory. (The Treasury of Merit)
    - What is purgatory?
        - An intermediate state after physical death in which you await the purification that is needed in order to enter heaven. For more see page 177.
- They begin teaching baptismal regeneration.
    - What is baptismal regeneration?
        - The doctrine that teaches that justification is not possible without being baptized.
- With all that is going on, we can see why a reformation was needed.
- Constantinople falls to Muslim forces in 1453 marking the end of the Middle Ages.

NOTES

An Introduction to The Reformation

"There are seasons in the lives of all when it is not easy, no not even for Christians, to believe that God is faithful. Our faith is sorely tried, our eyes bedimmed with tears, and we can no longer trace the outworkings of His love. Our ears are distracted with the noises of the world, harassed by the atheistic whisperings of Satan, and we can no longer hear the sweet accents of His still small voice. Cherished plans have been thwarted, friends on whom we relied have failed us, a professed brother or sister in Christ has betrayed us. We are staggered. We sought to be faithful to God, and now a dark cloud hides Him from us. We find it difficult, yea, impossible, for carnal reason to harmonize His frowning providence with His gracious promises."[1]

A. W. PINK

- When did the Reformation begin?
    - Many believe the Reformation began in 1517 when Martin Luther nailed his 95 theses to the door of the church in Wittenberg. It actually began prior to that.
    - The Reformation was a process which started much earlier in the 1500s.
- What central issues sparked the Reformation?
    - The sale of Indulgences
    - Headship

1. Pink. *The Attributes of God*

- Authority
  - Who is the head of the church?
    - Jesus is the head of the Church. All other doctrines (the five solas) flowed out of this point.

(**Sola Scriptura**) The Word of God alone is our authority for (**Sola Fide**) Faith alone by (**Sola Gratia**) Grace alone on the basis of (**Sola Christus**) the work of Christ alone for (**Soli Deo Gloria**) the Glory of God alone.

- Jan Hus was told to stop preaching by the pope because of his stance against the Roman Catholic Church. He said that he could not stop because God was his authority.

From John McArthur's book *Slave:*

> "Huss's major work, *De Ecclesia* (the Church), outlined his major disagreements with the Roman Catholic system of his day. It was read publicly in Prague in 1413, and it contained radical views. For instance, Huss taught that the church was made up of all the predestined believers of all ages. This contrasted with the official position of the Roman Catholic Church, which taught that "the pope is the head and the cardinals the body of the church." Common laypeople were not real members but only communed with the true church through the Lord's Table (which for them was limited only to the bread). But the primary reason John Huss was put to death is this: he taught that Jesus Christ alone is the head of the church."[2]

Martin Luther in his *Table Talks*:

> "The chief cause that I fell out with the pope was this: the pope boasted that he was the head of the church, and condemned all that would now be under his power and authority . . . Further he took upon him power, rule and authority over the Christian church, and over the Holy Scriptures, the Word of God; (Claiming that) no man must presume to expound the Scriptures, but only he, and according to his ridiculous conceits; so that he made himself lord over the church"[3]

---

2. MacArthur. *Slave*
3. Luther, Martin. *The Ideas that Have Influenced Civilization*. P. 119

- What famous writing sparked The Reformation? The Bible

- Going back to the Waldensians, they were a rebel group who put the Bible in the hands of the laypeople. The RCC didn't think that the lay people should be reading it for themselves. It is for this reason that it was kept in Latin. When the lay people could read it themselves, The Reformation was sparked.

  - How does this apply to revivalism today? The Reformation is the largest revival in our history. Was it sparked by emotionalism, manipulation, or an evangelical crusade? No, it was sparked by people being exposed to the truth of God by reading his Word.

  - Did the Reformation represent something new? No, refer back to the section we covered "Are the Solas Something New?"

  - Was the Reformation necessary?

- Until recently no Christian would even question if the Reformation was necessary. Today many question its necessity. This is due largely to an ignorance of theology, doctrine, and church history.

  - Why is unifying all churches a bad idea?

FORERUNNERS TO THE REFORMATION

Peter Waldo (1140–218)

- Peter Waldo laid the foundation for the sixteenth century Reformation. He was a merchant who under conviction realized that he was motivated by money and not the love of Christ. In response, he sold all of his possessions and began a life of radical service to Christ. He loved the Scriptures, especially the Gospels. He was obligated to read them in Latin, however he wanted others to read and hear them in their own language. Peter and two other men translated the Scriptures into the people's language (French and Italian).

- He condemned papal excesses and Catholic dogmas, including purgatory and transubstantiation.

  - What is **purgatory**?

- An intermediate state after physical death in which you await the purification that is needed in order to enter heaven. Punishment is involved in order to purify the person.
        i. Roman Catholics get this doctrine from the apocryphal book 2 Maccabees. They also twist canonical passages such as: 2 Timothy 1:18; Matthew 12:23; Luke 16:19–26; and Luke 23:43.
    - What is **transubstantiation**?
        - The unbiblical teaching that at the Lord's Supper, the wine becomes the literal blood of Jesus and the bread becomes the literal body of Jesus when placed in the mouth.

- Waldo began to preach the Scriptures in the town square rather than in church buildings after being denied the right to preach by the RCC.
- He was excommunicated by the RCC and his followers were persecuted as heretics.
- He was given the nickname Peter after standing against the RCC and preaching despite being told that he could not.
- He started the Waldensian movement.
    - Have you ever realized that like Waldo, you were idolizing something?
        - Money is a big one, but ask yourself this question: what consumes my thoughts? Scripture tells us to *"pray without ceasing"* in **1 Thessalonians 5:17**. Learning to pray to God, follow God, glorify God, and meditate on his Word throughout your day is a skill worth honing. Understand that it is by God's grace that you grow in this, so ask him to help you to make an idol of nothing and glorify the One True God. You may be surprised at what you find yourself doing.

Waldensians (1184–1500's)

- Following Waldo, the Waldenses began to preach in France and Italy in the town squares.
    i. They asked permission from the pope to preach. The pope asked if they believed in Mary the mother of Christ and they answered yes, uneducated on the Nestorian controversy and the nuances of what they affirmed. They were laughed at and considered heretics.
        a. This is an example of where theology got in the way of biblical truth, they simply didn't understand what the implications were because of their ignorance of church history.
- They practiced voluntary poverty, lay preaching, and believed in the authority of Scripture alone.
- They would carry copies of the Bible with them and would give them away to people. They believed that the Bible should never be sold. They referred to the Bible as the "Pearl of Great Price."
- They were greatly persecuted by the RCC and would often flee into the Alps to hide in order to survive.
- They assigned large portions of Scripture to different families to memorize in the event that they were overtaken, and their Bibles taken away. If this were to happen, they planned to gather and re-write the Bible from memory.
- This group joined the Reformers in the 1500s. They still exist today, sadly as a liberal denomination.
    - What are some ways that theology can get in the way of biblical truth, understanding, or like the Waldensians . . . action?
    - The Waldensians believed that the Bible should be free to people. Why are there so many versions available today?

John Wycliffe (1329–1384) (England)

- Wycliffe believed that Scripture alone was his authority and that the pope was the antichrist.
- His followers were known as the Lollards because they would often sing and hand out handwritten tracts to people with Scripture in English rather than Latin.
- He taught sola fide.
- He taught that clergy could marry.
- He denied baptismal regeneration.
- He opposed transubstantiation and the Mass.
  - What is the Mass? A Roman Catholic Church ceremony that involves Bible reading, prayer, sacrifice, hymns, symbols, gestures, and the partaking of bread and wine.

  "Perhaps the most notable, and most troubling, aspect of the Mass is the sacrament of the Eucharist. According to Paragraph #1336 of The Catechism of the Catholic Church (CCC), the Mass seeks to "re-present" Jesus as a sacrifice during the observance of the Eucharist. CCC Paragraph #1367 communicates that the atoning Sacrifice of Jesus and the Eucharist are one in the same. In other words, every time the Catholic Church observes the Eucharist during Mass, it is re-sacrificing Jesus."[4]

- Wycliffe opposed crusades, indulgences, and religious orders.
- He translated the Bible from Latin into English.
  i. The Wycliffe Bible and some of his commentaries are still available.
- He had close ties with the King which kept him from being killed by the RCC on several occasions.
- About fifty years after he died, the RCC dug up his bones and burned them.

---

4. Article from Pulpit and Pen. *"Is the Roman Catholic mass biblical?*

"The true Christian was intended by Christ to prove all things by the Word of God: all churches, all ministers, all teaching, all preaching, all doctrines, all sermons, all writings, all opinions, all practices. These are his marching orders. Prove all by the Word of God; measure all by the measure of the Bible; compare all with the standard of the Bible; weigh all in the balances of the Bible; examine all by the light of the Bible; test all in the crucible of the Bible. That which cannot abide the fire of the Bible, reject, refuse, repudiate, and cast away. This is the flag which he nailed to the mast. May it never be lowered!"[5] John Wycliffe

- Do you examine the Scriptures to see if what you have been taught by your favorite pastor/teacher is true?
- What did Jesus say was the greatest commandment? **Matthew 22:37** *"You shall love the Lord your God with all your heart, and with all your soul, and with all your mind."*
- In what way can the Lollards be an example to us?
- Would you feel comfortable singing or handing out gospel tracts in public?

Jan Hus (1369–1415)

- Hus pastored a church of approximately three-thousand people in Prague (Czech Republic).
- He taught that Christ was the head of the church.
- He openly denounced the sale of indulgences.
- He preached in the language of the people.
- He taught that the church consists of the total number of the predestined.
    i. The RCC taught at this time that only the clergy was part of the church.
- He distinguished between being in the church and being of the church.

---

5. Wycliffe, John. *Light from Old Times or Protestant Facts and Men*

- What is the visible and what is the invisible church?
  - The visible church refers to anyone who is present inside of the church building on any given worship service. The invisible church refers to true believers, those redeemed by Christ.
    i. Going to church does not make anyone a Christian.
- He denounced the moral failing of clergy, bishops and papacy from his pulpit. He was burned at the stake by the Roman Catholic Church because of this.

"Therefore, faithful Christian, seek the truth, listen to the truth, learn the truth, love the truth, tell the truth, defend the truth even to death."
Jan Hus

The Legend of Jan Hus

Hus is translated as Goose. The famous phrase "Your goose is cooked" comes from Hus being burned at the stake. Hus reportedly said, "Today you cook a goose, but in one hundred years a swan will rise whom you will not be able to silence." Luther would nail his 95 Theses to the church door one hundred years later.

Girolamo Savonarola (1452–1498) (Italy)

- Pope Alexander VI had five illegitimate children at this time from multiple women. Savonarola exposed publicly the pope's immorality. He was summoned by the pope because of this. He refused the summoning. He was excommunicated because he wouldn't appear before the pope. This didn't stop him however, he continued to preach in direct violation of the pope's order. Because he defied the pope, he was hanged, and his body burned by the Roman Catholic Church.
  - Is it okay to call out publicly false teachers like Girolamo did?

2 Timothy 3:16–17 *16 All Scripture is inspired by God and profitable for teaching, for reproof, for correction, for training in righteousness; 17 so that the man of God may be adequate, equipped for every good work.*

- Girolamo was sentenced to death under these charges:
    i. Free justification through faith in Christ.
    ii. Communion ought to be ministered under both kinds (clergy and laypeople).
    iii. Indulgences and pardons of the pope were of no effect.
    iv. Preaching against the filthy and wicked living of the cardinals and spirituality.
    v. Denying the pope's supremacy.
    vi. Affirming that the keys were not given to Peter alone, but unto the universal church.
    vii. Preaching that the pope did neither follow the life nor doctrine of Christ; for that he did attribute more to his own pardons and traditions than to Christ's merits; and therefore, he was antichrist.
    viii. Teaching the pope's excommunications are not to be feared, and that he who fears or flee them is excommunicated of God.
    ix. Preaching auricular confession is not necessary (confessions to clergy).
    x. Moving the citizens to uproar and sedition.

- Discuss some of these charges. Was Girolamo wrong in any of these?

> "O soul, do not let yourself be reduced to that point, but still, if you are so reduced, do not despair, take hold of these remedies. First, have recourse to the Crucified; consider the goodness of him who wanted to be crucified and to die to save you. Have great confidence in him, that, if you have recourse to him with a contrite heart, he will help you, even if you have committed thousands of sins. Consider how benevolently he pardoned the thief, and do not despair, but have faith that he will pardon you also, if you have recourse to him in all humility, for he has poured out his blood for you."[6] **Girolamo Savonarola**

---

6. Bentham. *Selected Writings of Girolamo Savonarola*

An Introduction to The Reformation

Jacques Lefevre (Jacob Faber) (1455–1536)

- Lefevre translated the Bible into French in 1528.
- He was a great influence on John Calvin who met with him between 1533–1534.
- He taught Sola Scriptura, Sola Fide, and Soli Deo Gloria.

> "Christ truly forgives our sins, setting us free from them in this life's pilgrimage . . . But he who trusts in works trusts in himself and leans on a cane which breaks of itself . . . By grace alone [*per solam gratiam*] can we be saved . . . For we are saved by his grace through faith—saved not because of ourselves, but by God's grace. For grace is a gift, not a work. And lest we should think that the faith by means of which we are justified is ours, *even this is God's gift*. Therefore, *we should attribute everything to God and nothing to ourselves*, and so we should glory neither in ourselves nor in works, but in God's grace and mercy alone."[7]

> "The apostle teaches us that we must look to God for the accomplishment of every good work that has been started, saying that it is for him to complete the work he has started . . . Accordingly, we can readily understand that *of himself man can do no good thing*, and that all who boast of their ability are in error and blaspheme against God when they attribute to themselves what belongs properly to God, *from whom comes our ability to do any good thing* . . . The apostle was quite right to be confident concerning the Philippians that God would grant them this grace to enable them to persevere to the end . . . Here, then, St. Paul causes us to understand how *good work in its entirety, from beginning to end, should be attributed to God*."[8]

- Is sanctification synergistic or monergistic? How would Lefevre answer this question?

    i. We have covered Synergism vs. Monergism. Here is a quick review:

    Synergism teaches that humans have the obligation and responsibility to cooperate with God in order to be justified and in the workings of sanctification. This was the RCC view.

---

7. Hughes. *Lefevre; Pioneer of Ecclesiastical Renewal in France*
8. Hughes. *Lefevre; Pioneer of Ecclesiastical Renewal in France*

Monergism teaches that justification is entirely the work of God. That man is dead and has the ability to do nothing, therefore is not able to take credit in any way for justification. This is the reformed view.

Desiderius Erasmus (1466–1536)

- Erasmus never leaves the RCC though he battles it from within. Perhaps wanting to change it rather than abandoning it.
- He wrote several books including:

The Praise of Folly which attacked Roman Catholic traditions and superstitions.

Novum Instrumentum and *Novum Testamentum* a Greek New Testament with translations and notes. It also exposed errors in the Vulgate.

> Erasmus: "But what do I speak of any one or the other particular kind of men, as if this self-love had not the same effect everywhere and rendered most men superabundantly happy? As when a fellow, more deformed than a baboon, shall believe himself handsomer than Homer's Nereus . . . Or to what purpose is it I should mind you of our professors of arts? Forasmuch as this self-love is so natural to them all that they had rather part with their father's land than their foolish opinions; but chiefly players, fiddlers, orators, and poets, of which the more ignorant each of them is, the more insolently he pleases himself, that is to say vaunts and spreads out his plumes . . . *the more foolish a man is, the more he pleases himself and is admired by others, to what purpose should he beat his brains about true knowledge, which first will cost him dear, and next render him the more troublesome and less confident, and lastly, please only a few*?"[9]

- What is Erasmus communicating to us in the above passage?

> Erasmus: "And next there come those that commonly call themselves the religious and monks, most false in both titles, when both a great part of them are farthest from religion, and no men swarm thicker in all places than themselves . . . By reason of these fooleries they not only set slight by others, but each different order, men otherwise professing apostolical charity, despise

9. Erasmus, *The Praise of Folly*

one another, and for the different wearing of a habit, or that 'tis of darker color, they put all things in combustion. And among these there are some so rigidly religious that their upper garment is haircloth, their inner of the finest linen; and, on the contrary, others wear linen without and hair next their skins. Others, again, are as afraid to touch money as poison, and yet neither forbear wine nor dallying with women. In a word, 'tis their only care that none of them come near one another in their manner of living, nor do they endeavor how they may be like Christ, but how they may differ among themselves . . ."[10]

- What is Erasmus pointing out in the above passage?

• Martin Luther and Erasmus butted heads over Erasmus's refusal to leave the RCC and Semi-Pelagian theology.

- Should a person stay at an apostate or heretical church to try to change it like Erasmus did?

REFORMERS

Martin Luther (1483–1546)

• Luther's father Huns was a successful miner. Huns wanted his son Martin to become a lawyer, so he funded much of Martin's education. Martin got his master's degree in law. He was enrolled in law school at Erfurt when on July 2nd, 1505, he was nearly struck by lightning. He cried out to his patron St. Anne "save me and I will become a monk." Fifteen days later he joined the Augustinian monastery. His father was furious that all the money he spent on Martin's education was suddenly lost.

• Johann von Staupitz was the head of the monastery that Luther joined. Luther was so gripped by his depravity and unworthiness before a holy God that he would confess his sins so frequently that Staupitz became annoyed. Luther confessed to Staupitz longer and more frequently than anyone else and would often even wake him in order to confess. Staupitz had to limit Luther's confessions for his own sanity and peace.

10. Erasmus, *The Praise of Folly*

- What is the doctrine of total depravity or moral inability?
- What is the difference between partial and total?

* Luther understood his depravity well, yet he did not understand moral inability.
    i. There is nothing you can do to satisfy God's perfect justice.

* Luther would perform extreme acts of penance such as laying on the cold floor in the winter without a blanket, whipping himself, and starving himself. This was done to such extremes that his body was permanently damaged.

Luther wrote: "If ever a monk got to heaven by monkery, I would have gotten there."

* He was ordained into the priesthood in 1507, began teaching theology at Wittenberg in 1508, and earned his doctorate in 1512.
* Luther's extreme sense of guilt and unworthiness could not be satisfied no matter what he did to himself or any effort he made to pay for his own sins. He thought surely a trip to Rome would do the trick, so in 1510 he traveled to Rome. He was very excited to arrive in Rome, but quickly became disillusioned by all of the corruption. The people of Rome had a saying: "If there is a hell, surely Rome is built on top of it."
* According to the RCC you had to be perfected in order to enter heaven. Luther realized that it was impossible for him to be perfected, therefore a sense of hopelessness consumed him. Finally he began to understand justification while studying **Romans** and **Galatians**.

Romans 1:16–17 is what seemed to be the key to Luther's turning: *For I am not ashamed of the gospel, for it is the power of God for salvation to everyone who believes, to the Jew first and also to the Greek. For in it the righteousness of God is revealed from faith to faith; as it is written, "But the righteous man shall live by faith."*

   i. He hated the phrase *"the righteousness of God"* because all he could see was his own condemnation. He viewed this as "the righteous standard of God." Through studying

Romans and Galatians, he finally came to understand that it isn't only the righteous standard of God but the righteous provision of God also.

- How is God's righteous standard satisfied?

  - The righteousness of God is satisfied by faith alone through grace, based on Christ's righteousness, by which we are justified because of his death, burial and resurrection on our behalf.

Martin Luther "At last, by the mercy of God, meditating day and night, I have heed to the context of the words, namely, "In it the righteousness of God is revealed, and it is written, 'He who through faith is righteous shall live.'" There I began to understand that the righteousness of God is that by which the righteous lives by a gift of God, namely by faith. And this is the meaning: the righteousness of God is revealed by the gospel, namely, the passive righteousness with which merciful God justifies us by faith, as it is written, "He who through faith is righteous shall live." Here I felt that I was altogether born again and had entered paradise itself through open gates. There a totally other face of the entire Scripture showed itself to me."[11]

- This is an expression of relief. The relief that every sinner should feel when they grasp the gospel and are saved.

  - Have you ever suddenly understood a Bible doctrine and the entire Bible came to life in a new way? If so, what Bible doctrine was it?

- Presuppositions are brought to Scripture and believed, even in the most intensive studies such as a monastery. However, until the Holy Spirit brings the text to life, understanding is impossible.

  - What presuppositions have you brought to Scripture?

- In 1517, Albert of Hohenzollern commissioned Johann Tetzel to sell indulgences in Germany. When Tetzel came to Wittenberg, it greatly angered Luther in which he responded with his 95 theses. His theses were intended for inter-church debate. It was written

11. Luther. *Preface to the Complete Edition of Luther's Latin Writings. Vol V.*

in Latin but was translated into German which exploded into the Reformation. He was angered by the corruption of Rome but also the injustice of the people who believed Rome and were giving their well-earned money for a scam.

    i. The scam continues today in a new light by health, wealth, and prosperity charlatans.

Tetzel's slogan: "As soon as a coin in the coffer rings, the soul from Purgatory springs."

    - Is there ever a time that anger is a correct response?
    - Have you ever been angered by false teaching just to realize later that it wasn't the teaching you were angry about but the brothers and sisters in Christ who were being deceived by it?

- In July 1519, Luther debated Johann Eck on papal authority. He appealed to the Scriptures and the church fathers.
- On June 15, 1520, a papal bull ordering Luther to recant within sixty days or face excommunication was issued. This is still a state religion, and to be excommunicated would be an act of treason against the government. Luther took the full sixty days to announce his decision. He understood what would likely happen to him, he wasn't ignorant of church history, he would more than likely be burned at the stake. On the sixtieth day he marched out into the town square with some of his students, built a bond fire, and burned the papal bull. It was his way of saying, "I am going to be burned, but first let me burn this to show my stance and my dedication to Christ".

    i. To burn someone was a symbol that they await hell fire, so he burns the papal bull!

- Luther wrote a response to the papal bull in which he called the pope "antichrist" who oversaw a church that was "the most lawless den of robbers, the most shameless of all brothels, the very kingdom of sin, death and hell."
- He began to understand what he would call the "Theology of the Cross." Human beings can do nothing to earn their own righteousness before God; nor can they add anything to the righteousness

provided for them through the Cross; any righteousness given to them comes from outside of them. It is an "alien righteousness."

   i. The RCC taught/teaches what Luther called the "Theology of glory." That even after the fall there remained some ability in man to achieve his own righteousness (through his own free will); and that sinners are saved by materially cooperating with the righteousness they receive from God. Thus, it is God's righteousness plus their own righteousness that saves them.

- He was excommunicated by Pope Leo X on January 3, 1521.
- He was summoned to **the Diet of Worms** (Diet meaning a council called by an emperor rather than a church) to make a defense of his teachings. He was promised safe passage. He agrees to go based on the promise of safe passage. Had he refused he would surely have been put to death.

   i. Some of his prayer is recorded the morning of this event: "My God, stand by me against all the world's wisdom and reason. Not mine but Yours is the cause. I would prefer to have peaceful days and to be out of this turmoil. But Yours, O Lord, is this cause. It is righteous and eternal. Stand by me, O God. In the name of your dear Son, Jesus Christ, who shall be my defense and shelter, yes, my mighty fortress, through the might and strength of Your Holy Spirit. Amen."

- When asked by the council whether or not he would recant, he replied. "Since your Majesty and your Worships desire a simple reply, I will answer ... Unless I am convinced by Scripture and plain reason, I do not accept the authority of popes and councils for they have contradicted each other. My conscience is captive to the Word of God. I cannot and I will not recant anything, for to go against conscience is neither right nor safe. God help me. Amen (Here I stand)."[12]

   i. He is saying this to the Emperor and his representatives and the pope and his representatives!

---

12. Luther. Diet of Worms. April 18, 1521

Matthew 10:28 *"Do not fear those who kill the body but are unable to kill the soul; but rather fear Him who is able to destroy both soul and body in hell."*

- The pledge to give him safe passage was honored at that time; however, he was declared a notorious heretic. This made it a crime to assist Luther or even provide him with food or shelter. They banned his writings and made it legal for anyone to kill him without consequence. On the way home he was "kidnapped" by Prince Frederick III of Saxony, who took him to the Wartburg Castle.
- He took the name Junker Jorge and began writing under this name.
- While at the Wartburg Castle, he translated the New Testament from Greek to German.
- Radical Anabaptists (the Zwickau Prophets) began causing trouble during this time in Wittenberg, including acts of violence. They were stirred by the Reformation and wanted a revolution. Luther returned to the city and preached against those who were inciting unrest and the city quickly returned to order.
    i. He was very concerned that the Reformation did not become a political revolution.

Luther preached: "Do you know what the Devil thinks when he sees men use violence to propagate the gospel? He sits with folded arms behind the fire of hell, and says with malignant looks and frightful grin: 'Ah, how wise these madmen are to play my game! Let them go on; I shall reap the benefit. I delight in it.' But when he sees the Word running and contending alone on the battlefield, then he shudders and shakes for fear."[13]

- Why should there be godly leadership in the church?

- Luther disagreed with priestly celibacy, so he married a woman named **Katharina von Bora**. This broke the cycle of priestly celibacy that had been in the church for centuries. Katie was a nun that Luther helped escape from the nunnery by hiding her and others in fish barrels. Prior to marrying Katie, Luther wrote: "I shall never take a wife, as I feel at present. Not that I am insensible to my flesh

---

13. Schaff. *History of the Christian Church*

or sex (for I am neither wood nor stone); but my mind is averse to wedlock because I daily expect the death of a heretic."[14] They had six children together. They had a great marriage, He referred to Katie as his "rib" and referred to his favorite book of the Bible (Galatians) as his "Katie."

- Why is biblical marriage a good thing?

• The radical Anabaptists were still stirring up the people, trying to turn the Reformation into revolution. They started what is known as the "Peasant War." One of the things they were demanding was communism.

Luther wrote in support of the military forces to put a stop to this war:

> "Therefore, let everyone who can, smite, slay, and stab, secretly or openly, remembering that nothing can be more poisonous, hurtful, or devilish than a rebel . . . For baptism does not make men free in body and property, but in soul; and the gospel does not make goods common, except in the case of those who, of their own free will, do what the apostles and disciples did in Acts 4. They did not demand, as do our insane peasants in their raging, that the goods of others—of Pilate and Herod—should be common, but only their own goods. Our peasants, however, want to make the goods of other men common, and keep their own for themselves. Fine Christians they are! I think there is not a devil left in hell; they have all gone into the peasants. Their raving has gone beyond all measure."[15]

- Is a violent Christian revolution ever the proper response?
- Was Luther correct in supporting the military to put an end to this revolution?

• In 1527 Luther's health took a turn for the worst and he thought that he may die. This year the black plague hit Wittenberg. It is during this time that Luther wrote that he had almost lost his faith, much like the cries of David in the Psalms. He understands that it is only by God's grace that he was persevered, and God preserved him and his faith. It is out of this mindset that Luther wrote his famous

---

14. Schaff. *History of the Christian Church*
15. Wilson and Herman. *Critical Thinking Using Primary Sources in World History*

hymn, "A Mighty Fortress." (He mentions this in his prayer that was recorded on page 189.)

- Have you been through a trial in which you felt like you could lose your faith?
- Why does God allow us to go through or put us through these things?

- By the year 1534 Luther had finished translating the entire Bible.
  i. This influenced Tyndale to translate the Bible into English.

- Luther disagreed with other reformers on Communion. He insisted on the real presence of Christ, while other reformers taught it is symbolic.
  i. The RCC view is called transubstantiation in which the wine and bread turn into the literal body and blood of Christ.
  ii. Luther's view is called consubstantiation in which there is a real presence of Christ in, above, and around the bread and wine.
  iii. Zwingli's view is the memorial view which is done in remembrance.
      a. Later this would be such a disagreement that it split the Reformation into Reformed and Lutheran distinctions that are still divided today over this topic.

- Martin's intense and passionate personality came out against everyone who disagreed with Scripture, and this included the Jews. He initially espoused kindness toward them, for the purpose of converting them. Later he grew hostile toward them because of their refusal to convert and their greed in the marketplace in which they were taking advantage of people in banking and by over pricing merchandise.
  i. Unlike the RCC, he did not blame the Jews for crucifying Christ.

An Introduction to The Reformation

- ii. He wrote a pamphlet against them toward the end of his life that was very harsh and considered by some to be antisemitic.

  - What is antisemitism? Hostility, prejudice, and discrimination against Jews.

- Luther's pamphlet was not intended to be antisemitic, but it was certainly too harsh. This was perfectly in line with his intense personality and passion for the truth of the gospel in which the Jews rejected and, in his eyes, blasphemed the deity of Christ. He was much harsher toward the RCC, popes, and really anyone who disagreed with him. Not to make excuses for him, he was a flawed man just like all men.

The best of men are still men at best.

- Because he was wrong in this area does not bring down all the other things he did and stood for.
- Luther did not hate the bloodline of the Jews; he hated their stubbornness, greed, and religion. That is the difference between being antisemitic or not. True antisemitism hates the Jews simply because they are Jews.

  - i. Despite his intentions, he had an impact on history that was dark on this matter.
  - ii. Let us consider our own sin and the impact it has to our little world around us.
  - iii. And let us not forget that God himself used Luther in a powerful way and not let this dark mistake he made taint the work God used him to accomplish.

- In 1542 his thirteen-year-old daughter Magdalena died. This was the greatest trial in Luther's life. It sent him into depression. At times he felt like he was going to break, yet God's strength undergirded him.

  - Have you ever felt like that?

        i. Many great leaders in the faith have felt this, and so will you at some point. Trials are meant for us to learn to lean on God and not on our own strength.

- Luther's last sermon was in February 1546. He was traveling to assist his siblings in a legal matter and died on February 18 in which his abused body finally gave out.

Ulrich Zwingli (1484–1531 Switzerland)

- Zwingli was highly influenced by the teachings of Erasmus and looked forward to reform taking place in the RCC.
- It was by God's sovereignty that Zwingli began reform at the same time as Luther, yet never hearing of Luther or any of his teachings at this point in time.
- He was a chaplain for Swiss troops.
    i. The pope used these troops for his own agendas in other countries. Zwingli was greatly opposed to the idea of his countrymen dying for the pope rather than serving their country.
- He was an expository preacher. He preached verse by verse almost through the entire New Testament.
    i. This is what stirred the hearts of the people, being exposed to the Word of God in such a deep way. They had never heard anything like this before.

> Zwingli: (from his sermon "On the Clarity and Certainty or Power of the Word of God.") The Word of God is so sure and strong that if God wills all things are done the moment that he speaks his Word. For it is so living and powerful that even the things which are irrational immediately conform themselves to it, or to be more accurate, *things both rational and irrational are fashioned and dispatched and constrained in conformity with its purpose.* The proof may be found in Genesis I: "And God said, Let there be light; and there was light." Note how alive and strong the Word is, not merely

ruling all things but *creating out of nothing* that which it wills. *With God, in fact, there is no such thing as past or future*, but all things are naked and open to his eyes. *He does not learn with time or forget with time, but with unerring knowledge and perception he sees all things present in eternity.* It is in time that we who are temporal find the meaning and measure of longness or shortness. Yet what seems long to us is not long to God, but eternally present.[16]

- Discuss some of the doctrines in the above excerpt.
- Because of his biblical preaching, indulgences in his country were done away with.
- When the plague hit Zurich, he refused to leave because he wanted to minister to the people. As a result, the plague nearly killed him in 1519.
  - i. Two-thousand out of seven-thousand people died in Zurich.

- He wrote a poem when he thought he was going to die: "Thy purpose fulfill: nothing can be too severe for me. I am thy vessel, for you to make whole or break to pieces. Since, if you take hence my spirit from this earth, you do it so that it will not grow evil and will not mar the pious lives of others."[17]
  - i. This clearly shows his understanding of the sovereignty of God. John Calvin gets most of the credit during the Reformation, because he so clearly pins the sovereignty of God in his *Institutes*. But here we see it very clear before the writings of Calvin. Calvin was influenced by this man.
    - How do you think the people felt to have a minister next to them on their deathbed, risking his own life to minister to them?

- Because he stayed rather than leaving when the plague struck, the people greatly loved and respected him.

---

16. Zwingli. *Zwingli & Bullinger*. Bromiley
17. Zwingli. *Radical Reformation*. Williams

- He preaches against all of the RCC abuses: indulgences, fasting, private confession, The Mass, icons, purgatory, and the intercession of the saints.
  - What is the intercession of the saints?
    - The belief that we should pray to people that the Roman Catholic and Easter Orthodox Churches have deemed to be saints. This also includes prayer to Mary and angels. The saints will intercede on our behalf.
  - What is the biblical definition of a saint? Anyone who is in Christ.[18]
- Zwingli is so committed to sola Scriptura that he forbids anything in church that is not explicitly taught in the Scriptures. This included music.

The Normative Principle teaches that unless Scripture explicitly prohibits something it is allowed. This was what Luther believed and taught.

The Regulative Principle teaches that unless the New Testament explicitly commands something it is forbidden. This is what Zwingli believed and taught.

  - What are the pros and cons of these two principles?

- Zwingli practices what he preaches and preaches against fasting on Lent. Afterwards, he and other priests broke the fast by eating smoked sausages in public.
- He petitioned the RCC to void mandatory celibacy. His request was denied; however, it didn't stop him from secretly marrying Anna Reinhard, which nearly caused a scandal when it was made public in 1524.

"For God's sake, do not put yourself at odds with the Word of God. For truly it will persist as surely as the Rhine [river] follows its course. One can perhaps dam it up for a while, but it is impossible to stop it."[19] Ulrich Zwingli (The dam being the RCC.)

---

18. Acts 9:13 and 32; Acts 26:10; Romans 1:7; Philippians 4:22
19. Zwingli. *Zwingli A reformed Theologian*. Courvoisier

- On January 29, 1523, in Zurich, he defended, in front of over six-hundred people, **Sixty-Seven Articles** of his evangelical belief in order to state his case that the church should become protestant. Below are the first ten of his sixty-seven articles.

    I. All who say that the gospel is invalid without the confirmation of the church err and slander God.

    II. The sum and substance of the gospel is that our Lord Jesus Christ, the true Son of God, has made known to us the will of his heavenly Father, and has with his innocence released us from death and reconciled God.

    III. Hence Christ is the only way to salvation for all who ever were, are and shall be.

    IV. Who seeks or points out another door errs, yes, he is a murderer of souls and a thief.

    V. Therefore all who consider other teachings equal to or higher than the gospel err, and do not know what the gospel is.

    VI. For Jesus Christ is the guide and leader, promised by God to all human beings, which promise was fulfilled.

    VII. That he is an eternal salvation and head of all believers, who are his body, but which is dead and can do nothing without him.

    VIII. From this follows first that all who dwell in the head are members and children of God, and that it is the church or communion of the saints, the bride of Christ, *Ecclesia catholica*.

    IX. Furthermore, that as the members of the body can do nothing without the control of the head, so no one in the body of Christ can do the least without his head, Christ.

    X. As that man is mad whose limbs (try to) do something without his head, tearing, wounding, injuring himself; thus when the members of Christ undertake something without their head, Christ, they are mad, and injure and burden themselves with unwise ordinances.

- The RCC sent Johann Faber to defend its position at this disputation. Zwingli won and was allowed to continue reformation in the city. This became the first Protestant city.

- On October 26, 1523, in Zurich, a second disputation was organized to address the Mass and Icons. There were over nine-hundred people who attended. Zurich made massive reforms including:
    i. Images were removed which included pictures, statues, and candles
    ii. Bones of saints were buried
    iii. Altars were replaced by tables
    iv. Organs in churches were dismantled
    v. Choirs were abolished
    vi. Gold and silver were melted down from relics and crucifixes
    vii. Monasteries were transformed into shelters and schools

While Luther wanted reformation to take place slowly, Zwingli was much more aggressive.

- On April 16, 1525, Zwingli performed the first protestant Lord's Supper in centuries. He served both elements to the people rather than just the bread. He also read Scripture in German rather than Latin.
- Zwingli began discipling a group of men. Together they began looking at the way certain Bible doctrines were being taught. These men agreed that infant baptism was not in the Bible and should not be practiced. This is where they differed from Zwingli who held to the RCC way of baptism. These men parted with Zwingli over a decision he made in which they believed that he followed the city council over biblical truth. It seemed to them that his final authority was government rather than the Bible.
- In Jan 1525 Zwingli debated his former students on the issue of baptism. The city sided with Zwingli and ordered the former students to baptize their children. They were also forbidden to meet for private Bible study and were threatened with banishment.
    i. These students became known as the Anabaptists.
- Twelve men met in the home of Felix Manz and performed believer's baptism for the first time recorded in centuries.

An Introduction to The Reformation

   i. They went house to house preaching believer's baptism.
   ii. They published pamphlets against Zwingli on baptism.

- In March 1526 the town issued a death penalty for rebaptism. As a result, many were drowned for practicing believer's baptism.
   i. Protestants killing protestants in what they considered a permanent baptism.
      - Is the separation of church and state a good idea?
- There were different movements of the Anabaptists. These in Switzerland were not violent and did not want communism like those in Germany.
- The tension between the RCC and the protestants eventually led to two wars, one of which Zwingli died in battle in the year 1531.
   i. He accompanied the army from Zurich to defend against five invading catholic cantons. He was a chaplain who carried a battle axe into war.
   ii. The RCC cut his body into pieces, burned them all and mixed his ashes with dung so that he could not have a grave.
      - Does America need a Reformation today?
      - If so, what are some of the things in today's church that need to be reformed?

Anabaptists (re-baptizers) also known as the Radical Reformers

- We have already seen that this title applies to groups of people that may believe entirely different things. The one thing that united them is that they all acknowledge believers' baptism. Below are four categories of anabaptists.

Anti-Trinitarian Rationalists

Michael Servetus

- We will learn about Servetus when we get to John Calvin in our study.

Spiritual Mystics

Caspar Schwenckfeld

- He believed in extra-biblical revelation from the Holy Spirit. His movement was a precursor to the modern Pentecostal movement.

Zwickau Prophets

- They attempted to bring spiritual change through political means. They claimed to be acting under the direct guidance of the Holy Spirit who was giving them divine revelation. Scripture was of secondary importance to these men. Their foundational authority was ultimately their own imagination. They believed that the Millennial kingdom could be brought about by purifying the church even by means of violence to accomplish this. We will see a similar idea emerge once again when we get to the charismatic movement.

Melchior Hoffman

- He was re-baptized in 1530 and predicted that Christ would return in 1533 and establish the New Jerusalem in Strasbourg, France.

Political Fanatics

Ulrich von Hutton

- He was a humanist and the leader of the Imperial Knights and led the Knights Revolt in Germany. He was defeated in 1522. He was a supporter of Martin Luther even though Luther preached against this revolt.

Thomas Muntzer

- He led the Peasants' Rebellion in Germany that Luther also came against. He was fighting for communism. He was defeated and killed.

Swiss Brethren

- These were Zwingli's students. They took his teachings on the regulative principle much further than Zwingli did.
- This was the group that sparked the anabaptist movement.
- The main issues they fought for were baptism and the separation of church and state.

Menno Simons (1496–1561)

- Menno was an anabaptist that started what today is called the Mennonite Church.
- His brother was killed as one of the anabaptist fanatics in battle. Menno was deeply affected. He was an avid student of Scripture and could see no place where Christians should ever revolt against the government and there was never a reason to kill another human being.
- He wanted nothing whatsoever to do with politics. This may have been a reaction to his brother being killed and the ugliness he could see in the violence between people who claimed to be Christians.
- He started teaching **pacifism**.
    - What is pacifism? The belief that a Christian should never take a human life. In some cases, it is believed this is true even in self-defense or the defense of family.
    - Is pacifism biblical?
- Menno wrote a book *The Blasphemy of John of Leiden*, which was a polemic against Leiden who self-proclaimed himself to be King David of New Jerusalem.
    i. Jan van Leyden (Leiden) was another anabaptist that believed Christ was about to return and that Munster, Germany was the New Jerusalem.

The death of Leiden and two other Anabaptists (Bernhard Krechting and Bernhard Knipperdolling): Leiden was attached to a pole by an iron spiked collar and his body ripped with red-hot tongs for the space of an hour. After Knipperdolling saw the process of torturing John of

Leiden, he attempted to kill himself with the collar, using it to choke himself. After that the executioner tied him to the stake to make it impossible for him to kill himself. After the burning, their tongues were pulled out with tongs before each was killed with a burning dagger thrust through the heart. The bodies were placed in three iron baskets and hung from the steeple of St. Lambert's Church and the remains left to rot. About fifty years later the bones were removed, but the baskets remained.

- Menno became recognized by the people as a great polemicist and gathered a large following.
- There is a book of anabaptist martyrs, much like *Foxe's book of Martyrs*, called the **Martyrs Mirror**.
- The anabaptists were persecuted by the RCC and the protestants.
    i. The protestants lumped them all into the category of radical and viewed them as undoing what they had worked so hard to do because they wanted to uproot the government.
- They were burned at the stake by the RCC and drowned by the protestants.
    - We should learn how to learn even from things that we would disagree with. Though we would disagree with the anabaptist in many areas, they were willing to die over what we would consider secondary issues. Would you be willing to die over secondary issues?

John Calvin (1509–1564) (France)

- Calvin was a second-generation Reformer.
- He is the most controversial reformer because his name is associated with a soteriology.
    i. In his time he was probably the least controversial.
    - What is soteriology? The method and specifics of how a person becomes justified.

Calvin's father wanted him to become a priest at first, but realizing that lawyers make more money, decided he should become a lawyer. He became a lawyer in 1532. It is while studying to become a lawyer that he was converted. He rarely talks about himself in his writings, but we find this in his commentary on the Psalms:

> "And first, since I was too obstinately devoted to the superstitions of Popery to be easily extricated from so profound an abyss of mire, God by a sudden conversion subdued and brought my mind to a teachable frame, which was more hardened in such matters than might have been expected from one at my early period of life. Having thus received some taste and knowledge of true godliness I was immediately inflamed with so intense a desire to make progress therein, that although I did not altogether leave off other studies, I yet pursued them with less ardor."[20]

- Has there been a time in your life that you were filled with an intense desire to make progress in your faith?
- If so, what caused that?

- Calvin learned Greek which was impactful for him when studying Scriptures.
- He was forced to flee France when he embraced reform.
- He wrote the first part of his famous work *The Institutes of the Christian Religion* in 1536. This book is the first systematic theology of the reformed church and went through several additions during the life of Calvin. Whether you're a fan of Calvin or not, this is a must read for any Christian. Begin with his section on prayer . . . do not try to read straight through it . . . that is not the intention of any systematic theology book.
- In 1536 he was traveling to Strasbourg, Germany but forced to go through Geneva in order to avoid French troops. **William Farel** pleaded with him to stay and help with reform there. Farel was a fiery reformer who would travel place to place and call people and catholic clergy to repentance and reform. Which got him into several fights because people would try to physically stop him. He was responsible for bringing the Waldensians into the Reformation.

---

20. Calvin. *A History of Christian Conversion.* Kling

Farel realized that he was not able to stay long term and wanted Calvin to stay and shepherd the church.

> Christianhistory.net: "With his brother and sister and two friends, John Calvin fled Catholic France and headed to the free city of Strasbourg. It was the summer of 1536; Calvin had recently converted to the "evangelical" faith and had just published The Institutes of the Christian Religion, which articulated his Protestant views. He was a wanted man."
>
> Word quickly passed to local church leader William Farel that the author of *The Institutes* was in town. Farel was ecstatic. He was desperate for help as he strove to organize a newly formed Protestant church in town. He rushed to the inn and pleaded with Calvin, arguing it was God's will he remain in the city.
>
> Calvin said he was staying only one night. Besides, he was a scholar not a pastor. Farel, baffled and frustrated, swore a great oath that God would curse all Calvin's studies unless he stayed in Geneva.
>
> Calvin, a man of tender conscience, later reflected on this moment: "I felt as if God from heaven had laid his mighty hand upon me to stop me in my course—and I was so terror stricken that I did not continue my journey."
>
> To this day, Calvin's name is associated, for good and for ill, with the city of Geneva. And Calvin's belief in God's election is his theological legacy to the church."

> John Calvin: "Being of a disposition somewhat unpolished and bashful, which led me always to love the shade and retirement, I then began to seek some secluded corner where I might be withdrawn from the public view; but so far from being able to accomplish the object of my be desire, all my retreats were like public spectacles. In short, whilst my one great object was to live in seclusion without being known, God so led me about through different turnings and changes, that he never permitted me to rest in any place, until, in spite of my natural disposition, he brought me forth to public notice."[21]

- Is a person's personality type ever an excuse to disobey The Great Commission?

---

21. Calvin, John. *John Calvin's Bible Commentaries: Psalms 1-35* P. 22

- His first few years were very hard as the reformer in the city. People would harass him, throw rocks at his house at all hours of the night, and even name their dogs after him.
- He drafted a set of morals which included things such as: no gambling, dancing, singing of immoral songs, and a curfew for the city. This set of morals was enforced which caused nonbelievers to hate him.
- Later the city turned on Calvin and Farel because they refused to let the city tell them how to take communion. They refused communion to a number of people who were not genuine Christians. They took this stand to show that they believed in the separation of church and state.
- In 1539 they were kicked out of town after being the reformers for two and a half years.
- Calvin continued to his original destination, Strasbourg, Germany. He really enjoyed Strasbourg. **Martin Bucer** was the reformer there . . . he was taught by Luther. He made Calvin the pastor of a French refugee church.
- In 1540 Calvin published his first commentary on Romans and got married.
- God sends Calvin back to Geneva even though he does not want to go in 1541.
    i. The city council realized they had made a mistake by running Farel and Calvin out of town. They write Bucer and ask for Calvin to return because they needed a strong theologian to counter the RCC. Strasbourg agreed to lend Calvin to Geneva for six months. Calvin spends the rest of his life there.
- The Sunday Calvin steps back into the pulpit to preach, he doesn't mention anything about what had happened. He simply opens his Bible to the very next verse where he left off two and a half years earlier in Romans and continues like nothing ever happened.
- He preaches six to seven times a week to the tune of over two-thousand sermons exposited verse by verse through the Scriptures.
- Calvin had a son who was born premature and died after a few days.

- Calvin's wife died after nine years of marriage which caused him great grief.
    - What keeps a believer sound in the midst of great tragedy?
- In 1546 a group of people known as the Libertines came on scene. They hated Calvin's strict moral ethical code.
    i. The man (Ami Perrin) who invited Calvin back was convicted of violating Geneva's dancing prohibition and became Calvin's main opponent and the leader of the Libertines.
- The Libertines wanted to be able to remain members of the church while indulging in whatever sin they were inclined to. One of these men placed a threatening letter on Calvin's pulpit, as a result he was sentenced to death by the city court which added fuel to the fire. The Libertines eventually took control of the city council.
- In 1553 opposition became so bad that Calvin asked to resign but was denied, probably because the city council enjoyed making his life miserable.
    - Have you ever wanted to give up on something that God providentially gave you to do?

It was during this time that a man was sentenced to excommunication from the church. This decision had to be approved by the city, however, the city would not approve the church's decision. The following Sunday Calvin refused to serve the man communion as recorded in the writing below:

> "His famous motto was embossed on the dark-red velvet pulpit cover: Soli Deo Gloria. Raising his voice and lifting up his hands, he exclaimed, in the words of St. Chrysostom: "I will lay down my life before these hands give the sacred things of God to those who have been branded as his despisers." A crowd of Libertines surged forward to the table. Calvin, descending from the pulpit stood before the table. With drawn sword a Libertine cried, 'Administer communion to us or you will die.' His head thrown back and his arms extended over the sacred elements, Calvin responded that although they might cut off his arms, shed his blood, and take his life, they would never

force him to give holy things to the profane and dishonor the table of his God."²²

  i. The men were ordered not to kill Calvin and communion was celebrated in profound silence under a solemn awe.

- The opposition came to an end in 1555 when the Libertines had to flee the city after a failed plot to burn down a house.

Did Calvin kill Michael Servetus?

- Servetus was a well-known heretic who opposed both the RCC and Protestants because he denied the Trinity. He wrote a book called "*On the Errors of the Trinity.*" According to Robert Godfrey, Calvin wanted to win him from his heresy and arranged a meeting, but Servetus did not show up. He continued to write against the Trinity, which was a very dangerous thing to do.

Calvin tried again to persuade him from his errors and warned Servetus that what he was espousing was lethal to his soul, dangerous to the Christian community, and would lead to his execution if arrested. Servetus didn't listen and published another book "*Restitution of the Christian Religion*" which was clearly a rebuttal to Calvin's "*Institutes.*"

- Servetus was arrested in France and was awaiting execution, but he escaped. He came to Geneva, probably to debate with Calvin, but was arrested and tried by the court. They wanted to burn him at the stake, but Calvin wanted a more humane execution, so he wrote to have him beheaded instead. They ignored Calvin and burned Servetus at the stake in 1553.
- Also, in the year 1553 Protestant refugees had to flee England because of Queen Mary I or "Bloody Mary" who made an attempt to stomp out the Reformation and reinstate the RCC system. Calvin welcomed the refugees including John Knox.

  i. These refugees later return to England and become known as the Puritans. John Knox returned to Scotland.

---

22. Article from The Banner of Truth. *The Reformers: The Secret Of Their Greatness.* Osterhaven

- Calvin established a school in Geneva where a man named Theodore Beza was head.
- Calvin was so dedicated to the preaching of God's word, that just before he died, he had men carry him on his bed to the pulpit to preach his last sermon. He preached from Ezekiel.
- He requested that there be no grave marker for fear that people would want to do some kind of hero worship because of the great public ministry God thrust upon him, even against his will.
  - How would Calvin feel about people today calling themselves Calvinists?
    i. He went through great lengths to be sure that people would not recognize him but glorify God . . . but like it or not, here we are.
- He did not come up with the TULIP acronym (see page 228). However, he did teach all of those things.
- Some of the key doctrines in Calvin's *Institutes*:
  i. Sola Scriptura
  ii. The Trinity
  iii. Divine Providence
  iv. Predestination
  v. Original sin
  vi. Justification by faith alone with obedience as fruit
  vii. Invisible /Visible Church
  viii. Only two sacraments: baptism and the Lord's Supper (memorial view)
  ix. A denunciation of RCC use of images and the denial of papal authority
  x. Prayer

Briefly go over each of these ten things.

THE ENGLISH REFORMATION

King Henry VIII (1491–1547) sparked the English Reformation politically. He wanted to divorce his wife, but the pope said no, so he divorced the RCC instead.

- He made reform and then backtracked because he was not really Protestant.

William Tyndale (1494–1536)

- Tyndale was an English reformer who lived under King Henry VIII.
- He completed the first Greek to English translation of the New Testament which was published in 1526.
    i. His Bibles were smuggled into England because the RCC would not allow laypeople to own Bibles. The Bishop of London, Cuthbert Tunstall, would seize Tyndale's Bibles and burn them publicly at St. Paul's Cathedral.
        - According to Scripture is there ever a time that a believer should deliberately disobey governmental law? No, unless the government is interfering with our obedience to God.[23]
- Much of the King James Bible is Tyndale's work.
- He was burned at the stake in 1536 by the RCC, two years before the Reformation began in England. He began to preach as the fires were lit, so they strangled him to shut him up.

"I call God to record against the day we shall appear before our Lord Jesus, that I never altered one syllable of God's Word against my conscience, nor would do this day, if all that is in earth, whether it be honor, pleasure, or riches, might be given me."[24]

William Tyndale

- Do you see God's Word being altered today?

---

23 Joshua 2:3–4; 1 Kings 18:4; Acts 5:29
24. Tyndale. *The Church Historians of England*

King Edward VI (1537–1553) followed Henry VIII. He made several reforms.

- He got sick at the age of fifteen. Just before he died, he chose his cousin, Lady Jane Gray as his heir.

Mary I (1516–1558) was Edward's half-sister. She resented Edward's decision to make Jane Gray the queen. She turned the powers that be against Jane Gray and had her deposed... becoming the queen herself. She worked to undo all of the reforms that Edward had made.

- *Foxe's book of Martyrs* was written in response to her bloody insurgency against the Protestants. She put to death around three-hundred Protestant leaders.
    i. Remember that many of the refugees fled to Geneva during this time.
- It was during this time that a group of men who were influenced by Luther and Wycliffe began to meet in a tavern called **The White Horse Inn** to discuss Reformation ideas. These men would all be martyred.

Elizabeth I (1533–1603) was the next Queen of England and embraced the Reformation allowing it to finally gain traction in England.

- The refugees who fled to Geneva return and become known as the Puritans. They were called the Puritans as a derogatory remark because their goal was to purify God's church.

THE SCOTTISH REFORMATION

John Knox (1510–572)

- Knox was a very fiery preacher whose reflection in art always has him seeming to fly out of the pulpit and his audience drawing back in shock at the power of his conviction.
- He found himself arrested while with a group of Protestants who had killed a cardinal for revenge after the cardinal had burned their

preacher at the stake. Knox had nothing to do with the killing, he was just visiting the outlaw Protestants.

- Why do bad things happen to good people?

- Knox was sentenced to a life of slavery in the gallows of a French ship. By God's providence he only served two years.
- He was severely beaten after refusing to kiss a sculpture of Mary, throwing it overboard and saying "Let our Lady now save herself. Let her learn to swim."
    i. This is a good example of how we should treat idolatry, throw it overboard.
- As he was on the ship looking across the water to Scotland he prayed: "Lord, give me Scotland or I die."
    - Does it seem like Knox had his mind fixed on his circumstances or on God's work?
- After being released from the slavery in the gallows, he returns to Scotland and is forced to flee because of Bloody Mary's reign of terror. This is when he spends time with Calvin in Geneva (1554–1559). He pastored the refugee church while in Geneva.
- When he returned to Scotland, he started the Presbyterian Church of Scotland.
- He confronts Mary the Queen of Scotland (a Roman catholic) to her face and makes her cry. He had been summoned by Mary because he had brought her marriage to Don Carlos up in one of his sermons. Prior to this he had been summoned by her because he had written a book against women in governmental power, which was a response against Bloody Mary. Mary of Scotland thought he was challenging her power as Queen, which put Knox in a very peculiar circumstance. Yet he stood his ground at her summoning. He was summoned three times by her because of things that he had said during his sermons.
    i. She plotted to kill her husband later and was imprisoned, which allowed Knox to bring full reform to Scotland.

- Discuss the following two John Knox quotes:

"I have never once feared the devil, but I tremble every time I enter the pulpit."

"As touching nature, I am a worm of this earth, and yet a subject of this commonwealth; but as touching the office wherein it has pleased God to place me, I am a watchman . . . For that reason, I am bound in conscience to blow the trumpet publicly."[25]

OTHER IMPORTANT EVENTS DURING THIS TIME

The Heidelberg Catechism (1563) (Germany)

- It was written at the request of Elector Frederick III. Frederick reached out to Zacharius Ursinus who was a professor of theology at the Heidelberg University, and Caspar Olevianus who was a preacher. They obtained the advice and cooperation of the entire theological faculty. Its intention was for instructing the youth and guiding pastors and teachers.

Excerpts from The Heidelberg Catechism

1. Q. What is your only comfort in life and death?

    A. That I am not my own, but belong with body and soul, both in life and in death, to my faithful Saviour Jesus Christ. He has fully paid for all my sins with His precious blood and has set me free from all the power of the devil. He also preserves me in such a way that without the will of my heavenly Father not a hair can fall from my head; indeed, all things must work together for my salvation. Therefore, by His Holy Spirit He also assures me of eternal life and makes me heartily willing and ready from now on to live for Him.

2. Q. What do you need to know in order to live and die in the joy of this comfort?

---

25. Koontz. *World Studies for Christian Schools*

A. First, how great my sins and misery are; second, how I am delivered from all my sins and misery; third, how I am to be thankful to God for such deliverance.

3. Q. From where do you know your sins and misery?

   A. From the law of God.

4. Q. What does God's law require of us?

   A. Christ teaches us this in a summary in Matthew 22: You shall love the LORD your God with all your heart, and with all your soul, and with all your mind. This is the great and first commandment. And a second is like it, You shall love your neighbor as yourself. On these two commandments depend all the law and the prophets.

5. Q. Can you keep all this perfectly?

   A. No, I am inclined by nature to hate God and my neighbor.

6. Q. Did God, then, create man so wicked and perverse?

   A. No, on the contrary, God created man good and in His image, that is, in true righteousness and holiness, so that he might rightly know God His Creator, heartily love Him, and live with Him in eternal blessedness to praise and glorify Him.

7. Q. From where, then, did man's depraved nature come?

   A. From the fall and disobedience of our first parents, Adam and Eve, in Paradise, for there our nature became so corrupt that we are all conceived and born in sin.

Faustus Socinus (1539-1604)

- Socinus was a theologian and one of the founders of the Unitarian Universalist Church.
- He is worth mentioning only because his ideas about the atonement are still around today.
- He published a book called "*On Christ the Savior*" in which he writes:

"Christ is Savior not because he suffered for our sins, but because he showed us the way to eternal salvation, which consists in our imitating him; and that he did not suffer to satisfy God's justice nor to appease his wrath."[26]

- Socinus' view became known as Socinianism.
- This is the view that if God punished Jesus in our place it would be an injustice because Jesus was innocent, and God cannot punish an innocent person.
- Advocates of Socinianism see Peniel Substitutionary Atonement as "cosmic child abuse." They believe that Peniel Substitutionary Atonement was invented by the reformers. (refer to page 84)
  - How can a perfectly just God punish an innocent person for the sins of others?
    - First, we must understand that Jesus was a willing sacrifice.

John 10:17-18 *"For this reason the Father loves Me, because I lay down My life so that I may take it again "No one has taken it away from Me, but I lay it down on My own initiative. I have authority to lay it down, and I have authority to take it up again. This commandment I received from My Father."*

- Second, we must understand that it was God's Law that we have broken so it is he who deems the means of reconciliation.

Psalm 115:3 *But our God is in the heavens; He does whatever He pleases.*

- Third, we must understand imputation of our sins to Christ.

2 Corinthians 5:21 *He made Him who knew no sin to be sin on our behalf, so that we might become the righteousness of God in Him.*

- Fourth, we must understand that Jesus wanted God to be glorified in the eyes of man because his name and glory had been trampled by us.

---

26. Wilbur, Earl Morse. *Our Unitarian Heritage*

John 17:1-5 *Father, the hour has come; glorify Your Son, that the Son may glorify You, 2 even as You gave Him authority over all flesh, that to all whom You have given Him, He may give eternal life. 3 "This is eternal life, that they may know You, the only true God, and Jesus Christ whom You have sent. 4 "I glorified You on the earth, having accomplished the work which You have given Me to do. 5 "Now, Father, glorify Me together with Yourself, with the glory which I had with You before the world was.*

- Fifth, we must understand that the entire Old Testament sacrificial system was pointing to Christ being the innocent lamb whose blood would be poured out for the sins of the people.

1 Peter 1:18-19 *knowing that you were not redeemed with perishable things like silver or gold from your futile way of life inherited from your forefathers, 19 but with precious blood, as of a lamb unblemished and spotless, the blood of Christ.*

You must work hard to not see penal substitutionary atonement in the Bible. We are really dealing with idolatry. Other views of the atonement are committing the same fallacy that Arminians do. They feel like they must defend God somehow because he is a type of monster if you adhere to views that they simply do not understand, and for that matter do not want to understand. If they are to learn to see the truth of Scripture, it must be by the Holy Spirit illuminating what they see as contradictory natures of God and showing them that his nature is all together perfect.

NOTES

An Introduction to The Puritans
1559–1688

- The name puritan was given to this group of people as a derogatory name because they wanted to purify the church. We will focus on the puritans in England mostly.
- It is during this time period that **King James** comes to power in 1603 and authorizes a Bible known by his name. The Puritans asked him to enforce the Millenary Petition, a petition signed by one-thousand puritan pastors to further reform the Anglican Church. King James ignores their petition.
    - What is the Anglican Church? The word "Anglican" means "of England." When King Henry VIII split off from the RCC, the Anglican Church began. It wasn't fully developed until 1662.
        - They hold to the Normative Principle of Worship (see page 196).
        - They have thirty-nine Articles of Religion.
        - They follow *The Book of Common Prayer*.
        i. In 1549, Archbishop of Canterbury, Thomas Cranmer, wrote *the book of Common Prayer* by translating Latin Catholic liturgy into English, and infused the prayers with Protestant reformed theology.
            - Most Anglicans had an Episcopalian form of church government, an RCC type of church liturgy and a Calvinistic form of soteriology.

From Anglican.org "Our belief is written down in the Holy Bible and the Articles of Religion [39 Articles]; our tradition is in part embodied in our Book of Common Prayer. The first Book of Common Prayer was produced in 1549. In it the Latin liturgy was radically simplified and translated into English, and for the first time a single 'use' was enforced throughout England. It has been revised numerous times since then, the most significant revision being the first, in 1552. All revisions since then, before the modern era, were very conservative revisions. The 1662 English Book of Common Prayer forms the historical basis for most Anglican liturgy around the world. While several countries have their own prayer books, all borrow heavily from the English tradition rooted in Cranmer's original work."

- Can you name English translations of the Bible prior to the King James?
    - Wycliff Bible 1380s
    - William Tyndale 1520s
    - The Great Bible 1538 the first authorized Bible (mostly the work of Tyndale and Myles Coverdale)
    - Geneva Bible 1560 (The first to add chapters, verses and study notes) (also largely based on Tyndale's work)
    - The Bishops Bible 1568 the second authorized Bible
- What does it mean that the Bible is authorized? An authorized Bible is one that has been authorized by the king to be translated into the common language.

- The Puritans did not like the Bishops Bible yet was forced to use it because it was authorized. They used the Geneva Bible in their own private study. They ask King James for a new authorized Bible, and he agrees because he did not like the Geneva Bible and the Bishops Bible was a bad translation. **Richard Bancroft** oversaw the translation which was a very thorough process using multiple committees, checks, balances, and agreement among the members of the committee.

- King James began persecuting the Puritans because he sided with the Anglicans.

i. He sent spies to prayer meetings. Preachers without a license were thrown into prison. Protestants received fines and were placed in dungeons for trying to reform the church any further than the boundaries the Anglicans had made for reform.

Charles 1 comes to power in 1625 and things go from bad to ugly for the Puritans.

- He married a Roman Catholic Queen (Henrietta-Marie de Bourbon). The Puritans had flashbacks of Bloody Mary.
- An Anglican Archbishop (**William Laud**) comes to power who despised the Puritans.
- Arminianism (Semi-Pelagianism) began to become popular in the Anglican Church which changed their view of soteriology.
- Laud outlaws any preaching on predestination.
    i. He couldn't remove it from the pages of Scripture, so he made it illegal to preach on.
- In the 1630s **the Great Migration** took place under the persecution of Charles I, which brought Puritans to the New World (America). They called themselves the Massachusetts Bay Colony.
    i. There had already been an earlier Migration in the 1620s to Massachusetts Bay. They called themselves the Plymouth Colony.
- During the English Civil War (1642–1651) the Puritans took power and set up a form of government.
- During the war, Puritan theologians met at Westminster and drafted the **Westminster Confession** in 1643.

Excerpts from the Westminster Confession of Faith

On Scripture: The authority of the Holy Scripture, for which it ought to be believed, and obeyed, depends not upon the testimony of any man, or church; but wholly upon God (who is truth itself) the author thereof: and therefore it is to be received, because it is the Word of God ... The whole counsel of God concerning all things necessary for his own glory, man's salvation, faith and life, is either expressly set down in Scripture, or by good and necessary consequence may be deduced from Scripture: unto which nothing at any time is to be added, whether by new revelations or the Spirit, or traditions of men.

On the Trinity: In the unity of the Godhead there be three Persons of one substance, power, and eternity: God the Father, God the Son, and God the Holy Ghost. The Father is of none, neither begotten nor proceeding, the Son is eternally begotten of the Father; the Holy Ghost eternally proceeding from the Father and the Son.

On the Doctrine of Predestination: Those of mankind that are predestinated unto life, God, before the foundation of the world was laid, according to his eternal and immutable purpose, and the secret counsel and good pleasure of his will, has chosen, in Christ, unto everlasting glory, out of his mere free grace and love, without any foresight of faith, or good works, or perseverance in either of them, or any other thing in the creature, as conditions, or causes moving him thereunto; and all to the praise of his glorious grace. As God has appointed the elect unto glory, so has he, by the eternal and most free purpose of his will, foreordained all the means thereunto.

- Do you agree with these points of the Westminster Confession of Faith?

- The **Westminster Catechisms** (long and short) are produced during this puritan government. The shorter catechism contains one hundred seven questions.
    - What is a Catechism and is this Roman Catholic? First, no it is not Roman Catholic.
        - A catechism is simply a summary of the principles of Christian religion in the form of questions and answers. Good catechisms are very useful for teaching people biblical doctrine and theology.

Excerpts from the Westminster Shorter Catechism

1. Q. What is the chief end of man? A. Man's chief end is to glorify God, and to enjoy him forever.
2. Q. What rule hath God given to direct us how we may glorify and enjoy him? A. The Word of God, which is contained in the Scriptures

of the Old and New Testaments, is the only rule to direct us how we may glorify and enjoy him.

3. **Q.** What do the Scriptures principally teach? **A.** The Scriptures principally teach, what man is to believe concerning God, and what duty God requires of man.

4. **Q.** What [who] is God? **A.** God is a Spirit, infinite, eternal, and unchangeable, in his being, wisdom, power, holiness, justice, goodness, and truth.

- In 1662 Charles II came to power, undoes all the Puritans' efforts and restores the Anglican Government. As a result, twenty-four hundred Puritan pastors are forced out of their churches in what is called **The Great Ejection.**

    i. They continue to preach as outlaws and become known as nonconformists.

PURITAN PASTORS TO BE FAMILIAR WITH

- What is a nonconformist? This term applies to English Protestants who would not conform to the doctrines or practices of the established Church of England.

"The Old English Puritan was such an one, that honored God above all, and under God gave every one his due. His first care was to serve God, and therein he did not what was good in his own, but in God's sight, making the word of God the rule of his worship. He highly esteemed order in the House of God: but would not under colour of that submit to superstitious rites, which are superfluous, and perish in their use. He reverenced Authority keeping within its sphere: but durst not under pretense of subjection to the higher powers, worship God after the traditions of men. He made conscience of all God's ordinances, though some he esteemed of more consequence.

He was careful in all relations to know, and to duty, and that with singleness of heart as unto Christ. He accounted religion an engagement to duty, that the best Christians should be best husbands, best wives, best parents, best children, best masters, best servants, best magistrates, best subjects, that the doctrine of God might be adorned, not blasphemed.

He was conscientious of equity as well as piety knowing that unrighteousness is abomination as well as ungodliness. He was cautious in promising, but careful in performing, counting his word no less engagement than his bond. He was a man of tender heart, not only in regard of his own sin, but others misery, not counting mercy arbitrary, but a necessary duty wherein as he prayed for wisdom to direct him, so he studied for cheerfulness and bounty to act."[1] John Gerre

Richard Baxter (1615–1691)

- Baxter was a nonconformist that wrote one of the best books on heaven ever published called *The Saints Everlasting Rest.*

"I preached as never sure to preach again, and as a dying man to dying men."

Richard Baxter

- What if preachers preached like this today? What if they were more concerned over people's souls than growing attendance?

"Remember the perfections of that God whom you worship, that He is a Spirit, and therefore to be worshipped in spirit and truth; and that He is most great and terrible, and therefore to be worshipped with seriousness and reverence, and not to be dallied with, or served with toys or lifeless lip-service; and that He is most holy, pure, and jealous, and therefore to be purely worshipped; and that He is still present with you, and all things are naked and open to Him with whom we have to do. The knowledge of God, and the remembrance of his all-seeing presence, are the most powerful means against hypocrisy."[2] Richard Baxter

- What is some of the theology Baxter brings out in the above quote? Discuss each point.

---

1. Grerre. *The Character of an Old English Puritan, or Non-Conformist*

2. Baxter, Richard. *A Christian Directory: or, A body of Practical Divinity, and Cases of Conscience*

John Bunyan (1628–1688)

- Bunyan was a nonconformist imprisoned for twelve years for preaching illegally. He wrote *The Pilgrim's Progress* while in prison.

"Pray often, for prayer is a shield to the soul, a sacrifice to God, and a scourge for Satan."

John Bunyan

- How is prayer a shield to the soul?
- How is prayer a sacrifice to God?
- How is prayer a scourge (to cause great suffering or a whip) for Satan?

"Fear, lest, by forgetting what you are by nature, you also forget the need that you have of continual pardon, support, and supplies from the Spirit of grace, and so grow proud of your own abilities, or of what you have received from God."[3] John Bunyan

- What is the root of what he is addressing in the above quote?

Matthew Henry (1662–1714)

- Matthew's father was a nonconformist pastor. Matthew was persecuted growing up as a Puritan. He wrote an expository commentary on the entire Bible.

"Extraordinary afflictions are not always the punishment of extraordinary sins, but sometimes the trial of extraordinary graces. "Matthew Henry

- What does he mean by this?

"Be careful if you make a woman cry, because God counts her tears. The woman came out of a man's ribs. Not from his feet to be walked on, not from his head to be superior, but from his side to be equal, under the arm to be protected, and next to the heart to be loved."[4] Matthew Henry

---

3. Bunyan. *A Treatise of the Fear of God*
4. Henry. *The Power of Transformation*. Lewinson

"It is easy to be religious when religion is in fashion; but it is an evidence of strong faith and resolution to swim against a stream to heaven, and to appear for God when no one else appears for Him."[5] Matthew Henry

- If it were possible for every person on the entire planet to all agree collectively on one thing, and that one thing was contrary to God's Word, who would be right?

John Owen (1616–1683)

- Owen was highly educated and scholarly. After the Restoration in 1662 he had to live like a fugitive in London just like all the other nonconformists. He was never arrested.
- He was friends with John Bunyan and loved to hear Bunyan preach. He fought hard to get Bunyan out of prison to no avail.
- He wrote numerous theological and practical works. He operated at a very high intellectual level and is hard to follow sometimes without pause.

> "That which we plead is, that the Lord Christ fulfilled the whole law for us; he did not only undergo the penalty of it due unto our sins, but also yielded that perfect obedience which it did require. And herein I shall not immix myself in the debate of the distinction between the active and passive obedience of Christ; for he exercised the highest active obedience in his suffering, when he offered himself to God through the eternal Spirit. And all his obedience, *considering his person*, was mixed with suffering, as a part of his exinanition [emptying] and humiliation; whence it is said, that "though he were a Son, yet learned his obedience by the things which he suffered." And however doing and suffering are in various categories of things, yet Scripture testimonies are not to be regulated by philosophical artifices and terms. And it must needs be said, that the sufferings of Christ, as they were purely penal, are imperfectly called his passive righteousness; for *all righteousness is either in habit or in action*, whereof suffering is neither; nor is any man righteous, or so esteemed, from what he suffers. Neither do sufferings give satisfaction unto the commands of the law, which require only obedience. And hence

---

5. Henry. *An Exposition of the Old and New Testament*

it will unavoidably follow, that we have need of more than the mere sufferings of Christ, whereby we may be justified before God, if so be that any righteousness be required thereunto; but the whole of what I intend is, that *Christ's* fulfilling of the law, in obedience unto its commands, is no less imputed unto us for our justification than his *undergoing the penalty of it* is."[6] John Owen

- Discuss some of the doctrines found in the above excerpt.

"However, this, on all hands, will, as I suppose, be agreed unto, that among the generality of professed Christians, the glory and power of Christianity are faded and almost utterly lost, though the reasons and causes thereof are not agreed upon; for however some few may please themselves in supposing nothing to be wanting unto a good state of things in religion, but only security in what they are and enjoy, yet the whole world is so evidently filled with the dreadful effects of the lusts of men, and sad tokens of divine displeasure, that all things from above and here below proclaim the degeneracy of our religion, in its profession, from its pristine beauty and glory. Religion is the same that ever it was, only it suffers by them that make profession of it. Whatever disadvantage it falls under in the world, they must at length answer for in whose misbelief and practice it is corrupted. And no man can express a greater enmity unto or malice against the gospel, than he that should assert or maintain that the faith, profession, lives, ways, and walkings of the generality of Christians are a just representation of its truth and holiness." John Owen *"Apostasy from the Gospel"*[7]

- What is Owen's main point of this passage?

Thomas Watson (1620–686)

- Watson was well-versed in Greek and Hebrew.
- He was imprisoned in 1651 and released later.
- He is considered to be the most articulate and readable of the Puritans. It is truly joyful to read his work.

---

6. Owen. *The Doctrine of Justification by Faith*. P. 141–142
7. Owen. *Nature and Causes of Apostasy from the Gospel*. P. 6

- Discuss each of these quotes from Watson:

"The pleasure of sin is soon gone, but the sting remains."[8]

"The glory of God is a silver thread which must run through all of our actions."[9]

"Lord I am content to be a loser, if thou be a gainer; to have less health, if I have more grace, and thou more glory."[10]

"As the silkworm, when she waves her curious work, hides herself under the silk, and is not seen; so when we have done anything praiseworthy, we must hide ourselves under the veil of humility, and transfer the glory of all we have done to God."[11]

"Who for a drop of pleasure would drink a sea of wrath?"[12]

OTHER IMPORTANT EVENTS ALONGSIDE THE PURITANS

- Roger Williams established the first Reformed Baptist colony in Providence, Rhode Island in the year 1636.

Arminianism

- Arminianism arose from the teachings of **Jacob Arminius** (1560–1609) in a response to Supralapsarianism, a doctrine articulated by Theodore Beza and Jerome Zanchius in the late 1500s.
- In order to understand Arminianism, let's look at some of the views developed concerning God's decrees:

It should be noted that both Supralapsarianism and Infralapsarianism are held in reformed circles. Both agree that God decreed all things

---

8. Watson. *A Body of Divinity*
9. Watson. *A Body of Divinity*
10. Watson. *A Body of Divinity*
11. Watson. *A Body of Divinity*
12. Watson. *A Body of Divinity*

before the foundation of the world, they disagree on what order he decreed them, however.

Supralapsarianism: God decreed to elect some for salvation and elect most for eternal condemnation before the creation of all things.

Infralapsarianism: God decreed to save some and pass over most after he decreed the fall of man by Adam.

Arminianism: God looked through the corridors of time to see who would choose him and elected those.

Supralapsarianism	Infralapsarianism	Amyraldism	Arminianism
Decreed to elect some, reprobate the rest	Decreed to create	Decreed to create	Decreed to create
Decreed to create	Decreed to permit fall	Decreed to permit fall	Decreed to permit fall
Decreed to permit fall	Decreed to elect some, pass over the rest	Decreed to provide salvation sufficient for all (hypothetical universalism)	Decreed to provide salvation sufficient for all
Decreed to provide salvation	Decreed to provide salvation	Decreed to elect some, pass over the rest	Call all to salvation
Calls the elect to salvation	Calls the elect to salvation	Calls the elect to salvation	Elect those who believe

Synod of Dort (1618–1619) (Netherlands) Dutch Reformed Church responds to Arminianism and their Five Articles of Remonstrance (1610) (See below)

- **The five points of Calvinism** were developed at this synod (church council).

1. Total Depravity
2. Unconditional Election
3. Limited Atonement
4. Irresistible Grace
5. Perseverance of the Saints

- Arminius dies but his followers issue a response to supralapsarianism called **The Five Articles of Remonstrance** (1610).

1. Against total depravity, that man is able of himself to exercise saving faith
2. Against irresistible grace, that God's grace can be rejected by man
3. Against limited atonement, that the atonement was unlimited in its intention
4. Against unconditional election, that divine predestination is conditional (based on God's foreknowledge of man's response), not absolute
5. Against the perseverance of the saints, that it is possible for believers to fall from grace and lose their salvation

Comparison Chart

The Five Points of Arminianism	The Five Points of Calvinism
1. *Free Will or Human Ability* Although human nature was seriously affected by the fall, man has not been left in a state of total spiritual helplessness. God graciously enables every sinner to repent and believe, but He does not interfere with man's freedom. Each sinner possesses a free will, and his eternal destiny depends on how he uses it. Man's freedom consists of his ability to choose good over evil in spiritual matters; his will is not enslaved to his sinful nature. The sinner has the power to either cooperate with God's Spirit and be regenerated or resist God's grace and perish. The lost sinner needs the Spirit's assistance, but he does not have to be regenerated by the Spirit before he can believe, for faith is man's act and precedes the new birth. Faith is the sinner's gift to God; it is man's contribution to salvation.	**1. *Total Inability or Total Depravity*** Because of the fall, man is unable of himself to savingly believe the gospel. The sinner is dead, blind, and deaf to the things of God; his heart is deceitful and desperately corrupt. His will is not free, it is in bondage to his evil nature, therefore, he will not—indeed he cannot—choose good over evil in the spiritual realm. Consequently, it takes much more than the Spirit's assistance to bring a sinner to Christ—it takes regeneration by which the Spirit makes the sinner alive and gives him a new nature. Faith is not something man contributes to salvation but is itself a part of God's gift of salvation—it is God's gift to the sinner, not the sinner's gift to God.
2. *Conditional Election* God's choice of certain individuals unto salvation before the foundation of the world was based upon His foreseeing that they would respond to His call. He selected only those whom He knew would of themselves freely believe the gospel. Election therefore was determined by or conditioned upon what man would do. The faith which God foresaw and upon which He based His choice was not given to the sinner by God (it was not created by the regenerating power of the Holy Spirit) but resulted solely from man's will. It was left entirely up to man as to who would believe and therefore as to who would be elected unto salvation. God chose those whom He knew would, of their own free will, choose Christ. Thus the sinner's choice of Christ, not God's choice of the sinner, is the ultimate cause of salvation.	**2. *Unconditional Election*** God's choice of certain individuals unto salvation before the foundation of the world rested solely in His own sovereign will. His choice of particular sinners was not based on any foreseen response or obedience on their part, such as faith, repentance, etc. On the contrary, God gives faith and repentance to each individual whom He selected. These acts are the result, not the cause of God's choice. Election therefore was not determined by or conditioned upon any virtuous quality or act foreseen in man. Those whom God sovereignly elected He brings through the power of the Spirit to a willing acceptance of Christ. Thus God's choice of the sinner, not the sinner's choice of Christ, is the ultimate cause of salvation.

Comparison Chart

The Five Points of Arminianism	The Five Points of Calvinism
3. *Universal Redemption or General Atonement* Christ's redeeming work made it possible for everyone to be saved but did not actually secure the salvation of anyone. Although Christ died for all men and for every man, only those who believe on Him are saved. His death enabled God to pardon sinners on the condition that they believe, but it did not actually put away anyone's sins. Christ's redemption becomes effective only if man chooses to accept it.	**3. *Limited Atonement or Particular Redemption*** Christ's redeeming work was intended to save the elect only and actually secured salvation for them. His death was a substitutionary endurance of the penalty of sin in the place of certain specified sinners. In addition to putting away the sins of His people, Christ's redemption secured everything necessary for their salvation, including faith which unites them to Him. The gift of faith is infallibly applied by the Spirit to all for whom Christ died, therefore guaranteeing their salvation.
4. *The Holy Spirit Can be Effectually Resisted* The Spirit calls inwardly all those who are called outwardly by the gospel invitation; He does all that He can to bring every sinner to salvation. But inasmuch as man is free, he can successfully resist the Spirit's call. The Spirit cannot regenerate the sinner until he believes; faith (which is man's contribution) precedes and makes possible the new birth. Thus, man's free will limits the Spirit in the application of Christ's saving work. The Holy Spirit can only draw to Christ those who allow Him to have His way with them. Until the sinner responds, the Spirit cannot give life. God's grace, therefore, is not invincible; it can be, and often is, resisted and thwarted by man.	**4. *Irresistible Grace or The Efficacious Call of the Spirit*** In addition to the outward general call to salvation which is made to everyone who hears the gospel, the Holy Spirit extends to the elect a special inward call that inevitably brings them to salvation. The external call (which is made to all without distinction) can be, and often is, rejected; whereas the internal call (which is made only to the elect) cannot be rejected; it always results in conversion. By means of this special call the Spirit irresistibly draws sinners to Christ. He is not limited in His work of applying salvation by man's will, nor is He dependent upon man's cooperation for success. The Spirit graciously causes the elect sinner to cooperate, to believe, to repent, to come freely and willingly to Christ. God's grace, therefore, is invincible; it never fails to result in the salvation of those to whom it is extended.

Comparison Chart

The Five Points of Arminianism	The Five Points of Calvinism
5. Falling from Grace Those who believe and are truly saved can lose their salvation by failing to keep up their faith, etc. All Arminians have not agreed on this point; some have held that believers are eternally secure in Christ—that once a sinner is regenerated, he can never be lost.	**5. Perseverance of the Saints** All who are chosen by God, redeemed by Christ, and given faith by the Spirit are eternally saved. They are kept in faith by the power of Almighty God and thus persevere to the end.

This chart is taken from fivesolas.com

"I might say it like this: you can tell if someone is an Arminian or a Calvinist by how they answer the question 'What was the decisive cause of your faith in Christ?' So, you go up to somebody, and you ask, 'What was the decisive cause of your faith in Christ? Was it God, or was it yourself?' The Calvinist says, 'The decisive cause of my faith was God,' and the Arminian says, 'The decisive cause of my faith in Christ was myself.'"[13] John Piper

Molinism

- Molinism was introduced in the 1500s. Its intention is to be a view of God that is neither Arminian nor Calvinistic.
- It was introduced by Luis de Molina (1535-1600) and Pedro da Fonseca (1528-1599).
- They have their own flower acronym (in response to TULIP) which is the ROSES.
    i. This acronym doesn't seem to be standardized. The acronym below was taken from Brian Chilton who is a self-professing Molinist.[14]

---

13. Piper. Article from Desiring God: *Watershed Differences Between Calvinists and Arminians*
14. The Christian Post. Article. What is Molinism

R Radical depravity takes the place of the Calvinist doctrine of total depravity. Radical depravity holds that humans are depraved to the point that they cannot save themselves. However, this depravity does not remove one's divine image given to them by the Creator. Thus, the human being is unable to save oneself, however this does not mean that he or she could not respond to God's grace when given.

O Overcoming grace replaces irresistible grace. Rather than holding that a person cannot respond to God's grace, Molinists hold that God's grace is able to overcome the depraved human condition leading to a place where the person can respond positively or negatively to God's free offer of grace.

S Sovereign election replaces the unconditional election portion of TULIP. Molinists hold that God knows each person so completely that he knows how each person will respond in certain circumstances (e.g., Pharaoh's hardened heart in Exodus). Thus, God elects to save those whom he knows will respond to his grace, but this knowledge does not come from the person, but rather within the mind of God. God knows everything about everyone before anything was created. See point three for a further description of the Molinist's view of divine sovereignty.

E Eternal assurance. Rather than emphasizing the perseverance of the saints, which can be construed to mean that not everyone who makes a profession of faith will persevere, the Molinist (at least many Evangelical Molinists) holds that a person's salvation is assured because of the working of God in the person's salvation. God's promises are always true.

S Singular redemption. The last S of Molinism's ROSES replaces limited atonement in TULIP. This doctrine holds that Christ's death was powerful enough to cover the sins of the world, but only applies to those who respond to God's grace by faith. Thus, Christ's atoning work was sufficient to save the world, but efficient to save only the elect.

- They also teach the doctrine of "Middle Knowledge" to define God's omniscience.
  - How do you balance God's sovereignty and man's free will? If given a set of circumstances a person has the power to choose to do or not to do something, how can this be consistent with sovereignty? Well..."middle knowledge" of course.

- Middle knowledge teaches that given an array of possible outcomes, God sees all options and choices so he knows what they would freely choose in every possible circumstance.
  - Is it possible for God to learn something? (you can apply this question to Arminianism as well)
  - What does it mean that God is omniscient?

Covenantalism

- What is covenant theology?
  - It is a framework or hermeneutic for interpreting Scripture more so than a theology.
  - It looks at Scripture through the frame of the covenant of works, the covenant of grace, and the covenant of redemption.
    i. The covenant of redemption is made among the three persons of the Trinity to elect, atone for, and save a group of people in whom they have chosen.
    ii. The covenant of works is the first covenant God made to man. **Genesis 2:16-17 16 *The Lord God commanded the man, saying, "From any tree of the garden you may eat freely; 17 but from the tree of the knowledge of good and evil you shall not eat, for in the day that you eat from it you will surely die." God promises eternal life to Adam as long as he is obedient.*
    iii. The covenant of grace was given when Adam failed to keep the covenant of works. In this covenant God freely offers to sinners' eternal life and salvation through faith in Jesus Christ.
- Covenantalism was systematized in the Netherlands in the mid-1600s.
- Because of their framework or hermeneutic, covenantalism views Israel in the Old Testament, as the church. They do not view the church as starting in the book of Acts. It is for this reason this is

referred to as "replacement theology" or supersessionism by people outside of this camp.

  i. Most people that hold to covenantalism are amillennialist. They must spiritualize all of the verses that are concerning Israel and a future millennial kingdom because they believe that Jesus fulfilled these prophecies at his first advent.

      a. Remember amillennialism was developed in the fourth century and was not the historic view of Christians before this time.

  ii. More scholarly amillennialist would not agree to being called replacement theologians. They would say that rather than the church replacing Israel they see no distinction because both Jew and Gentile are under one covenant.

- The most beneficial thing that covenantalism brings to the table is an intense desire to see God working in every verse of the Bible from Genesis to Revelation. All Scripture is pointing to Christ.

    - Must you adhere to covenantalism in order to be "reformed"? No

    - What does the word "reformation" mean? To (re)-<u>form</u> that which was (de)-formed.

    - What was the main thing that had be deformed? Sola-Scriptura and Sola-fide

        i. Eschatology wasn't on the reformers radar; they were more interested in primary doctrines and bringing the Word of God to the people. True reform of what was taught by the apostles and earliest church fathers would be premillennialism, but that isn't a requirement to be reformed either.

        ii. The reformation wasn't about hermeneutics it was about perspicuity.

    - What is perspicuity? The things clearly seen in Scripture.

Dispensationalism

- Dispensationalism was also developed during this time. People in this camp think that it is much like a continuation of the reformer's work.
    i. John Nelson Darby popularized and systematized it in the 1800s.
- It is a further development of premillennialism.
- Dispensationalism rightly takes a literal, grammatical, historical hermeneutic consistently throughout Scripture.
- Dispensationalism believes that the church began in the book of Acts.
- Dispensationalism makes the distinction between Israel and the church, seeing a literal fulfilment of the promises God made to them in the Old Testament. He fulfills this by "the Day of the Lord" (Joel 2:1; Acts 2:20) or the Tribulation found in the book of Revelation, to bring the Jewish people back to himself. He preserves a remnant of them through the Tribulation and brings them into the Millennial Kingdom in which all of his promises to them are fulfilled.
    i. If dispensationalism stopped there it would be good, but things get out of hand from that point and many people in this theology over complicate Scripture greatly. Some begin making distinctions that are simply not in the Bible.
        a. Dispensationalism makes a distinction between the new covenant for the church and the new covenant for Israel.
        b. A distinction between the kingdom of God and the kingdom of heaven.
        c. A distinction between placing some of Jesus's teaching for this age and some for the Millennial Kingdom.
        d. They started making distinctions between books of the Bible, some are for the Jews and some are for the church.
        e. Some make a distinction in the way Jews are saved vs Gentiles.

f. Some believe all Jews are saved.
g. There can be as few as three and as many as eight dispensations.
h. There is classical dispensationalism, modified dispensationalism and progressive dispensationalism.
i. Most believe in 7 dispensations:

1. Innocence (Genesis 1–3) Adam and Eve before they sinned
2. Conscience (Genesis 3–8) First sin to the flood
3. Civil Government (Genesis 9–11) After the flood
4. Promise (Genesis 12–Ex. 19) The Law is given
5. Law (Exodus 20–Acts 2:4) Moses to the cross
6. Grace (Acts 2:4–Rev. 20:3) Cross to the millennial kingdom
7. Millennial Kingdom (Rev. 20:4–6) The rule of Christ on earth

- Because of popular books and movies concerning eschatology, some dispensationalists have spun out of control with newspaper exegesis and seeing fulfilled prophecies in almost everything.
    i. The emotions of people lacking in the understanding of biblical doctrine and theology has been stirred, which opens the door even wider for book sales and movie deals.
        a. There are some who call themselves dispensational for the purpose of writing books and making money by tugging on the emotions of people by using scare tactics and other things. They make a mockery of God and use his name in vain.
    ii. Unfortunately, and unjustly so, because of the wackiness of many of these things dispensationalism has been placed in the category with unicorns and fairy tales by many churchmen.

- Dispensationalism is good when dealing with eschatology alone, yet simply overcomplicated and sometimes not biblical in all of its distinctions.
- The most beneficial thing that dispensationalism brings to the table is a literal, grammatical, historical hermeneutic.

- If it were possible to summarize what the Bible is about by two distinctions what would you say they would be? The attributes of God and the work of Christ.

1689 Second London Baptist Confession of Faith

- This confession was written by Particular (Reformed) Baptists.
- It was based on the Westminster Confession of Faith and the Savoy Declaration with modifications concerning baptism and church government.
- It was first introduced in 1677 but wouldn't be until 1989 that it was accepted at the General Assembly where as many as one hundred eight churches were represented.
- The First London Baptist Confession was completed and printed in 1644.
  - What was the Savoy Declaration? It was basically the Westminster Confession of Faith with modifications and omissions. There was one chapter added (chapter 20). It was a conglomeration of John Owen and Thomas Goodwin who led a committee to make these changes.

NOTES

The Great Awakening

- After Martin Luther died, Lutheranism became characterized by polemical opposition to any other system, whether Roman Catholic or Reformed. This led to dead orthodoxy.
  - What is dead orthodoxy?

Revelation 2:2-5 explains this well: *2 'I know your deeds and your toil and perseverance, and that you cannot tolerate evil men, and you put to the test those who call themselves apostles, and they are not, and you found them to be false; 3 and you have perseverance and have endured for My name's sake, and have not grown weary. 4 'But I have this against you, that **you have left your first love**. 5 'Therefore remember from where you have fallen, and repent and do the deeds you did at first; or else I am coming to you and will remove your lampstand out of its place—unless you repent.*

  - Dead orthodoxy is losing your *first love*. What does that mean? Becoming mechanical in the things you do for God.

- A **dead church** must not be confused with an **exciting church**, as if because something is exciting it is alive. Look at **Revelation 3:1-2** *1 "To the angel of the church in Sardis write: He who has the seven Spirits of God and the seven stars, says this: 'I know your deeds, that **you have a name that you are alive, but you are dead**. 2 'Wake up, and strengthen the things that remain, which were about to die; for I have not found your deeds completed in the sight of My God.*

- **Pietism** was a reaction to dead orthodoxy which emphasized genuine spiritual experience, holy living, and inward transformation. Rather than do you believe the creeds, the emphasis was on are you born again?

- - Was this a proper reaction or an overreaction?

- Pietism swung too far in some cases to a form of legalism or the other way into emotionalism, with less emphasis on doctrine.
    - i. Unfortunately, this was a cracked door that has been kicked wide open in today's church.
    - - Why is emotionalism bad for the church?
    - - Why is a lack of doctrine bad for the church?

THE AGE OF ENLIGHTENMENT

- - What do you know about The Age of Enlightenment?

- The Age of Enlightenment begins in 1650 after **Rene Descartes** published a book called *Discourse on the Method*. It ends around 1800.
- "I think therefore I am" became the worldview.
    - i. Up till this point, people thought about the world in terms of biblical revelation and church tradition. These were the structures in which the world was governed. At this point the world view became that of reason.

Rationalism

- - What is rationalism?
    - ◆ Rather than the Bible and church tradition being the guide for government and life in general, now rational thinking, nature, and science become the driving forces on how the world is viewed.

- Rationalism was a structure built on the foundation of Aristotle's work that was re-discovered when they were translated into other languages in the 1600s. This was the first step toward modernism that hit in 1900 and postmodernism that would come later.

- What is modernism?
  - **Modernism** was the re-examining of anything that could potentially hold back the progress of modern society, such as religion.
- What is postmodernism?
  - **Postmodernism** is relativism, or truth is reasoned by each individual, so each person has their own truth and that is ok. There are no absolutes. This was an application of Einstein's Principle of Relativity taken from the laboratory and applied to a world view.

- Rationalism overtakes Pietism in the mid-1700s.
- There is a reaction to Rationalism during this time called **Romanticism.**
  - What is Romanticism? It is a view that emphasizes feelings, art, music, and beauty.
  - How does Rationalism and Romanticism have an impact on the church today?

- Rationalism is seen even in some modern Bible commentaries where the writer tries to explain away the miracles of Christ and the apostles.
- Some of the effects on world view during this time were:

Philosophy became for the sake of philosophy rather than for the sake of better understanding religion.

Science became secular, where before it was done by religious men.

- Romanticism led to Pantheism, Transcendentalism, and the New Age Movement that hit in the twentieth century.
  - What is Pantheism? The belief that God consists of and is in all things (trees are god etc.).
  - What is Transcendentalism?

- The belief that people and nature are inherently good. People can find truth through their own intuition and imagination.

- What is the New Age Movement?
    - It is basically the merging of Eastern mysticism with Christianity. Their belief and doctrine are hard to define because they are not dogmatic and embrace an assortment of different theologies.
    - There are two basic beliefs: Evolutionary Godhood and Global Unity.

    i. Evolutionary Godhood is basically the belief that the next step in the evolutionary process will be spiritual rather than physical. This is why they try to push this physical body closer to the next evolutionary process by means such as: astral projection (out of body experiences); contacting spirits; using crystals to purify your body's and mind's energy systems; and visualization to impute health. This also teaches that mankind is divine so you can create your own reality. You can also enhance your life through your own person.

    ii. Global Unity consists of three divisions: Man with Man; Man with Nature; and Man with God.

    a. We will learn our divine relationship with one another by achieving harmony, love and acceptance Man to Man.
    b. Nature is god, so people can unite by getting in tune with, by nurturing nature and being nurtured by nature. The name "Gaia" has been given to the earth, and she is to be revered and respected.
    c. In order to realize our own goodness, people must see themselves as divine by nature which will unite the collective purpose of love and development.

- Romanticism affected not only laity but pastors who became more concerned with philosophy, science, and recreation than spiritual renewal.

The Great Awakening 243

- The world view became secular and will remain so.
- Philosophers such as John Locke (1632-1704) and David Hume (1711-1776) attacked the heart of the gospel by teaching Platonic philosophy and deism.
  - What is deism?
    - God is far away, setting waiting for what will happen in his creation. Reason and observation of the natural world are sufficient for the understanding of God and revelation is not needed.
- The church was in a steep spiritual decline. Satan was working hard to confuse and distort all of the biblical truth that was made clear by the Reformation. The children of the Puritans who came to America for religious freedom began to become indifferent to religion. They became focused on the development of a new world. The gospel was considered out of date and spiritual zeal was regarded as fanaticism. Christian life came to mean a moral life of good works. In other words, a return to Law.
  - Busyness has been an excuse in the disregard of the things of God. How hard do you try to make time for God in life's busyness?
  - What distracts you from the admiration, worship, and service to God that you should be engaged in?

SOLOMON STODDARD BECAME THE PASTOR OF THE CHURCH IN NORTHAMPTON, MASSACHUSETTS.

- He was the grandfather of Jonathan Edwards.
- He noted the growing spiritual decline and lack of interest in the church and spiritual things in New England. In response he attempted to incorporate "nominal Christians" into the life of the church by what was called the **Halfway Covenant**. The Halfway Covenant allowed partial church membership for people who followed the rules and creeds of the church, even if they did not profess to be converted. He wanted a larger audience in the church because

people had grown uninterested. He thought people would come if they were members. As a result, the church in New England grew cold, nominal, and dead.

- Stoddard was not a bad preacher; he just made a mistake at this point.

  - Have you ever, like Stoddard, tried to help God out? What is that called? Unbelief!
  - Is God faithful?

- Faithfulness is an attribute of God.

"God is true. His Word of promise is sure. In all his relations with his people God is faithful. He may be safely relied upon. No one ever yet really trusted him in vain. We find this precious truth expressed almost everywhere in Scriptures, for his people need to know that faithfulness is an essential part of the Divine character. This is the basis of our confidence in him. But it is one thing to accept the faithfulness of God as a divine truth, it is quite another to act upon it."[1] A.W. Pink

- We sometimes want to humanize God. We think that because we have been unfaithful to him, he will be unfaithful to us because that is what we deserve. This may be unintentional but is evident in our actions. God is faithful to us even when we are not faithful to him.

Deuteronomy 7:9 *"Know therefore that the Lord your God, He is God, the faithful God, who keeps His covenant and His lovingkindness to a thousandth generation with those who love Him and keep His commandments"*

- A Great Awakening was much needed, and really began in England with what is called the "Evangelical Revival." George Whitefield (1714-1770), John Wesley (1703-1791) and Charles Wesley (1707-1788) are men that God used to start a great revival that impacted not only Europe, but America as well.

---

1. Pink. *The Attributes of God*

JOHN WESLEY (1703-1791) (ENGLAND)

- Wesley's father was an Anglican minister who was very Arminian and moralistic.
- Charles was his younger brother born two years later.
- In 1709 John Wesley was rescued from a fire at St. Andrews Church, which later he would see as a key moment in his life where God "plucked him from the fire" and set him apart for special service.

GEORGE WHITEFIELD (1714-1770) (ENGLAND)

- George Whitefield was very poor and could not afford a university education, so he became an errand boy for the students of Oxford in order to pay his way.
- He would preach over eighteen hundred sermons between England and America. Between his sermons and talks it is estimated that he taught the Bible as much as one-thousand times a year, totaling much more than eighteen thousand times.
  - How much time do you waste being entertained?
  - How much time should we give to learn about the Creator of all things, our Lord and Savior Jesus Christ, the Trinity, the Attributes of God, and solid biblical doctrine?
- Whitefield was a very powerful preacher.

Pembroke College in Oxford

- The unconverted Whitefield is invited by the Wesley brothers to be a member of the "Holy Club" that they had started, because Whitefield prayed three times a day and fasted weekly.
  - i. The Wesley brothers admit they thought they were converted because they were very moralistic. They realized later that they were not converted.
  - ii. This "Holy Club" was mockingly called the Methodist (extreme methods).

- Whitefield becomes converted by reading a book he borrowed from the Wesley brothers called "*The life of God in the Soul of Man* by Henry Scougal" in which he learned he "must be born again or be damned." He realized that external actions were not the means of justification. This was the spark that ignited the Evangelical Revival. This is similar to the story of Martin Luther.
    i. Like Luther, Whitefield also suffers ill health because of the severe discipline he put his body through trying to earn salvation.
- John and Charles leave Oxford, England for a mission's trip to Georgia in 1735. They are still not converted but are trying to earn salvation.
    - Do we have unconverted pastors, teachers, and missionaries today? We should pray for these men to be converted.
- Charles Wesley returns to England five months after their arrival.
- John flees America in 1738 after a woman he was dating marries a different man because John refuses to commit to her. John refuses to allow her to take communion and is sued by the woman's new husband. On the ship back to England he meets a group of Moravians by God's providence.
    - What is God's providence? God the good Creator of all things, in his infinite power and wisdom upholds, directs, disposes, and governs all creatures and things until their ultimate end.

"The providence of God is *Regina mundi*, 'the queen and governess of the world: it is the eye that sees, and the hand that turns all the wheels in the universe. God is not like an artificer that builds a house, and then leaves it, but like a pilot he steers the ship of the whole creation."[2] Arthur Pink

   i. **The Moravians** were influenced by John Huss and the Pietists who emphasize the gospel's power to pierce and transform the sinner's heart.
   ii. Wesley attends a Moravian meeting in that same year and

---

2. Pink. *The Attributes of God*

hears them reading from Luther's commentary on Romans (justification by faith alone) and his heart is "strangely warmed." He becomes converted.

- Charles is also converted and is famous for the thousands of hymns he wrote.
    - Can you name some of his hymns?
- Whitefield begins to draw thousands of people to hear him preach.
    i. Whitefield was doing something different; he was preaching outdoors and even moving around to preach to anyone who would hear him.
- He traveled to America in 1739 and preached to thousands in New York and Philadelphia.

Benjamin Franklin attended one of his meetings in Philadelphia because he heard reports of Whitefield preaching to tens of thousands of people and did not believe he could be heard by that many at once. Franklin walked away from Whitefield until he could no longer hear him and calculated the area of a semi-circle centered on him. Allowing two square feet per person he realized that Whitefield really could be heard by tens of thousands of people in the open air.

Franklin stated that when he would go to hear Whitefield preach, he would leave his money at home for fear that under such powerful preaching he would give all of his money away.

- Whitefield was a Calvinist for lack of better words and believes God's sovereignty is the catalyst which drives him. Preaching to all who would listen in order to stir the hearts of the elect. He believed that the fields are full of God's elect, and it was his great joy to go and find them.
    - What does it mean that God is sovereign? That God is in control of all things.

> "There is no attribute more comforting to His children than that of God's Sovereignty. Under the most adverse circumstances, in the most severe trials, they believe that Sovereignty has ordained

their afflictions, that Sovereignty overrules them, and that Sovereignty will sanctify them all. There is nothing for which the children ought more earnestly to contend than the doctrine of their Master over all creation—the Kingship of God over all the works of his own hands—the Throne of God and his right to sit upon that Throne. On the other hand, there I no doctrine more hated by worldings, no truth of which they have made such a football, as the great, stupendous, but yet most certain doctrine of the Sovereignty of the infinite Jehovah. Men will allow God to be everywhere except on his throne. They will allow him to be in his workshop to fashion worlds and make stars. They will allow him to be in his almonry to dispense his alms and bestow his bounties. They will allow him to sustain the earth and bear up the pillars thereof, or light the lamps of heaven, or rule the waves of the ever-moving ocean; but when God ascends his throne, his creatures then gnash their teeth, and we proclaim an enthroned God, and his right to do as he wills with his own, to dispose of his creatures as he thinks well, without consulting them in the matter; then it is that we are hissed and execrated, and then it is that men turn a deaf ear to us, for God on his throne is not the God they love. But it is God upon the throne that we love to preach. It is God upon his throne whom we trust."[3] Charles Spurgeon

Sarah Edwards (Jonathan Edwards' wife): "Many, very many persons in Northampton date the beginning of new thoughts, new desires, new purposes, and a new life, from the day on which they heard him (Whitefield) preach of Christ and this salvation."

- Whitefield returned to England in 1741. John Wesley didn't like Whitefield's Calvinistic soteriology, so animosity began to grow between them. They both grew up in an Anglican home that was Arminian, yet Whitefield was convinced by Scripture of God's sovereignty in election while Wesley remained Arminian.

    i. The Methodist Church splits into an Arminian branch and a Calvinistic branch.

- Wesleyanism is still found in the Nazarene Church today.

- Wesley believed that sinless perfection is attainable in this life (he never claimed to have reached it). He called this the "second blessing." John Fletcher, Wesley's successor, would refer to this second blessing

3. Spurgeon. *Sermon on Matthew 20:15*

experience as a "baptism of the Holy Spirit," in which a deeper life experience was expected to those who seek it. Later Charles Finney would associate the baptism of the Spirit with ecstatic experiences and "unutterable gushings" of praise. This paves the way for the Pentecostal association of tongues with the baptism of the Spirit and the entrance into a deeper form of the Christian life.

- What should the objective be in growing in sanctification . . . perfection or to glorify God? Sometimes nuances can steer a ship off course.

- Whitefield wrote a letter to Wesley: "What a fond conceit is it to cry up **perfection**, and yet cry down the doctrine of **final perseverance**. But this, and many other absurdities, you will run into, because you will not own **election**. O that you would study the covenant of grace! . . . O that you would not be too rash and precipitant! If you go on thus, honored sir, how can I concur with you? It is impossible. I must speak what I know . . . I must preach the gospel of Christ, and that I cannot now do, without speaking of election."[4]

  i. Whitefield's point was that Wesley had a contradiction in teaching that a person could reach sinless perfection and yet lose their salvation.

- If it is by your own efforts that your salvation is held together, who gets the glory?

- Can a Christian be assured that they are held tight by God in salvation, and that he will not release his grasp?

"The children of God would be troubled, though their grace should not fail, if their privileges should be cut off; but you are sure of both. God will maintain a spark, and the seed remaineth, and the privileges of grace are sure too. This was figured under the law. An Israelite could never wholly alienate his title to the land: Lev25:23 'The land shall not be sold for ever; for the land is mine, for ye were strangers and sojourners with me.' His title to the land shall not be quite cut off, 'it shall not be sold for ever;' which was a type of our spiritual inheritance in Christ, which cannot be alienated from us."[5] Thomas Manton (A Puritan pastor in his sermons on John)

4. Whitefield. *The Works of the Reverend George Whitefield*. P. 212
5. Manton. *The complete Works of Thomas Manton*. P. 309

- Again, Whitefield wrote: "Dear sir, for Jesus Christ's sake, consider how you dishonor God by denying election. You plainly make salvation depend not on God's free grace, but on man's free will. And if thus, it is more than probable, Jesus Christ would not have had the satisfaction of seeing the fruit of his death in the eternal salvation of one soul. Our preaching would then be vain, and all invitations for people to believe in him, would also be in vain."[6]

    i. His point being that if salvation depended on man's free will, no one would ever choose God, and even if one wanted to choose God, there is a potential that no one would. Kind of like Jesus rolling the dice.

    - If God didn't interfere with man's will, then why would anyone pray for the salvation of someone?

- Despite the differences they had in doctrine, they remained friends and allies in the faith, while ministering separately.
- Wesley took Whitefield's form of preaching and preached in the open, impacting thousands of people for the gospel.
- Wesley wrote a book called "*The Almost Christian*" in which he makes the case that the greatest dangers to the Christian faith is anything that falls short of full commitment. God gave us God's all; we are called to offer back the whole of ourselves . . . all we are and all we have-as a living sacrifice to God.

It is important to understand that no one at this point in church history ever planned an event called a revival. The two greatest revivals happened simply by the clear preaching of the gospel and people responded in a great way.

JONATHAN EDWARDS (1703-1758)

- Edwards was born the same year as John Westley.
- His father, Timothy Edwards and grandfather, Solomon Stoddard, whom we already talked about, were both pastors.

6. Whitefield. *Readings in Historical Theology*. Lay. P. 339

The Great Awakening

- Jonathan met George Whitefield which had a great effect on his ministry. These two together are the instruments God uses for the Great Awakening in America.
- Some believe that Edwards was the greatest theological mind that America has ever produced.
- He entered Yale College in 1716 at the age of twelve years old. While at Yale he experienced an illness in which he thought he was going to die at the age of sixteen years old.
- His life was changed when he came to understand the sovereignty of God as a beautiful thing. His lack of understanding God's sovereignty prior to this made God out to be hateful.
  - Have you ever put human conditioning on God when attempting to understand His sovereignty?
- When he was eighteen years old, he wrote seventy personal resolutions as a desire to please God in everything. Listed below are twelve of them.

1. Resolved, that I will do whatsoever I think to be most to God's glory, and my own good, profit and pleasure, in the whole of my duration, without any consideration of the time, whether now, or never so many myriads of ages hence. Resolved to do whatever I think to be my duty and most for the good and advantage of mankind in general. Resolved to do this, whatever difficulties I meet with, how many soever, and how great soever. (This ties into number four)
   i. This is where John Piper gets his Christian Hedonism. Edwards believed that his greatest good, profit and pleasure came from glorifying God.
2. Resolved, to be continually endeavoring to find out some new contrivance and invention to promote the aforementioned things.
3. Resolved, *if ever I shall fall and grow dull*, so as *to neglect to keep any part of these Resolutions*, to *repent* of all I can remember, *when I come to myself again.*
4. Resolved, never to do any manner of thing, whether in soul or body, less or more, but *what tends to the glory of God*; nor be, nor suffer it, if I can avoid it.

5. Resolved, never to lose one moment of time; but improve it the most profitable way I possibly can. (This ties into number four)
6. Resolved, to live with all my might, while I do live. (This ties into number four)
7. Resolved, never to do anything, which I should be afraid to do, if it were the last hour of my life.
8. Resolved, to act, in all respects, both speaking and doing, as if nobody had been so vile as I, and as if I had committed the same sins, or had the same infirmities or failings as others; and that I will let the knowledge of their failings promote nothing but shame in myself, and prove only an occasion of my confessing my own sins and misery to God.
9. Resolved, to think much on all occasions of my own dying, and of the common circumstances which attend death.
10. Resolved, when I feel pain, to think of the pains of martyrdom, and of hell.
11. Resolved, when I think of any theorem in divinity to be solved, immediately to do what I can towards solving it, if circumstances do not hinder.

    - What kind of thinking is this called? Critical thinking

    The church is in desperate need of critical thinkers.

12. Resolved, if I take delight in it as a gratification of pride, or vanity, or on any such account, immediately to throw it by.

- He became the pastor of Northampton, Massachusetts after his grandfather (Solomon Stoddard) died.
- He began preaching against Arminianism in 1731 with a sermon titled "God Glorified in Man's Dependence" in which he expresses God's sovereignty in salvation.

> "Hence those doctrines and schemes of divinity that are in any respect opposite to such an absolute and universal dependence on God, derogate from his glory, and thwart the design of our redemption. And such are those schemes that put the creature in God's stead, in any of the mentioned respects, that exalt man into the place of either Father, Son, or Holy Ghost, in any thing

pertaining to our redemption. However, they may allow of a dependence of the redeemed on God, yet they deny a dependence that is so absolute and universal. They own an entire dependence on God for some things, but not for others; they own that we depend on God for the gift and acceptance of a Redeemer, but deny so absolute a dependence on him for the obtaining of an interest in the Redeemer. They own an absolute dependence on the Father for giving his Son, and on the Son for working out redemption, but not so entire a dependence on the Holy Ghost for conversion, and a being in Christ, and so coming to a title to his benefits. They own a dependence on God for means of grace, but not absolutely for the benefit and success of those means; a partial dependence on the power of God, for obtaining and exercising holiness, but not a mere dependence on the arbitrary and sovereign grace of God. They own a dependence on the free grace of God for a reception into his favor, so far that it is without any proper merit, but not as it is without being attracted, or moved with any excellency. They own a partial dependence on Christ, as he through whom we have life, as having purchased new terms of life, but still hold that the righteousness through which we have life is inherent in ourselves, as it was under the first covenant. Now whatever scheme is inconsistent with our entire dependence on God for all, and of having all of him, through him, and in him, it is repugnant to the design and tenor of the gospel, and robs it of that which God accounts its luster and glory."[7]

- In 1733 revival broke out and grew through 1739. The Great Awakening had begun.
- In 1741 he preached "Sinners in the Hands of an Angry God," in which many people responded to God with great anguish over their sins. Under the weight of this message people became so convicted they had a physical reaction. People were crying out loud, collapsing onto the floor, and groaning in agony over their guilt before a holy God.

The main points to this message:

    i. There is no want (or lack) of power in God to cast wicked men into hell at any moment.

---

7. Edwards. *Sermons of Jonathan Edwards*. P. 15–16

ii. They deserve to be cast into hell; so that divine justice never stands in the way, it makes no objection against God's using his power at any moment to destroy them.

iii. They are already under a sentence of condemnation to hell.

iv. They are now the objects of that very same anger and wrath of God, that is expressed in the torments of hell.

v. The devil stands ready to fall upon them and seize them as his own, at what moment God shall permit him.

vi. There are in the souls of wicked men those hellish principles reigning, that would presently kindle and flame out into hell fire, if it were not for God's restraints.

vii. It is no security to wicked men for one moment, that there are no visible means of death at hand.

viii. Natural men's prudence and care to preserve their own lives, or the care of others to preserve them, do not secure them a moment.

ix. All wicked men's pains and contrivance they use to escape hell, while they continue to reject Christ, and so remain wicked men, don't secure them from hell one moment.

x. God has laid himself under no obligation by any promise to keep any natural man out of hell one moment.

Excerpt from "*Sinners in the Hands of an Angry God*": The God that holds you over the pit of hell, much as one holds a spider, or some loathsome insect over the fire, abhors you, and is dreadfully provoked: His wrath towards you burns like fire; He looks upon you as worthy of nothing else, but to be cast into the fire; He is of purer eyes than to bear to have you in his sight; you are ten thousand times more abominable in his eyes, than the most hateful venomous serpent is in ours. You have offended him infinitely more than ever a stubborn rebel did his prince; and yet it is nothing but his hand that holds you from falling into the fire every moment. It is to be ascribed to nothing else, that you did not go to hell the last night; that you was suffered to awake again in this world, after you closed your eyes to sleep. And there is no other reason to be given, why you have not dropped into hell since you arose in the morning, but that God's hand has held you up. There is no other reason to be given why you have not gone to hell, since you have sat here in the house of God, provoking his pure eyes by your sinful wicked manner of attending his solemn worship. Yea, there is nothing else that is to be given as a reason why you do not this very moment drop down into hell. O sinner! Consider the fearful danger you are in: it is a great furnace of wrath, a wide and bottomless pit, full of fire of wrath, that you are held over in the hand of that God, whose wrath is provoked and incensed as much against you, as against many of the damned in hell. You hang by a slender thread, with the flames of divine wrath flashing about it, and ready every moment to singe it, and burn it asunder; and you have no interest in any Mediator; and nothing to lay hold of to save yourself, nothing to keep off the flames of wrath, nothing of your own, nothing that you ever had done, nothing that you can do, to induce God to spare you one moment. And now you have an extraordinary opportunity, a day wherein Christ has thrown the door of mercy wide open and stands in calling and crying with a loud voice to poor sinners; a day wherein many are flocking to him, and pressing into the kingdom of God. Many are daily coming from the east, west, north and south; many that were very lately in the same miserable condition that you are in, are now in a happy state, with their hearts filled with love to him who has loved them, and washed them from their sins in his own blood, and rejoicing in hope of the glory of God. How awful is it to be left behind at such a day! . . . Therefore, let everyone that is out of Christ, now awake and fly from the wrath to come. The wrath of Almighty God is now undoubtedly hanging over a great part of this congregation. Let everyone fly out of Sodom: "Haste and escape for your lives, look not behind you, escape to the mountain, lest you be consumed."[8]

- What does it mean that God is just?

- Edwards also focused on heaven and love; this is just one of his more popular sermons.
- Conservative pastors fought against the Great Awakening because of the emotions people were expressing under the weight of conviction.
    i. Edwards had a lecture and published a book called *The Distinguishing Marks of a Work of the Holy Spirit*. He makes the case that emotions neither prove nor disprove

---

8. Edwards. *Sinners in the hands of an Angry God*

a genuine revival. There is worldly sorrow that leads to no change in behavior, and there is godly sorrow that leads to genuine repentance. He teaches that you must wait to see if there is any evidence of fruit.

- What is the difference between worldly sorrow and godly sorrow?

    ii. He preached a sermon called "Religious Affections" in response to the conservative pastors. He was concerned because he took what they had to say seriously:

"Christian practice is the sign of signs, in this sense, that it is the great evidence which confirms and crowns all other signs of godliness. There is no one grace of the Spirit of God, but that Christian practice is the most proper evidence of the truth of it . . . Practice is the proper proof of the true and saving knowledge of God: as appears by that of the apostle already mentioned, 'Hereby we know that we know him, that we keep his commandments.' It is in vain for us to 'profess that we know God, if in works we deny him,' Titus 1:16. And if we 'know God, but glorify him not as God;' our knowledge will only condemn, and not save us, Romans 1:21. The great note of that knowledge which saves and makes happy, is, that it is practical; John 8:17, 'If ye know these things, happy are ye if ye do them': Job 28:28. 'To depart from evil is understanding.'"[9]

- In 1748 he came into conflict with the "half-way covenant" of his church. He would not let non-believers partake in communion, even if they had been baptized as infants. As a result, his church fires him.

In 1750 he became a pastor in Stockbridge, Massachusetts and a missionary to the Housatonic Indians.

---

9. Edwards. *The Works of Jonathan Edwards.* P. 217

NOTES

The Second Great Awakening

1792–1820s

- What is the difference between revival and revivalism? **Iain Murray** wrote a book on this that is very helpful.
- The Reformation Revival and the First Great Awakening Revival were all a result of Scriptural teaching being rediscovered. Exposition and clear teaching of justification by faith alone in Christ alone by grace alone, through Scripture alone for the glory of God alone. It was unplanned, unexpected, and was brought into fruition by God.
- The Second Great Awakening begins much like the other revivals, an unexpected move of the Holy Spirit on the hearts of thousands of people. However, it shifts to something else toward the end.
- Influenced by the Great Awakening, pastors begin to look at the emotional response associated with John Edwards' message "Sinners in the hands of an angry God."
    i. They apparently didn't read his book" *Religious Affections*" and thought they could use certain tactics to create emotional responses in order to get more confessions of faith. They thought they could plan a revival on certain dates.
- Long revival meetings lasting days were discovered effective in getting someone to make a confession of faith.
- Music became a means of manipulation playing on the emotions.
- Encouraging people to respond physically became effective.

The Second Great Awakening

- Peer pressure building into a climactic moment was used to get people to make the decision which was viewed as a conversion.
- The goal became numbers rather than actual conversions. Success was measured now by the number of confessions.
- This is what Iain Murray calls "revivalism."
- A shift is made from personal revival, which is a long process of complete change of an individual by the work of the Spirit . . . to a momentary decision.
- Evangelists begin to be more like salesmen than expositors of the Bible.
- The First Great Awakening was much smaller and did not last as long; three to five years compared to twenty-five or so years.
- The First Great Awakening was primarily Puritans while the Second included Baptists, Methodists, Episcopalians, and others.
- Some of the men of the First Great Awakening started a college in New Jersey, which would later be known as Princeton. Jonathan Edwards was the president for a few years. It is from Princeton that the Second Great Awakening begins.

John Witherspoon (one of the signers of the Declaration of Independence) was the president of the college during this time. Revival broke out among the students and many were converted and became pastors.

John McMillan was one of the students that later went on to be a leader of Presbyterian Churches in Pennsylvania.

He writes:

> "I never saw that I was a lost, undone sinner, exposed to the wrath of a justly offended God, and could do nothing for my own relief. In this situation I continued until I entered College at Princeton, in the spring of 1770. I had not been long there, until a revival of religion took place among the students, and I believe, at one time, there were not more than two or three but what were under serious impressions. On a day which had been set apart by a number of the students to be observed as a day of fasting and prayer,—while the others were at dinner, I retired into my study, and while trying to pray, I got some discoveries of Divine things, which I had never had before. I saw that the Divine law was not only holy, just and spiritual, but that it was

good also, and that uniformity to it would make me happy. I felt no disposition to quarrel with the law, but with myself, because I was not conformed to it. I felt that it was now easy to submit to the Gospel plan of salvation and felt a serenity of mind to which I had hitherto been a stranger. And it was followed by a delight in contemplating God's glorious perfections in all his works. I thought I could see God in everything around me."[1]

- Discuss some of the interesting portions of this quote.
- This revival spilled out into every Christian denomination. Circuit riding preachers log thousands of miles riding from settlement to settlement preaching the gospel.
    i. They were not able to build churches fast enough for the expansion of America into the West. The only church many of these people would have are these circuit riding evangelists riding into town every so often.
- The preachers of the First Great Awakening had all been Calvinistic, most of the Preachers of the Second G.A. were Methodist influenced by John Wesley. They began to teach that Calvinism was a dangerous error.
    - Why do some people see Calvinism as dangerous?

America was in steep spiritual decline not only because of a lack of churches but because of the Revolutionary War (1775–1783).

- In the early 1800s **James McGready** held a communion service that started what is known as a camp meeting, where people would travel as much as one hundred miles prepared to camp on the ground. This became very popular across Kentucky and much of the country. These camp meetings on one hand were good, but on the other became a catalyst for doctrinal error, theological and spiritual abuses, and emotional and hysterical accesses. The restraint that they felt inside of a church building was not present in the outdoors. People began to fall down as if dead at these meetings, which led to disorder increasing and becoming the norm.

---

1. McMillan. *Annuals of the American Pulpit*

The Second Great Awakening

- - Is disorder something we find canonical Christians engaged in? Yes, and they were chastised by Paul in **1 Corinthians**.
  - Is it wise for new believers to become preachers, teachers or leaders?
  - Does Scripture say we must worship God with our whole emotions?
  - In disorderly and emotionally driven services what is lacking? The mind and biblical exegesis.

- The First Great Awakening was: Biblical Exegetical Preaching = Emotion = Fruit (the evidence of a changed life). The goal was a changed life.
- The Second Great Awakening became Preaching = Emotion which was seen as fruit. What is missing? Evidence. The goal was an emotional response to make a decision, so preaching changed to reflect this outcome.

    i. The altar call was introduced for the first time.

- This is all a result of Arminianism (Semi Pelagianism). If justification is solely based on a person's free will to choose, then why not manipulate that person to choose, and by any means necessary?
- Preaching became man centered because its end goal became an emotional response . . . ***what you do*** rather than the end goal being to show people they are wicked to the core and need a savior named Jesus and we should glorify him because of ***what he has done***.

  - What attribute of God is essential for proper evangelism? The holiness of God

> "He only is independently, infinitely, immutably holy. In Scripture He is frequently styled "The Holy One": He is so because the sum of all moral excellency is found in him. He is absolute Purity, unsullied even by the shadow of sin. "God is light, and in him is no darkness at all" (1 John 1:5). Holiness is the very excellency of the Divine nature: the great God is 'glorious in holiness' (Ex. 15:11). Therefore do we read, 'Thou art of purer eyes than to behold evil, and canst not look on iniquity' (Haab. 1:13). As God's power is the opposite of the native weakness of

the creature, as His wisdom is in complete contrast from the least defect of understanding or folly, so his holiness is the very antithesis of all moral blemish or defilement . . . It is this, supremely, which renders him lovely to those who are delivered from sin's dominion."[2] Arthur Pink

- Many Christians begin evangelism with God's love. This is where you should end.
  - Many Christians do not understand God's holiness, why?
    - First, it is rarely taught because many teachers are lacking in knowledge and have been influenced by Arminianism in which emotion is the driving force.
    - Second, because God's holiness is frightening.

"The holiness of God is traumatic to an unholy people."[3] R.C. Sproul

- What is holiness? It means set apart or entirely different. God is entirely different than us. His standard is perfect and pure and that is frightening.

"Do you see that we spend our entire lives veiling ourselves from the true character of God? Our natural bent, our natural inclination, is to hide ourselves from him, because we know instinctively that as soon as the holy appears it exposes and reveals anything and anyone who is not holy by virtue of that standard."[4]

"We have a justification for every sin that we commit. We are masters of self-deceit."[5] R.C. Sproul

For more resources on the Holiness of God I recommend: Isaiah 6; Exodus 19:16—20:21: Exodus 33:18–23: Exodus 34:29–35: Leviticus 10:1–3; 2 Samuel 6:1–7: *The Holiness of God* by R.C. Sproul; *Knowing God* by J.I. Packer; *The Attributes of God* by Arthur Pink

Charles Finney (1792–1875)

- Finney was a Presbyterian preacher who became a revivalist.

2. Pink. *The Attributes of God*
3. Sproul. Ligonier: Ligonier Teaching Series: *The Holiness of God: Lecture 2*
4. Sproul. Ligonier: Ligonier Teaching Series: *The Holiness of God: Lecture 2*
5. Sproul. Ligonier: Ligonier Teaching Series: *The Holiness of God: Lecture 2*

- Finney came to see "new measures" necessary for revival which included:

    i. The encouragement of physical response (falling on the floor, etc.) to preaching
    ii. Women speaking in worship
    iii. Meetings lasting long hours and many days
    iv. Inviting individuals to "submit to God" and prove it by a "humbling" action such as standing up, kneeling down, or coming forward to "the anxious seat" (or altar call).

- Calvinists had always preached that you must cry out to God for him to give you a new heart. Finney changed this, taking Arminianism to its logical conclusion:

A sermon he titled "Make yourselves a New Heart": "I will show you what is intended in the command of the text. It is that man should change the governing purpose of his life. A man resolves to be a lawyer; then he directs all his plans and efforts to that object, and that, for the time is his governing purpose. He directs all his efforts to that object and so **has changed his heart** . . . It is apparent that the change now described, effected by the simple volition of the sinner's mind through the influence of motives, is a sufficient change, all that the Bible requires. ***It is all that is necessary to make a sinner a Christian***"[6]

    i. If you can convince someone to be a lawyer, you can convince someone to be a Christian.
    ii. The gospel becomes a door to door salesman technique.
    iii. Conversion isn't a gift from God but a gift to God. It isn't something God does but something you do.

    - Who gets the glory here?

- He taught that revival could be planned rather than being an unexpected work of God.

Iain Murray wrote:

---

6. Quoted in review in *Biblical Repertory and Theological Review* (1832) P. 295

"It was now claimed as proven that the use of 'the anxious seat', and its attendant teaching, always saw the multiplication of converts; and the argument went, as such a result could not be without the working of divine power, God must be setting 'his seal to the doctrines that were preached and to the means that were used'. What was indisputable was the making 'conversion' a matter of instant, public decision, with ascertainable numbers immediately announced in the religious press, produced a display of repeated 'successes' on a scale never before witnessed. Numbers seen to be responding were claimed as more than sufficient evidence for the rightness of the changes in practice and teaching"[7]

- The number of confessions were undeniable, so Finney's new measures became the most popular method for preachers to use.
- When his new measures were challenged by pastors and Christians, they would point to the number of confessions as a way to say, "who are you to judge, look at these results."
    i. This argument is still used today.
        a. If numeric results show God's approval, I guess we all need to be Muslims.
- Finney was influenced by a man named **Nathaniel W. Taylor** (an Arminian) who was motivated to make the gospel more palatable due to attacks from Unitarians.

Iain Murray wrote: "The solution . . . was to assert that sin and guilt can only be attributed to men's voluntary choices. All that needs to be changed in the unconverted man is his will, not his nature. As Taylor's biographer observed, the doctrine of total depravity was central in the Unitarian attack on orthodoxy, and in departing from that doctrine Taylor and his New Haven colleagues were trying to 'restate Calvinism in more acceptable terms.'"[8]

- Finney took this further in which he reinterpreted the atonement of Christ.

---

7. Murry. *Revival and Revivalism*
8. Murry. *Revival and Revivalism*

Iain Murray wrote: "According to [Finney's] view, Christ's death was not a payment of debt on behalf of those whose sins he bore; it was rather an action to satisfy public justice, making it safe and possible for God to forgive those who repent and believe. So the act that secures forgiveness is man's, not Christ's. 'The atonement itself does not secure the salvation of any', wrote Finney. 'When a sinner repents that state of feeling makes it proper for God to forgive him'"[9]

    i. This denies Federal Imputation or Federal Headship.

    ii. God's forgiveness is based on the sinner's response rather than the finished work of Jesus at the Cross.

- The Presbyterian church split over Finney's methods into what was known as the "Old School" and the "New School."

- Finney guaranteed that his new measures would yield results: "**The prayer of faith is always answered** by the specified blessing prayed for. We see that **pious parents can render the salvation of their children certain**. Only let them pray in faith and be agreed as touching the things they shall ask for, and God has promised them the desire of their hearts." (Source Dr. Nathan Busenitz Lecture 21 of Historical Theology II)

  - What are some of the problems with this statement? "Always answered" this seems like Word of Faith before there was a Word of Faith Church.

    - He is attributing emotional manipulation to faith. You can talk someone into making a confession, and if you make a confession God will give you that desire.

  - What does **Psalms 37:4** mean?

"Delight yourself in the Lord; And He will give you the desires of your heart."

   - *Delight in the Lord*. If you *delight in the Lord* fully and truly then what do you no longer delight in? The things this world has to offer. In other words, God will change your desires to the things that are holy.

9. Murry. *Revival and Revivalism*

- What is the problem with placing all of the weight of prayer always being answered on the person's faith?
    - First, it leaves no room for God's sovereignty. He may be taking you or the person you're praying for through a trial or even chastisement.
    - Second, when your prayers aren't answered it is because you are a failure.

Despite Finney's claims, his efforts failed in two ways. First, to produce more genuine Christians. Second, revival ceased.

> Iain Murray: "Finney's claim that success proved the rightness of his cause could be tested by facts; the facts, however, reveal evidence contrary to Finney's thesis. In the early 1830s Finney repeatedly asserted that if preachers adopted his convictions there would be continuous revival. Many men did adopt them and the practices that went with them but the revival that 'would never cease' never came. On the contrary, the Second Great Awakening, which had begun under doctrinal preaching different from his own, came to an end and no protracted meetings could recall it. The excitement of 1831 seems to have been the point of termination."[10]

- Murray points out four things as to why Finney's new measures were accepted (and still are):
    i. Visible, numeric success which trumped the need for a biblical defense.
    ii. Christians wanted to see visible success and were excited when people were affected.
    iii. These were introduced in a time of true revival, therefore was seen as a part of that.
    iv. The success of his methods over trumped the clear harm that was done to the church.

---

10. Murry. *Revival and Revivalism*

NOTES

Liberalism and The Higher Critics

Augustine: "You ought to say plainly that you do not believe the gospel of Christ. For to believe what you please, and not to believe what you please, is to believe yourselves, and not the gospel."[1]

Martin Luther: "The Holy Ghost is the all-simplest writer that is in heaven or earth; therefore, his words can have no more than one simplest sense, which we call the Scriptural or literal meaning."[2]

John Calvin: "Let us know that the true meaning of Scripture is the genuine and simple one and let us embrace and hold it tightly. Let us boldly set aside as deadly corruptions, those fictitious expositions which lead us away from the literal sense."[3]

- What is liberal theology? Christianity without the Bible.

- With the Age of Enlightenment and the rise of rational skepticism, the Bible came under attack. The Bible began to be looked at as just another book, which should be evaluated based on science and rational thinking. This led to the view that the Bible was a non-literal book. That it was only good for teaching moral or other lessons to benefit your life, like any book can do.

- Below are a few examples of liberal higher critics of the Bible during the nineteenth century that influenced a mass of people.

---

1. Augustin. *St. Augustine of Hippo Writings*

2. Luther. Article. Preaching.com. *Pattering Your Preaching with God's Authority*. Ken Burge

3. Calvin. *Institutes of the Christian Religion*

JOHANN GOTTFRIED EICHHORN (1753-1827) (GERMANY)

- He concluded that the Hebrew Scriptures had passed through several authors or editors before coming to their final form.
- He assumed everything supernatural recorded in the Old Testament could be explained through naturalistic means.
- He explained away miraculous events and concepts about God as being simply accommodations to an ancient way of thinking, which had no real value for modern society.
  - Have you heard any of these arguments from people today? How do we deal with these?
  - Who is the ultimate author of Scripture? The Holy Spirit
  - Did the scribes edit the Scripture?

First, we should understand that the process of copying Scripture was not an easy one.

  i. Clean animal skins are all that could be used, both to write on, and to bind manuscripts.
  ii. Each column of writing must be between forty-eight, and no more than sixty lines.
  iii. The ink must be black and made a particular way.
  iv. They must verbalize each word aloud while they are writing.
  v. They must wipe the pen and wash their entire bodies before writing the word "Yahweh (YHWH)," every time they write it.
  vi. A review of the copy must be done within thirty days, and if as many as three pages required corrections, the entire manuscript had to be redone.
  vii. The letters, words, and paragraphs had to be counted, and the document became invalid if two letters touched each other. The middle paragraph, word and letter must correspond to those of the original document.

viii. The copies must be stored only in sacred places, such as synagogues.
  ix. No document containing God's Word could be destroyed, so they were stored or buried in a genizah—a hiding place, usually a synagogue or Jewish cemetery.

Second, how many manuscripts are available for us to examine today?

- Over twenty-five thousand copies in various languages.
- Almost six thousand in the original language.
- There are also around thirty-six thousand quotes from church fathers that when brought together almost the entire Bible is quoted.

- When all of these are compared how many errors are found? Around two hundred thousand, but ninety nine percent of those are leaving a letter out of a word or a grammatical error. The remaining one percent has no doctrinal significance.

To answer the question did the scribes edit the Scripture . . . yes. It has been determined that the book of Mark had an ending added to it. It originally ended at 16:8. Verses 9–20 was probably added to close the book, even though it was left open intentionally. There is no contradiction in doctrine in this added ending. Mark is the only book of the Bible that has been determined to have something added to it or changed from all of the copies examined by countless critics.

FRIEDRICH SCHLEIERMACHER (1768–1834) THE FATHER OF LIBERAL THEOLOGY

- Friedrich was introduced to historical criticism at the University of Halle and became skeptical of the Christian faith in which he already had doubts.
- In a letter to his father who was an Army Chaplain he wrote: "Faith is the regalia of the Godhead, you say. Alas! Dearest father, if you believe that without this faith no one can attain to salvation in the next world, nor to tranquility in this—and such, I know, is your belief—oh! Then pray to God to grant it to me, for to me it is now lost.

I cannot believe that he who called himself the Son of Man was the true, eternal God; I cannot believe that his death was a vicarious atonement."[4]

- He became a chaplain at a hospital in 1794. A minister who does not believe that Jesus is the true God.
- He became a theology professor of Halle in 1804.
- He wanted to hang on to his Christian heritage but did not believe the Bible was true. He was influenced by Romanticism.
    i. He taught that the essence of Christianity is not in historical fact or in moral ethics, but in subjective feeling.
        - Would you say the essence of Christianity is any of these three things?
- He wrote two books: *On Religion*, and *The Christian Faith* in which these ideas were spewed.

> Life Magazine March 8th, 1968: "If God is not dead, how can man prove that he lives? Rational proofs cannot convince the skeptic; the Bible alone is authority only to the convinced believer; the demythologized universe no longer points to an unseen creator. One approach to an answer that appeals more and more to modern Protestant thinkers is the undeniable evidence of religious experience—the intuition men have of their dependence upon God. The popularity of this insight, in turn, leads back to the study of Friedrich Schleiermacher. (later in the article) ... Schleiermacher answered that faith is not based on doctrine or reason but upon man's "feeling of absolute dependence" and what he called "a sense and taste for the Infinite." Man, he argued, could never define or explain God, only his own experience of the divine. To Schleiermacher, church doctrines were primarily articulations of religious feelings, and he scandalized German Protestantism in his early writings by coolly appraising Christianity not as a faith with a unique monopoly on truth but simply as "the highest and purest" of the world's many religions. Skirting the question of Christ's divinity, he defined Jesus as "the completion of the creation of man."

---

4. Schleiermacher. *The Universalist Quarterly and General Review Volume 25*. P. 397

- If man were to invent a God would that God be holy? If you answer yes, you do not understand God's holiness.
- If man were to invent God, would salvation be obtained by works or by something out of your control like faith, which is by grace that you only receive and cannot earn?

DAVID FRIEDRICH STRAUSS (1808–1874)

- He was considered to be the pioneer of the "quest for the historical Jesus" in which the "Jesus of history" is recovered and differentiated from the mythological Jesus of the Bible.
- His book *The Life of Jesus* caused a firestorm in 1835 in which he argued that Jesus's miracles were simply mythical accounts.
  - Would the apostles and church fathers die for mythical accounts?
    i. I am unaware of any originator of a religion that has ever died for their faith other than Jesus and his apostles. Muhammed fell ill and died. Joseph Smith was shot, Buddha died of food poisoning, etc.

Charles Darwin published his *Origin of Species* during this time (1859) which added to the criticism.

ALBRECHT RITSCHL (1822–1889)

- Ritschl is known as the father of the social gospel.
  - What is the social gospel? Social issues become primary and equal to or greater than the biblical gospel.
- He taught that you could have Christianity without the Bible because it is based on good moral ethics.
- He taught that faith did not need to be based on historical facts, but rather on the value judgments of the believing community.
- He taught that Christianity is defined by what one does in society, in terms of ethical conduct. The gospel is not about personal salvation

from sin but about redeeming society through social work, "fatherhood of God and brotherhood of man." What would Jesus do rather than what did Jesus do.

JULIUS WELLHAUSEN (1844-1918)

- Wellhausen challenged the authorship of biblical books such as the Pentateuch. He claimed the Pentateuch was not written by Moses but many authors. This sparks criticism of other books like Isaiah that critics claimed was written by three authors, etc. This was all done in the name of being "scholarly," in reality, it was only a result of unbelief. Biblical criticism became a competition of cleverness rather than being scholarly.

ADOLF VON HARNACK (1851-1930)

- Harnack came up with the idea of peeling back layers of Christianity like an onion or corn to get through all of the Greek influence. He denied miracles, angels, and demons, apocalyptic elements and anything supernatural. He claimed that anything supernatural was, in reality, only Greek influences through years of the Bible being copied by various scribes.

J.I. Packer: "If we pursue theological knowledge for its own sake, it is bound to go bad on us. It will make us proud and conceited. The very greatness of the subject matter will intoxicate us, and we shall come to think of ourselves as a cut above other Christians because of our interest in it and grasp of it."[5]

- World war would shatter liberal theology for a time, yet today it has taken over many denominations entirely.
    i. We see it in guys like Rob Bell who teaches there is no hell, we see the acceptance of women pastors, the acceptance of homosexuality in the church and behind the pulpit, the embracing of other religions and other such things.

---

5. Packer. *Knowing God*

Richard Niebuhr in his book *The Kingdom of God in America* said, when referring to Liberalism, "God without wrath brought men without sin into a kingdom without judgment through the ministrations of a Christ without a cross."[6]

- What are some of the lessons we should learn from Liberal Theologians and Higher Critics?
    - Do not water down the gospel in order to reach people.
    - It only takes one generation to lose the gospel.
    - There is only one true gospel, and anything added or taken away is not the gospel at all.
    - Skepticism of God's Word is not being noble or "being real," it is sin.
    - There is a difference between skepticism and a quest for truth.
  i. Liberalism, skepticism, and the social gospel are dominating in America today.

- In America the church was divided between three groups: The liberalist, the fundamentalist, and the indifferentist. In many ways it remains this way.
- Liberalism became the dominant view in all of the main-line denominations in the early twentieth century. It brought unity over social issues while at the same time doctrinal ignorance to Scripture. Fundamentalists and conservatives left or in some cases were kicked out of liberal churches. This created the **fundamental denominations** who wanted to maintain doctrinal and theological purity and teach a clear gospel.
- Liberalism denies inerrancy and infallibility, a battle over inerrancy will take place later.
    - What is the difference between inerrancy and infallibility?
        - Inerrancy means without error.
        - Infallibility means incapable of making an error or mistake.

6. Niebuhr. *The Kingdom of God in America*

NOTES

The Cults and Heretics of the Nineteenth and Twentieth Centuries

"But false prophets also arose among the people, just as there will also be false teachers among you, who will secretly introduce destructive heresies, even denying the Master who bought them, bringing swift destruction upon themselves. Many will follow their sensuality, and because of them the way of the truth will be maligned; and in their greed they will exploit you with false words; their judgment from long ago is not idle, and their destruction is not asleep."

2 Peter

THE RESTORATIONIST MOVEMENT

- What was the restorationist movement?
    - A movement in the early 1800s that attempted to restore the church to the patterns of the New Testament.

Alexander Campbell (1788–1866) and **Barton Stone** (1772–1844).

- The Restorationist Movement was pioneered by Alexander Campbell and Barton Stone.
- They believed creeds divided Christianity.
- They believed confessions, creeds, and church history had corrupted the church. They wanted to get back to the first-century church.
    - Do creeds and confessions divide the church? Yes and no

The Cults and Heretics of the Nineteenth and Twentieth Centuries 277

- ◆ Doctrine will always divide, why? Because we are all sinners.
  - Should we throw out doctrine?
    - ◆ To throw out doctrine would be impossible but to get away from historical biblical doctrine is probably heresy. In other words, if you get away from creeds and confessions you will still be teaching your own doctrine and when left unchecked by the thousands of Christians who came before you, you will be prone to heresy.
- Campbell and Stone wanted to unite all people into one denomination which they called the Church of Christ of the Disciples of Christ.
  - What do the Church of Christ believe?
    - ◆ The church of Christ gets more right than they do wrong. However, they believe in Baptismal Regeneration which is heresy if taken to its logical conclusion. Some of their members believe they are the only true denomination therefore the only true believers.
- This is the platform that Satan used to start many cult movements. Getting back to the first-century church by using prophets or prophetesses to bypass eighteen hundred years of church history. They actually get back to early church heresies.

Mormons (Latter-Day Saints) (A regurgitation of Gnosticism and parallels Islam)

- What do you know about Mormonism?

- This is an offshoot of the Church of Christ that split to follow Joseph Smith. They call themselves the Church of *Jesus* Christ.

Joseph Smith (1805–1844)

- He claimed in 1827 that he dug up a book of thin golden plates near Palmyra, New York. He published a book in which he translated these plates from Egyptian Hieroglyphs to English in 1830 called *the Book of Mormon.*
    i. The Rosetta Stone had not been discovered yet . . . no one knew how to translate Hieroglyphs.
    ii. Smith claimed that these gold plates went back to heaven after he translated them.

- *The Book of Abraham,* which is about Abraham and Isaac, exposes Mormons as a fraud.
    i. Explorers who collect and sell real Egyptian artifacts came through America. Some of Smith's followers got excited and purchased hieroglyphs for Smith to translate. He spent two years translating the hieroglyphs of these scrolls into *the Book of Abraham* in which was adopted as scripture and added to *the Pearl of Great Price* for the Mormons. The scrolls he translated survive. After the Rosetta Stone was discovered they were translated accurately discovering that it had nothing to do with Abraham or Isaac.

- Smith was shot and killed.
    - What do Mormons believe?
        - Mormons believe that Jesus is one of many gods and is the physical offspring of a relationship between God and Mary.
        - If you are a good Mormon, you can become a god.
        - They have a works-based soteriology.
        - They add other books to the Bible.
        - They believe in polygamy.

Seventh Day Adventists (A regurgitation of the Judaizers)

- What do you know about the Seventh Day Adventists?

* It was founded by **William Miller** (1782–1849).
* Miller became a deist after being influenced by their morality. Later he was emotionally struck by the idea of Jesus being an atonement for our sins while reading a sermon. He began to question deism. His deist friends challenged him to justify his newfound faith. He did so by trying to harmonize what they saw as contradictions in the Bible. He had a particular interest in eschatology. He falsely predicted that Jesus would return to earth twenty-three hundred years after Ezra's return to Jerusalem which would be 1843. When that didn't happen, he changed it to 1844, when that didn't happen, he said he was correct, except Jesus came into his heavenly sanctuary rather than earthly. Miller said that Jesus stood up from where he was seated next to the Father, went into the heavenly sanctuary and began a second work of atonement called the "heavenly atonement".
* Miller was influenced by a prophetess named Ellen G. White.

  - What do Seventh Day Adventists believe?
    * They believe in the Heavenly Sanctuary, which is a secondary atonement.
    * They believe in soul sleep.
  - What is soul sleep? The belief that when a person dies his soul is in a sleep-like state until the resurrection.
    * They believe in annihilationism.
    * They believe you must worship on Saturday and keep other Mosaic laws.
  - Why do you think so many people have set the date of Christ's return when it is apparent in Scripture that no one knows the day or the hour?

Christian Science (The Church of Christ, Scientist) (Modern Gnosticism)

- What do you know about Christian Science?

  - It was founded by **Mary Baker, Glover, Patterson, Eddy** (1821–1910).

    "Mrs. Eddy was chronically sick growing up, with many ailments including paralysis, hysteria, seizures and convulsions. At 22, she married her first of three husbands, George Glover, who died within 6 months from yellow fever. Following Glover's death, she began to be involved in mesmerism (hypnosis) and the occult practices of spiritualism and clairvoyance. Still ill, she married Daniel Patterson in 1853, a dentist and homeopathic practitioner. It was during this time she met mental healer Phineas P. Quimby (1802–1866), whose influence would shape her belief of Christian Science. Quimby believed that illness and disease could be cured through positive thoughts and healthy attitudes, by changing one's beliefs about the illness. She claimed that Quimby cured her; she suddenly improved, but later the symptoms returned."[1]

- What does Christian Science believe?

  - They emphasize healing by mental assent to truth that denies the reality of both illness and matter.
  - They deny the reality of matter, evil, and sickness. These things are simply delusions of our senses.
    i. This is very appealing to sick people.

"We acknowledge that the crucifixion of Jesus and his resurrection served to uplift faith to understand eternal Life, even the allness of Soul, Spirit, and the nothingness of matter." (Christianscience.com)

  - Women can become pregnant by supreme concentration alone, because all matter is an illusion.
  - They believe death is an illusion and people only die because that is what they believe they should do.

---

1. Tucker. *Another Gospel.* P. 155

"It is also encouraging to realize that in our efforts to overcome death we are not fighting something real. What we are dealing with is the belief in death's reality. To the degree that we recognize the utter falsity of this belief we progress in overcoming our fear of it."[2]

"His (Jesus) crowning achievement was his victory over death and materiality in his own experience. As our Way-shower, Jesus expected us to follow his example."[3]

- This is an offshoot of the Church of Christ. The First Church of Christ, Scientist, of Boston became the mother church.
- Christian Science is neither Christian nor science.

Jehovah's Witnesses (A regurgitation of Arianism)

- What do you know about the Jehovah's Witnesses?

- They were founded by **Charles Taze Russell** (1852–1916).
- In 1879 he began publishing a magazine called *Zion's Watch Tower and Herald of Christ's Kingdom*.
- He taught that there would be a heavenly resurrection of 144,000 and that the dead in that group existed in soul sleep.
- He taught that Jesus received his divinity after his resurrection.
- He taught that the Holy Spirit is not a person but a force of God's power.
- He thought the end of the world was World War 1.
  - What do Jehovah's Witnesses believe?
    - They deny the divinity of Christ.
    - They have their own bible which is called *the New World Translation*.
    - They have predicted the return of Christ multiple times.
    - They have a works-based soteriology.

2. Aug. 1974 Issue of *The Christian Science Journal*
3. Aug. 1974 Issue of *The Christian Science Journal*

- How do you witness to these types of people?
- In seeing the mutability of man, is it comforting to know that God is immutable?
- What does it mean that God is immutable?

> "God is immutable in His essence. His nature and being are infinite, and so, subject to no mutations. There never was a time when He was not; there never will come a time when He shall cease to be. God has neither evolved, grown, nor improved. All that He is today, He has ever been, and ever will be. 'I am the Lord, I change not' (Mal. 3:6), is His own unqualified affirmation. He cannot change for the better, for He is already perfect; being perfect, He cannot change for the worse. Altogether unaffected by anything outside Himself, improvement or deterioration is impossible. He is perpetually the same."
>
> "God is immutable in His attributes. Whatever the attributes of God were before the universe was called into existence, they are precisely the same now, and will remain so forever. Necessarily so; for they are the very perfections, the essential qualities of His being. Semper idem (always the same) is written across every one of them. His power is unabated, His wisdom undiminished, His holiness unsullied. The attributes of God can no more change than deity can cease to be. His veracity is immutable, for His Word is 'forever settled in heaven'"[4] A.W. Pink

Discuss the following question by filling in the blank a character of God:

- What does it mean that God's _____ is unchangeable? (love, justice, promises, etc.)
- What can we learn from the cults?

---

[4]. Pink. *The Attributes of God*

NOTES

The Keswick Movement and its Theology

- What is Keswick (KEZ-ik) Theology, also known as "Higher Life"?
  - Keswick Theology (1875–1920s) has a distinctive way of viewing justification and sanctification.
  - It teaches that justification and sanctification happen at different times in the believer's life which creates two "classes" of Christians.
    i. There are Christians who are saved but haven't begun the process of sanctification and there are Christians who have matured into beginning the journey of sanctification.
      - They believe that most Christians are living in a defeated life and the secret to a deeper or victorious Christian life is consecration followed by Spirit-filling.
- The founders of the Charismatic movement were influenced by this movement. Being filled with the Spirit is the next level or class of Christian.
- The Keswick motto was "Let go and let God."
  - Have you ever heard this motto? What are its implications?
    - It indicates that God can't do anything unless you let go, which renders him powerless against the human will. Some believers think of this as letting go of worry.

- - Sanctification is accomplished by letting go and letting God rather than praying for God to give you the grace you need to become more holy and applying that to action.
  - It promotes a type of passiveness or quietism.
- What is quietism?
  - Quietism is a type of mysticism that attempts to achieve peace and spiritual perfection by thinking of God and divine things.
- What should a believer do with their worry, let go and let God? No, we should pray and read Scripture about the sovereignty of God.

- This movement was influenced by John Wesley, John Fletcher, and Adam Clarke.
   i. Christian leaders who have held to this theology include Billy Graham, Oswald Chambers, and Hudson Taylor.
- Wesley taught that you could reach sinless perfection from willful sin, which is another type of elite Christian. Taking Wesley's teaching further, Keswick theologians began to teach that you can become justified and not be sanctified. Sanctification was something you can obtain at a later time.
- They do not believe in striving for the faith or struggling in our sanctification.
- They do not believe in the mortification of sin like the reformed view of sanctification.
  - What does it mean to mortify sin?

"So, the apostle, Col. iii. 5, 'Mortify therefore your members which are upon the earth.' Whom speaks he to? Such as were 'risen with Christ,' verse 1; such as were 'dead' with him, verse 3; such as whose life Christ was, and who should 'appear with him in glory,' verse 4. Do you mortify; do you make it your daily work; be always at it whilst you live; cease not a day from this work; be killing sin or it will be killing you. Your being dead with Christ virtually, your being quickened with him, will not excuse you from this work."[1] John Owens

- They believe that you are either in the flesh or in the Spirit and there is no gradual change. This is a form of perfectionism. You are either walking perfectly in the Spirit or you are in the flesh, which is okay because either way you are a Christian.

Category 1 Christians	Category 2 Christians
Free from the penalty of sin but not its power	Free from the penalty of sin and its power
Live in defeat	Live in victory
Jesus is Savior but not Lord	Jesus is Savior and Lord

Andy Naselli: (the Author of *Let Go and Let God?*)

"Keswick misunderstands the nature of the flesh, Keswick's error is not in speaking of two natures in the believer but in how it speaks of those natures, namely, its view of the sinful nature or flesh. Like the Chaferian view, the Keswick view incorrectly understands the flesh to be an equally powerful nature alongside the believer's new nature: both natures are unchanging entities within the believer, and only one is in total control at any given moment. Thus, the flesh either controls the believer or is counteracted by the Spirit. According to Keswick theology, a believer in category 1 "lives" in the flesh. It is all or nothing. Believers are either 'in the flesh' or 'in the Spirit.'"[2]

Andy Naselli: "Keswick theology chronologically separates justification from progressive sanctification by emphasizing a crisis of consecration subsequent to justification that enables genuine progressive sanctification. This essentially divides Christ as one whom people can "take" as their Justifier without "taking" him as their Sanctifier. From the moment of justification, progressive

---

1. Owens. *Of the Mortification of Sin in Believers*
2. Naselli. *Let Go and Let God?*

sanctification is experientially actual for all believers, not merely potential or possible."[3]

- Have you ever heard someone say something like: "I was saved as a child but didn't surrender to Christ till I was older?" This is the influence of this theology.

• Keswick theology views "abiding in Christ" as a Category 2 believer. An experience that is deeper and more intimate with Christ. Those that do not abide in Christ are carnal believers.

  i. Scripture teaches that if you are not abiding in Christ you are lost. **John 15 1-10**

• Today, some of the distinctives between Keswick theology and Reformed theology is seen in the Lordship salvation vs. Free Grace controversy. John MacArthur published a book in 1988 called *The Gospel According to Jesus* that caused a firestorm between these two camps. There is a lot of confusion passed on from the proponents of Free Grace to those they have taught about what Lordship Salvation is. Lordship salvation is not making Jesus Lord in order to be saved but the opposite. **Because you are saved**, Jesus is Lord of your life and there is fruit you bear as evidence. This is Lordship salvation and is the biblical model.

  - What does it mean that you are sanctified?
  - What does it mean that you are being sanctified?
  - What does it mean that you will be sanctified?

---

3. Naselli. *Let Go and Let God?*

NOTES

The Charismatic Movement

"And yet some people actually imagine that the revelation in God's Word is not enough to meet our needs. They think that God from time to time carries on an actual conversation with them, chatting with them, satisfying their doubts, testifying to His love for them, promising them support and blessings. As a result, their emotions soar; they are full of bubbling joy that is mixed with self-confidence and a high opinion of themselves. The foundation for these feelings, however, does not lie within the Bible itself, but instead rests on the sudden creations of their imaginations. These people are clearly deluded. God's Word is for all of us and each of us; He does not need to give particular messages to particular people."

JONATHAN EDWARDS

> Note: We will be looking at the charismatic movement in a polemical way. There are some churches that belong to this movement that have the essentials correct. There are true Christians in this movement, but they have really become the fringe as the most popular charismatic leaders are heretics and charlatans. Because of a lack of separation and accountability charismatics all get lumped into the same category. Polemics and accountability are desperately needed in this movement and a true separation needs to happen before the entire movement gets swept into heresy.
>
> A note to you if you are in this movement: If you have made it this far in this study, I dare say you may belong to the fringe. If you skipped everything else, please go through the rest of this study before getting into this chapter. I pray that you will carefully examine what is being

done and said in your own movement and glorify God by igniting the love of biblical truth, doctrine, and careful study of theology. I pray that you will hold people under the label "charismatic," who are obvious heretics, accountable and separate them from Christianity as you would a Mormon or Jehovah's Witness.

A note from the author: I was part of the charismatic movement for over thirty-five years. It is for this reason that I may seem to be more polemical concerning this movement than I am with other movements.

- There are three key movements in the charismatic church: Pentecostalism, Charismatic Renewal, and the Third Wave. Charismatics are still under the Restorationist Movement. They are trying to get back to the church in Acts and bypassing all of church history.
- Leading up to the three waves of Pentecostalism was a group from England known as the **Quakers** (founded in 1652) and later a group known as the **Shakers**.
- They were called Quakers and the Shakers because of the violent tremblings and quakings they experienced during worship.
- They spoke in tongues, sang in tongues, manifested holy laughter, practiced being slain in the spirit, dancing in the spirit, and being drunk in the spirit.
- All Shakers were allowed to prophesy, and all prophecies were considered inspired, so their doctrines are hard to follow.
  - If something is inspired by God, shouldn't it be added to the Bible? God's Word is timeless and always true, so if he spoke to someone and they didn't add what he said to the pages of the Bible wouldn't they be robbing all Christians of his timeless truth? If there were more truth to be found other than what is found on the pages of holy Scripture wouldn't all people need to know that truth? Do you understand the seriousness of saying "thus says the Lord" if it is not what God is speaking? Do you understand that that person is putting themselves on the same level as an apostle or prophet? What does the Bible say should happen to a false prophet? Deuteronomy 18:20

- The Shakers believed in what **George Fox** (the founder) called Inner Light in which God spoke to you and directed you within yourself, not from biblical teaching.

Note: This sounds much like Hinduism and Buddhism may have influenced him.

- They believed that sex was only for procreation within marriage. Even within marriage sex without the intention of procreation was considered lust, so separate bedrooms were the norm.
- They had no ordained clergy; anyone could teach.
- They did not believe in the Trinity. They believed that God is both male and female. The Holy Spirit is Christ and separate from Jesus who was a male manifestation of God.
- A woman named Ann Lee became their leader because she was believed to be a female manifestation of God and the second coming of Christ. Ann Lee came to America and started the Shaker movement here which influenced this type of so-called worship.
  - What is complementarianism? Men and women have different but complementary roles and responsibilities.
  - According to 1 **Timothy 2:12-14** should a woman exercise authority over a man in the church?

12 But I do not allow a woman to teach or exercise authority over a man, but to remain quiet. 13 For it was Adam who was first created, and then Eve. 14 And it was not Adam who was deceived, but the woman being deceived, fell into transgression.

The Vermont Journal wrote an article on Feb. 14th 1786 " on the Shakers: " They carry on very frequent dialogues with both angels, devils, and departed fouls—a party of them being employed now in preaching to the Indians and Negroes who have died since the beginning of time, in the respective languages of those nations;—others are engaged in like benevolent employ with the dead of other nations."

The New York Daily Herald wrote an article on June 8th, 1853 about attending a Shaker worship service: [a young woman] "suddenly commenced spinning round like a humming top. Her head soon began to jerk to and fro . . . At another time one of the females commenced speaking in a tongue which seemed a compound of all known and unknown languages . . . They have amongst them here a female who is regarded as possessing the gift of prophecy, and she is consulted when any important matter is to be undertaken."

IS HINDU WORSHIP SIMILAR TO CHARISMATIC WORSHIP?

- There are countless examples of Gurus and the Kundalini spirit. We will be looking at two examples:

Sri Ramakrishna (1836–1886) a Kundalini Yoga Guru

- Sri "reached a depth of God-consciousness that transcends all time and place."
- People flocked to him including philosophers, theologians, atheists, agnostics, Christians and Muslims.

"He daily went into 'samahdi,' a trance in which one involuntarily falls down unconscious and enters a rapturous state of super-conscious **bliss** complete with **beautiful visions** and often involving astral projection. These states could last anywhere from a few minutes to several days and were often accompanied by uncontrollable laughter or weeping. He could send others into this state with a single touch to the head or chest.[1]

  - Does a demonic experience feel demonic according to the excerpt above?

Swami Muktananda (1908–1982) a Kundalini yoga guru

- In 1947 he received the Kundalini Spirit.
- He was slain in the spirit and could see past and future events.
- He passed the spirit on by the laying on of hands.
- Physical manifestations included uncontrollable laughing, roaring, barking, hissing, crying, shaking, etc.

1. Article. John Rice. Spiritual Counterfeits Project. Citing Warren Smith: *Holy Laughter or Strong Delusion*. 1994. Vol. 19.2

"Many felt themselves being infused with **feelings of great joy and peace and love**. At other times the *'fire'* . . . was so overwhelming they would find themselves involuntarily hyperventilating to cool themselves down"[2]

- Are any of these things found in the charismatic movement?

- Speaking in tongues has been practiced in Hinduism for a thousand years. Clearly these manifestations were demonic.
- We have to ask questions:
  - Are the manifestations found in the Charismatic movement satanic like these?
  - Was the Kundalini spirit simply counterfeiting the real work of God?
    i. One of the charismatic arguments is that Satan can counterfeit real movements of God. We will be looking at its roots to see if this is from God.
  - What are the biblical examples for this type of behavior?
  - Was the Charismatic movement founded by solid Christian men who were doctrinally pure and were at the next level of Christianity? Let's look at its founders:

CLASSICAL PENTECOSTALISM (THE FIRST WAVE)

Charles Parham (1873–1929)

- Parham was the founder of the Pentecostal movement. He formulated classical Pentecostal theology in Topeka, Kansas in 1901. He was rooted in the Wesleyan Holiness movement which taught that believers could experience a "second blessing" by being baptized in the Holy Spirit, in which they enter a deeper, more holy phase of the Christian life.

---

2. Article. John Rice. Spiritual Counterfeits Project. Citing Warren Smith: *Holy Laughter or Strong Delusion.* 1994. Vol. 19.2

Note: Keep in mind he already bought into Arminian soteriology and with that the idea that nominal Christians can exist. Wesleyans believe you can reach a place of sinless perfection or being totally sanctified.

- He had a group of students that he encouraged to read the book of Acts and pray that they could experience the baptism of the Holy Spirit just like the believers did in the book of Acts. A young lady named **Agnes Ozman** began to speak in what was determined by the witnesses to be Chinese. Others began to follow, and it was recorded that over a dozen languages were recorded being spoken.
    i. They were convinced by the book of Acts that tongues consisted of real foreign languages.
- Parham told newspapers that missionaries can now be sent into other countries without learning their languages. As a result, several Pentecostals went into foreign countries relying on the new gift they had received, being like the people in the book of Acts. They all returned disappointed and disillusioned because no one could understand them at all.
- Agnes Ozman began to write in tongues, along with many others which is documented in many historical books and websites. See below for her writing in Chinese:

The Charismatic Movement

- It is important to note that they believed that just as in the days of the Bible, speaking in tongues was **an actual language** for the purpose of evangelizing foreign people.
- Investigations went into these claims because of the enormous media storm that stirred, all to conclude that no one was speaking actual languages that claimed to be speaking actual languages like they did in the book of Acts.
- As these languages were proven to be false it became a matter of experience rather than the Bible for Parham and his students.
    i. They believed that their experience was real, so the Bible must be re-interpreted to match their experience. Thus, the conclusion became, it must be the tongues of angels rather than actual languages like the book of 1 Corinthians.
        - Is it dangerous to take something you have experienced personally and impose it on Scripture? What is that called?
        - Can an experience be something worked up within your own mind because you desperately want it to be true?

Note: You would think angels would all speak one language, but over twelve were recorded.

- Were tongues in **1 Corinthians** the language of angels?

13:1 *If I speak with the tongues of men and of angels, but do not have love, I have become a noisy gong or a clanging cymbal.*

- If tongues of men are intelligent communication, this would be applied to angels as well. If angels speak to men, it is always understandable. Look at the next two verses to see the context of what this is concerning:

2 If I have the gift of prophecy, and know all mysteries and all knowledge; and if I have all faith, so as to remove mountains, but do not have love, I am nothing. 3 And if I give all my possessions to feed the poor, and if I surrender my body to be burned, but do not have love, it profits me nothing.

- This is not a passage showing that speaking in tongues is an angelic language. This is a passage showing that *if* I was perfect and even knew **all the *mysteries*** and had ***all knowledge*** that exists yet have

no *love*, *I am nothing*. This is a hyperbole statement to get the point across that anything done without love being at its core, is useless.

- What about **Romans 8:26**, what are the *"groanings too deep for words"* the Holy Spirit intercedes for us?

    i. The word "groanings" is the Greek word "stenagmos" which means "gushings of the heart." This is not actual words.

- Cult groups that spoke in tongues, prophesied, and had visions prior to the charismatic movement include: The Shakers, Hindus, Mormons, and Irvingites.
- The Charismatic movement is entirely based on experience over biblical truth which forces you to read into (eisegesis) Scripture rather than exegete (draw the true meaning out of) Scripture.
- Parham desired to destroy denominational distinctions.
- He taught annihilationism.
- He taught two separate creations. Adam and Eve were of a different race than people who lived outside of the Garden of Eden. The first race of men did not have souls and were destroyed in Noah's Flood.

    - Is this found anywhere in Scripture and if not, where did this idea come from? This is another example of his eisegesis.

- He taught that those who spoke in tongues were the "bride of Christ."

    - Does it say anywhere in Scripture that you must speak in tongues to be saved? This is another example of his eisegesis.

- He taught that physical healing was always God's will. Parham went on to participate in faith healings, in which many people died due to not seeking medical treatment.

    - Why is physical healing not always God's will?

- He was arrested for having a homosexual relationship.

- He created a scam in which he raised money to go to the Holy Land and retrieve the Ark of the Covenant and the tabernacle. He never went and claimed that he was mugged, and the money was stolen.[3]
- It was reported that eventually he joined the Ku Klux Klan in 1910.

William J Seymore (1870–922)

- Seymore was a student of Parham.
- He took Parham's ideas to Los Angeles and started the Azusa St. Revival.
- They (Azusa leaders) believed they could wield the Holy Spirit like a sword, or command Him to do things.

Eyewitness account:

> "I found men and women lying on the floor in all shapes . . . (they were) jabbering all at one time in what they called unknown tongues. While I was praying, one of the workers took hold of me and said, 'Holy Ghost, we command Thee to go into this soul'. The workers were jabbering and shaking their hands over me, and a demonic power (as I now know) took possession of me, and I fell among the people on the floor and knew nothing for ten hours. When I came to my senses, I was weak, and my jaws were so tired they ached. I believed then that this power was of God. They said I was wonderfully blessed, and the leader sent me from one place to another so that I could jabber in tongues."[4]

  - Does this reflect an inkling of an understanding of the holiness of God?
    i. Commanding a deity or spirit is only found in the occult.

- There was no order to the services and the Bible was rarely preached:

> "The meetings began in the mornings and continued for at least 12 hours. There was no order of services and usually no one leading. People sang at the same time but "with completely different syllables, rhythms, and melodies" (Ted Olsen, "American

3. Article. Democrat and Chronicle. Rochester, New York. Feb. 1st, 1902
4. White. *Demons and Tongues*

Pentecost," Christian History, Issue 58, 1998). The services were characterized by much confusion: dancing, jumping up and down, falling, trances, slaying in the spirit, "tongues" jerking, hysteria, strange noises, and "holy laughter" One visitor described the meetings as 'wild, hysterical demonstrations.' The seekers would be seized with a strange spell and commence a gibberish of sounds." A Time reporter noted that the participants "work themselves into a state of mad excitement in their peculiar zeal." There was little or no order to the Azusa Street services. Whoever felt "moved by the spirit" to speak, would do so. Seymour rarely preached. Instead, much of the time he kept his head covered in an empty packing crate behind the pulpit. He taught the people to cry out to God and demand sanctification, the baptism with the Holy Ghost, and divine healing"[5]

- Thousands of spiritualist mediums, hypnotists, and other occultist groups flocked to Azusa St.

". . . spiritualists and mediums from the numerous occult societies of Los Angeles began to attend and to contribute their seances and trances to the services."[6]

- Seymore became concerned and wrote to Parham for help. Parham visited Azusa and was shocked at what he saw and heavily rebuked it. Parham's wife recorded in his biography what he witnessed at Azusa: "hypnotic influences, familiar spirit influences, spiritualistic influences, mesmeric influences, and all kinds of spells and spasms, falling in trances, etc."[7]

- Perham told Seymore to remove the spiritualists and occultists from the services but Seymore refused claiming that "our Lord said to his worker to let the tares and wheat grow together and that at the end of the age they will be separated."

K.B. Napier: "Parham tried to counter the evil at Azusa Street by holding parallel meetings elsewhere, to deliver people from possession by demons."[8]

5. Synan. *The Holiness Pentecostal Movement in the United States*
6. Synan. *The Holiness Pentecostal Movement in the United States*
7. Liardon. *God's Generals*
8. Article. *Azusa Street: The Birth of a Lie*

The Charismatic Movement

- There was doctrinal division at Azusa St. which led to the formation of several churches:
    i. The Church of God in Christ
    ii. The Assemblies of God
        a. The United Pentecostal Church came out of the Assemblies of God church in 1914 when they split over baptizing in Jesus name only. They hold to modalism.
    iii. The Pentecostal Church of God

Sister Aimee McPherson (1890–944)

- She founded the Foursquare Church in 1923 in Los Angeles.
    i. Calvary Chapel (Chuck Smith) sprung from the Four-Square Church.
        a. The Vineyard Churches (John Wimber) sprung from Calvary Chapel.
- She was married three times.
- She allegedly faked her own kidnapping (for thirty-six days) in what people speculate was either for an affair with her radio engineer or for publicity.
- She died of a drug overdose.
- Her god seemed to be the god of love without holiness and a god that was impotent rather than omnipotent.
- Her message was more on imperatives rather than indicatives like almost all teachers in the charismatic movement.
    - What is the difference between an imperative and an indicative and why is understanding this important to the way the Bible is taught?
        - These are both verb moods.
        - An imperative is a command and is used in Scripture to tell us what we should do, overcome, or bear.

- An indicative refers to certainty or actuality and is used in Scripture to tell us what God has done, is doing or will do.
  - Should the majority of a pastor's sermon be an imperative or an indicative?
    - What did Jesus do or what should you do? This is Law vs. gospel.
  - Most Charismatic sermons are geared toward an imperative. How is this different than what the Judaizers, Roman Catholics, Mormons, or Jehovah's Witnesses do?
    i. A gospel sermon will have both imperatives and indicatives, but the object of it will be on what Jesus Christ has done, is doing, and will do . . . not on you. Too much application is not a good thing. If a sermon is written with application (imperative) in mind, it misses the whole point of Scripture. We need more gospel not more Law. Law should be used to necessitate the gospel, not to lay a burden upon a people who cannot bear its weight.

CHARISMATIC RENEWAL (THE SECOND WAVE) (1960)

Dennis Bennett (1917–1991)

- Bennett was an Episcopal Pastor in California who on Easter Sunday in 1960, said that he received the baptism of the Holy Spirit in which he could speak in tongues. This was reported by Time Magazine and Newsweek which threw Charismatics into the spotlight across the country. Soon the Roman Catholic church dove into the Charismatic Renewal as well as many mainline denominations such as Anglicans, Lutherans, and the Reformed. This led to many leaving these churches to start independent churches.

The Word of Faith Movement

- This movement was developed by men and women such as:

E. W. Kenyon (1867-1948); Kenneth Hagin (1917-2003); Kenneth Copeland; Benny Hinn; Joyce Meyer; and Joel Osteen

- They teach that words have power. You cannot say that you or anyone else is sick because that will bring it into fruition.
- You can speak things into existence because we are all little gods according to this heresy. This includes both good and bad things: money, houses, planes, etc. can be yours if you have enough faith and speak the right words. You can rebuke weather, sickness and disease. You have to be careful not to speak harm on loved ones because your words have power and will come true.

Kenneth Hagin: "You are as much the incarnation of God as Jesus Christ was. Every man who has been born again is an incarnation."[9]

Kenneth Copeland: "I say this with all respect, so that it don't upset you too bad, but I say it anyway . . . when I read the Bible where He says, I AM, I say yes, I AM TOO!"[10]

Kenneth Copeland: "Am I a god? Man was created in the god class, was not created in the animal class, it was the god class. He has a uniqueness about him that even angels do not have . . . Now Peter said by exceeding great and precious promises, you become partakers of the divine nature. Alright, are we gods? We are a class of gods."[11]

Benny Hinn: "God came from heaven, became a man, made man into little gods, went back to heaven as a man. He faces the Father as a man. I face devils as the son of God. Quit your nonsense! What else are you? If you say, I am, you're saying I'm a part of Him, right? Is he God? Are you His offspring? Are you his children? You can't be human! You can't! You can't! God didn't give birth to flesh . . . You said, "Well, that is heresy." No, that's your crazy brain saying that."[12]

- These men and women will not receive correction and quote **Psalms 105:15** out of context when criticized . . ."Touch not the Lord's

---

9. Almodiel. *Tanong At Sagot.* P. 84
10. Believer's Voice of Victory Broadcast, 7/9/1987
11. Praise the Lord, TBN, 2/5/1986
12. Our Position in Christ #2: The Word made Flesh: Orlando Christian Center, 1991: Videotape #255

anointed." What does this verse literally mean? To not physically harm or kill the Lord's anointed.

- Are pastors and elders obligated to call out false teachers? Yes

(Matthew 7:15; Acts 20:28–29; Matthew 16:6; Philippians 3:2, 3:18; Romans 16:17; 1 Corinthians 5:11; 2 Thessalonians 3:6,14; 2 Timothy 3:5; 2 John 10; 1 Timothy 5:19–20; 2 Timothy 4:10, 1:15; 1 Timothy 1:19–20; 2 Timothy 2:17)

- This is an altogether different religion; this is not Christianity. This is the highest form of blasphemy and should be in the category of witchcraft.
- They teach that a lack of faith hinders God from working miraculously.
    - Why is this such a vile doctrine?
        - First, it makes man sovereign and God weak. It reduces God to be a slave of man. It elevates man and renders God impotent.
        - Second, it puts all of the pressure on the sick person who doesn't have enough faith to be healed.
        - Third, going to the doctor is sometimes looked at as lacking faith. Many people have died refusing to go.

SIGNS AND WONDERS (THE THIRD WAVE) (1980s)

- This is difficult to systematize. Much of this teaching is intertwined together.
- One of the ideas that began to be taught is that in the New Testament church, prophecy no longer had to be infallible. Basically, the interpretation by a modern prophet of what the Holy Spirit was saying could be miscommunicated or entangled with human error. Prophecies that did not come to pass were no longer a problem. In addition, they were no longer held accountable to the Old Testament standard of the penalty of false prophecy. The standard had changed. A person can now prophesy falsely but not be a false

prophet. They often use 1 Corinthians 14:29 as a proof text which they take out of context. The context of this verse is Paul setting the standard of an orderly worship service. You must read into the text to come away with the idea that this teaches that it is ok to prophesy something God did not say.

Deuteronomy 18:10-22 *"There shall not be found among you anyone who makes his son or his daughter pass through the fire, one who uses divination, one who practices witchcraft, or one who interprets omens, or a sorcerer,11 or one who casts a spell, or a medium, or a spiritist, or one who calls up the dead. 12 "For whoever does these things is detestable to the LORD; and because of these detestable things the LORD your God will drive them out before you. 13 "You shall be blameless before the LORD your God. 14 "For those nations, which you shall dispossess, listen to those who practice witchcraft and to diviners, but as for you, the LORD your God has not allowed you to do so. 15 "The LORD your God will raise up for you a prophet like me from among you, from your countrymen, you shall listen to him. 16 "This is according to all that you asked of the LORD your God in Horeb on the day of the assembly, saying, 'Let me not hear again the voice of the LORD my God, let me not see this great fire anymore, or I will die.' 17 "The LORD said to me, 'They have spoken well. 18 'I will raise up a prophet (This is speaking of Jesus, Acts 3:22) from among their countrymen like you, and I will put My words in his mouth, and he shall speak to them all that I command him. 19 'It shall come about that whoever will not listen to My words which he shall speak in My name, I Myself will require it of him. 20 'But the prophet who speaks a word presumptuously in My name which I have not commanded him to speak, or which he speaks in the name of other gods, that prophet shall die.' 21 "You may say in your heart, 'How will we know the word which the LORD has not spoken?' 22 "When a prophet speaks in the name of the LORD, if the thing does not come about or come true, that is the thing which the LORD has not spoken. The prophet has spoken it presumptuously; you shall not be afraid of him.*

Jeremiah 14:14-16 *14 Then the Lord said to me, "The prophets are prophesying falsehood in My name. I have neither sent them nor commanded them nor spoken to them; they are prophesying to you a false vision, divination, futility and the deception of their own minds. 15 "Therefore thus says the Lord concerning the prophets who are prophesying in My name, although it was not I who sent them—yet they keep saying, 'There will be* no sword or famine in this land'—by sword and famine those prophets shall meet their end! 16 "The people also to whom they are prophesying will be thrown out into the streets of Jerusalem because of the famine and the sword; and there will be no one to bury them—neither them, nor their wives, nor their sons, nor their daughters—for I will pour out their own wickedness on them.

Ezekiel 13:6-9 6 "They see a falsehood and lying divination who are saying, 'The Lord declares,' when the Lord has not sent them; yet they hope for the fulfillment of their word. 7 "Did you not see a false vision and speak a lying divination when you said, 'The Lord declares,' but it is not I who have spoken?" ' " 8 Therefore, thus says the Lord God, "Because you have spoken falsehood and seen a lie, therefore behold, I am against you," declares the Lord God. 9 "So My hand will be against the prophets who see false visions and utter lying divinations. They will have no place in the council of My people, nor will they be written down in the register of the house of Israel, nor will they enter the land of Israel, that you may know that I am the Lord God.

- The Third Wave was developed by three men: Peter Wagner, John Wimber, and Mike Bickle.

C. Peter Wagner (1930–2016)

- In 2001 he claimed God had given apostles to the church again, and he is one of them.
- He claimed he is the one who stopped mad cow disease in Europe after he rebuked it.[13]

John Wimber (1934–1997)

- He was a former Quaker who started the Vineyard Church.
- He defends the RCC claims of healings through relics. He wanted the RCC and Protestants to unite. At a Vineyard pastors' conference, he apologized to all RCC on behalf of the Protestants. (source *Charismatic Chaos* by John MacArthur)

---

13. Wagner. *Wrestling with Alligators, Prophets, and Theologians.* P. 243

Mike Bickle

- He is the founder of the International House of Prayer.
- He was influenced by the heretical Latter Rain Movement which was started by false prophets **Bob Jones** and **Paul Cain** of the **Kansas City Prophets.**
- The Latter Rain Movement believed in what they called **"Joel's Army"** (Joel 2:1–11) an elite force of Christians in the end times that will take the world by storm using supernatural power and defeat the Antichrist.
  - What is the "army" of Joel 2?
    - It could be referring to the army of Revelation 9:16–19.
  - Can and does God control Satan and demons? Yes

  Job 1:6–12; Matthew 4:1

*Judges 9:23 Then **God sent an evil spirit** between Abimelech and the men of Shechem; and the men of Shechem dealt treacherously with Abimelech,*

1 Samuel 16:14 Now the Spirit of the Lord departed from Saul, and an evil spirit from the Lord terrorized him.

- God is sovereign over all things and all things have a purpose in God's creation.
  - What is the theological term that views Satan's power equal with God's? Dualism (The Yin and the Yang)

> Bickle: "We're not absent for the great tribulation, now listen carefully, the church causes the great tribulation. What I mean by that—it's the church, it's the praying church under Jesus' leadership that's loosing the judgment in the great tribulation in the way that Moses stretched forth his rod and prayed and loosed the judgments upon Pharaoh. The church in the tribulation is in the position that Moses was before Pharaoh but it won't be a Pharaoh and Egypt, it'll be the great end time Pharaoh called the antichrist and the book of Revelation is a book about the judgments of God on the antichrist loosed by the praying church"[14]

14. Bickle and International House of Prayer: *The Latter Rain Redivivus.* Bob

- The Third Wave teaches that God cannot do anything without us giving him permission to do it. They believe that God always wants to do abundant and remarkable miracles, but he is kept from doing so by the fear and unbelief of Christians.

Psalms 136:6 *Whatever the Lord pleases, He does, In heaven and in earth, in the seas and in all deeps.*

- These men and their followers believe that signs and wonders are a normal thing for them and authenticates their movement. Anyone can prophesy, anyone can heal, they claim they can read minds and raise the dead. They believe that any church body of believers who does not do those things and condemn their movement are Pharisees. So, they will not receive correction and look at true believers as instruments of Satan.
- With thousands of claimed healings and miracles, not one has been verified.
  - Which brings up another question, can Satan work miracles?

2 Thessalonians 2:8-9 *Then that lawless one will be revealed whom the Lord will slay with the breath of His mouth and bring to an end by the appearance of His coming; that is, the one whose coming is in accord with the activity of Satan,* **with all power and signs and false wonders, and with all the deception** *of wickedness for those who perish, because they did not receive the* **love of the truth** *so as to be saved.*

- They believe signs and wonders are the evangelistic means God uses today, so they often go out into public to pray for people to be healed yet forsaking the gospel message. They travel all over the world to teach people how to do signs and wonders, yet the gospel is absent. They have started schools to teach people how to do signs, wonders, and even prophesy.
- They believe that a lack of faith hinders God from working miraculously.

DeWaay. Also see THE FORERUNNER SCHOOL OF MINISTRY—MIKE BICKLE *The Book of Revelation The Revelation of Jesus: Bridegroom King and Judge (Rev. 1)* by Mike Bickle

New Apostolic Reformation (NAR)

"I needed a name ... For a couple of years, I experimented with 'Post denominationalism'. The name I have settled on for the movement is the New Apostolic Reformation."[15] C. Peter Wagner,

- The NAR is hard to follow because they are very loose in their theology. It seems that almost anything goes as long as you slap the name Jesus at the end of it.
- It is called the NAR because they believe there is a large wave of new apostles that are here today to reform the church into what it should be.
- Some of the leaders of this movement include:

Lou Engle (The Call and Azusa Now crusades); Bill Johnson (Bethel Church in Redding California); Bill Hamon (Christian International); Rick Joyner (MorningStar Ministries); and Todd White (Lifestyle Christianity)

- They believe that sound biblical exegesis, well defined doctrine, and theological studies will bring Christians into bondage, rendering them Pharisees.
    i. Satan does not want you to know who the true Living God is, he wants you to create an idol and worship that instead.
- They teach "**Kingdom Now**" theology which is the belief that the same supernatural things that happen in the kingdom of Heaven also happen on earth if you will only have enough faith. This is also tied in with dominionism and the 7 Mountain Mandate that we will take a look at in a moment.
- There is an aspect of deism in this theology as well. They believe that God lost control of his creation when Adam sinned, and God has been trying to reestablish control by seeking a special group of believers. This theology also encompasses "Joel's Army."

---

15. Wagner. *The New Apostolic Churches.*

- Jesus's Kingdom is "now" in part and it is up to us to usher it in fully by showing the power of the kingdom today by supernatural signs and wonders that will convince people to declare Jesus is Lord.
- They believe that since we have the same Holy Spirit indwelling us, we have the same access to heaven and can work the same, and even greater miracles than Jesus.

> "Jesus is the example for us to duplicate-in fact, we should *literally* be doing "greater works than Him." This means we should all expect to raise the dead and heal anyone we want to at anytime. There are no leaders in the NAR who are actually doing these things, but they make great claims of having extraordinary power and ability. And if you buy their books/DVDs/conference tickets they promise to give you the 'secret formula.' This is the Theology of Glory, as opposed to the Theology of the Cross."[16] Steven Kozar

- Kingdom now theology ascribes to an eschatological system called "The 7 Mountain Mandate."

The 7 Mountain Mandate that must be **conquered** to usher in the return of Christ is:

Religion, Family, Education, Government, Media, Arts & Entertainment, and Business.

In other words, **Christians must take over the world** in order to usher in the second coming of Christ.

- They believe Jesus was truly man but not truly God because he emptied himself completely and relied totally on the power of the Holy Spirit. This is known as "kenosis", a very heretical doctrine.
    - Could Jesus have atoned for our sins if he wasn't truly God?

Bill Johnson: "He [Jesus] performed miracles, wonders, and signs, as a man in right relationship to God . . . not as God. If He performed miracles because He was God, then they would be unattainable for us."[17]

---

16. *The New Apostolic Reformation Cornucopia of False Doctrine, Dominionism, Charismania and Deception*

17. Johnson. *When Heaven Invades Earth*

- The reason they embrace kenosis is because they believe that all that Jesus did, we should be able to do and do better. Why? Because they twist John 14:12:

"Truly, truly, I say to you, he who believes in Me, the works that I do, he will do also; and greater works than these he will do; because I go to the Father."

  - What are the *greater works* that the apostles and Christians throughout history have done than Jesus?
    - Spread the gospel of Jesus. The works that Jesus did is not referring to miracles, but ministry. Jesus's ministry was very small regionally, but through believers his work and message has spread to all parts of the world.

- They believe that there is a new super Christian that walks the earth now called the "**New Breed.**"
- Guys, like Todd White and Todd Bentley, will manifest Christ (they are sometimes called the Manifested Sons of God) here on earth with powerful signs, wonders, and judgments, greater than Jesus did, to cleanse the church and the world of all sin so that Christ can return. The signs and wonders these men perform is the beginning of a great end-time revival.

Bill Johnson: "We will carry the Elijah anointing in preparing for the return of the Lord in the same way that John the Baptist carried the Elijah anointing and prepared the people for the coming of the Lord."[18]

  - In the Old Testament what were miracles for?
    - To authenticate the prophet. In the New Testament what were miracles for? To authenticate Christ and the apostles . . . ultimately to authenticate Scripture. So, what would signs and wonders and miracles be for today?

Luke 11:29 *As the crowds were increasing, He began to say, "This generation is a wicked generation; it seeks for a sign, and yet no sign will be given to it but the sign of Jonah.*

---

18. Johnson. *When Heaven Invades Earth*

- What is the definition of a miracle and is it the same as providence?
  - When a theologian refers to a miracle it is something very specific and not broad like thought of today.
  - Miracles in the Bible were always instant, verified, public, and pointing to God.
  - Providence is God's will that is carried out, sometimes supernaturally, that may not be instant, may not be public, may not be verified, but will still point to God.
    i. With this definition we see that miracles as defined do not happen today and have not happened since the last apostle died. What is truly providence is confused with miracles.
- Will there be miracles in the future? Yes, according to the book of Revelation. What will that be authenticating? Jesus's second coming.

- Back to the question, if miracles authenticate something what would it be authenticating today after we have a completed canon of Scripture?
  - Would it be their message? Would it be their prophets? Would it be their prophecies?
  - If this is the case, wouldn't we need to be adding books to the Bible?

- If God speaks directly to people today, the canon was never closed, and God's message was not complete.
  - Wouldn't God be using people who had a correct understanding of Scripture, who had a pure understanding of the gospel and whose ultimate goal was to teach that clearly? Wouldn't he use people who believed in the biblical Jesus rather than creating an idol of the one they want to worship?

- This movement is simply the New Age Movement repackaged under the banner of Christianity.

"Although God is giving new revelation to his Prophets/Apostles they will make many mistakes in the process and that's okay, but following the Bible too closely makes you a "religious" and narrow-minded Pharisee. In the NAR, using your mind is generally bad but having a mystical and subjective experience is very good."[19] Steven Kozar

- This movement is also bent on teaching people to declare, bind, and command rather than the biblical concept of prayer. It seems Satan will use any trick to keep people from humble prayer. In the RCC he deceived people into praying to saints and Mary rather than God. In this movement he has deceived people into declaring, binding, and commanding rather than humbly falling on their knees and praying to God as Scripture teaches us to do.

CONTINUATIONISM, CESSATIONISM, AND RESTORATIONISM

- What is Continuationism? The supernatural miraculous gifts of the Spirit as recorded in the New Testament are still available to believers today.

- These gifts include speaking in tongues, prophecy, raising the dead, and healing.
- In some cases, continuationists believe in modern apostles, interpretation of dreams, and reading minds. Some also believe in miraculous signs and wonders such as barking like dogs, being slain in the Spirit, and sucking the anointing out of dead saints' graves.
- Scholarly Continuationist will argue that miraculous gifts were given to edify the church and that is what they still are for today. They will argue that there is no scriptural evidence to support Cessationism.

  - What is Cessationism?

---

19. *The New Apostolic Reformation Cornucopia of False Doctrine, Dominionism, Charismania and Deception*

- The supernatural miraculous gifts of the Spirit were for the pre-canonical Christians only and have ceased; not being available today.
- These supernatural gifts were to authenticate the message until we had a completed canon of Scripture at which time they stopped because no other message needed to be authenticated. Jesus performed supernatural signs and wonders not only to authenticate his message, but himself as being God.

  i. Like today, there were many false teachers running around; how would you know who to believe?
  - Today we have a measuring stick to measure the teacher or preachers message called what?

- Most Cessationists still believe that God performs miraculous things through providence.
- He still heals, but there is not a gift of healing that someone wields around like a sword.
- He still answers prayer.
- If he chooses to work miraculously through the Holy Spirit in a supernatural way he can, however this isn't in any way the norm.
- Concentric Cessationists believe that the miraculous gifts have ceased in the mainstream church but appear in unreached areas as an aid to spreading the gospel.
- There is no argument from church history that satisfies the continuation of supernatural gifts, the office of prophet, the office of apostle, or any other claim made by so called continuationists. They claim that these things ceased in the fourth century because the church went apostate. They claim that these gifts were restored during the sixteenth or nineteenth century . . . depending on who you ask.
  - The understanding of what they claim does not place them in the category of continuationists but the category of what? Restorationists

Belfast News Letter Oct 28, 1831 "He [James Irving] commenced by observing that manifestations of the Spirit in the gifts of prophecy and of tongues, had been the subject of historical record during the first three centuries, but from that period up to the present time, they had *ceased* to be the subject of historical record. It has, however, been the opinion of himself and of others that these manifestations might be renewed, and accordingly they had prayed to the Lord to **restore them** . . .

  i. James Irving and his followers called the Irvingites were a gnostic cult.

- On a positive note concerning Charismatics . . . they believe in the power of the Holy Spirit. Yes, they take it too far, but those of us outside of this camp often overlook the power and work of the Holy Spirit that is essential to our faith. Another positive lesson we could learn from the Charismatics is the freedom to worship. Again, they go way too far, but we who are outside of their camp are afraid to move, lift our hands, or cry out to God as we should . . . because of our fear of what others will think of us. Because we do not want to be associated with the Charismatics we stew in our pride and remain rigid. We must be careful to not overcorrect what we see to be wrong and we must not look down on another's response of worship that is found within the boundaries of Scripture.

  - What is the chief end of man? To glorify God and enjoy him forever. If your gaze is fixed upon anything other than this, you are in grave error. Unfortunately, many in the charismatic movement have fixed their gaze upon experiences, emotions, and the supernatural.
  - Would the Holy Spirit want you to have your eyes fixed on him or on Christ?

NOTES

Fundamentalism and Evangelicalism in America

"Be well instructed in theology, and do not regard the sneers of those who rail at it because they are ignorant of it. Many preachers are not theologians, and hence the mistakes which they make. It cannot do any hurt to the most lively evangelist to be also a sound theologian, and it may often be the means of saving him from gross blunders. Nowadays, we hear men tear a single sentence of Scripture from its connection, and cry 'Eureka! Eureka!' as if they had found a new truth; and yet they have not discovered a diamond, but a piece of broken glass... Let us be thoroughly well acquainted with the great doctrines of the Word of God."[1]

CHARLES SPURGEON

MAJOR ISSUES THE CHURCH FACED

- The rise of the social gospel happened in America in the late 1800s and early 1900s.

    - What is the social gospel? Rather than a person needing to be saved from the wrath of God, they need to be saved from social issues such as poverty, medical needs, and lack of provisions.

- Science became aware that drinking alcohol in excess is bad for you. In response the churches in America push for prohibition.

---

1. Spurgeon. *Lectures to My Students*

- Christian based organizations began such as City Rescue Missions, Goodwill, YMCA, and the Salvation Army in order to meet social needs of the mass immigration to America.
- Washington Gladden (1836–1918) wrote a series of books trying to apply Christian principles to the social and economic situations in the United States.
- Missions to other countries went from spreading the gospel to building hospitals, etc.
- Charles Sheldon (1857–1946) wrote a book "*In His Steps, What Would Jesus Do?*" 100,000 copies were sold within a few months. In this book he taught that Jesus was a good moral man, so when you face a situation you should say "what would Jesus do?"
    i. The question isn't WWJD but what did Jesus do. WWJD teaches moralism rather than the gospel. Moralism is another word for what? The Law. The proper view of sanctification fixes our eyes on Jesus, not ourselves. Do we as believers want to be like Jesus? Yes, but in his kingdom, we must learn this is only accomplished by leaning upon him and his work and not ours.
- The social gospel is still a major problem today.
- The Restoration Movement was in full swing:

1832 Alexander Campbell and Barton Stone (Churches of Christ)

1805–1844 Joseph Smith (Mormons)

1827–1915 Ellen White (Seventh Day Adventists)

1852–1916 Charles Russell (Jehovah's Witnesses)

1873–1929 Charles Parham (Pentecostalism)

- America was affected by Charles Darwin who taught evolution and Friedrich Nietzsche who promoted atheism.
- Modernism was the world view in which science, not God, was seen as absolute truth. In the midst of all these things the Fundamental Churches began to rise.

THE NIAGARA CREED (1878)

- The Niagara Creed and its fourteen doctrinal principles were established by a group of conservative Bible scholars that would later be called fundamentalism. These scholars put away their doctrinal differences to fight together against this barrage of false ideas and doctrines coming against God's church. Their common tie was sola Scriptura and sola fide.
- They soon were faced with a decision to make, much like the Reformers, to leave their denominations that were plummeting into liberalism or stay and try to change them from the inside.
- The founders of this movement were James Brooks (1830–897), Milton Stewart (1838–1923), and Lyman Stewart (1840–923).

James Brooks was a Presbyterian pastor and a leader of the Niagara Bible Conference.

Milton and Lyman (1840–923) Stewart were Presbyterian businessmen who funded the writing and distribution of much of the materials produced by the Niagara Bible Conference.

The Niagara Creed

"We believe that the world will not be converted during the present dispensation, but is fast ripening for judgment, while there will be a fearful apostasy in the professing Christian body; and hence that the Lord Jesus will come in person to introduce the millennial age, when Israel shall be restored to their own land, and the earth shall be full of the knowledge of the Lord; and that this personal and premillennial advent is the blessed hope set before us in the gospel for with we should be constantly looking."

The Fourteen Points of the Niagara Creed: We believe in ...

1. The verbal, plenary inspiration of the Scriptures in the original manuscripts
2. The Trinity
3. The creation of man, the fall into sin, and total depravity
4. The universal transmission of spiritual death from Adam
5. The necessity of the new birth

6. Redemption by the blood of Christ
7. Salvation by faith alone in Christ
8. The assurance of salvation
9. The centrality of Jesus Christ in Scriptures
10. The constitution of the true church by genuine believers
11. The personality of the Holy Spirit
12. The believer's call to a holy life
13. The immediate passing of the souls of believers to be with Christ at death
14. The premillennial second coming of Christ

- In 1910 Five Fundamentals were added: We believe in . . .

1. The inerrancy of Scripture
2. The virgin birth and deity of Jesus Christ
3. The substitutionary atonement through God's grace and human faith
4. The bodily resurrection of Jesus Christ
5. The authenticity of Jesus's miracles

    - Do you disagree with any of these points and if so, why?

- Between 1910–915 authors from many denominations (Presbyterians, Methodist, Baptist, and Independents) wrote articles to expound upon the Five Fundamentals in what is called "The Fundamentals."

Philip Mauro: "The living Word shall continue to be the discerning companion of all who resort to it for the help which is not to be had elsewhere in this world of the dying. In going to the Bible, we never think of ourselves as going back to a book of the distant past, to a thing of antiquity; but we go to it as to a book of the present—a living book. And so indeed it is, living in the power of an endless life, and able to build us up and to give us an inheritance among all them that are sanctified."[2]

- Discuss the above quote.

2. Mauro. *Life in the Word: The Fundamentals*

MODERNISM VS. FUNDAMENTALISM WAS AT THE CENTER OF EVOLUTION VS. BIBLICAL CREATIONISM

- In 1925, John Scopes (Tennessee) was put on trial for teaching evolution in public school. Scopes was found guilty. However, the trial turned public opinion against Fundamentalists.
- Liberal churches believing evolution was science began to view the creation account of Scripture entirely differently, which led to other creation views:

    i. Theistic Evolution

    - What is theistic evolution? The idea that God created the world through evolution rather than six literal days.

    ii. The Gap Theory

    - What is the gap theory?
        - The idea that a large gap of time can be found between Genesis 1:1 and 1:2. There was another world that existed during this gap that was destroyed, and God re-created it in the six days described in Genesis.

    iii. Genesis being a book of poetry rather than historical fact.

    - Does Genesis belong in the poetry genre?
        - No, it is an historical account but let's pretend it is poetry, would that change the infallibility of God's Word? Would you change the meaning of it to mean something other than what it actually says? If so, wouldn't the translation be relative?

- Ultimately all mainline denominations went liberal. Fundamentalists were seen as "country bumpkins" and split off to form other denominations.

Charles Spurgeon (1834–1892)

- Though Spurgeon isn't from America, we must mention this man and the impact felt by his ministry.
- Spurgeon was a reformed Baptist and considered the "Prince of Preachers." He preached to over ten million people.
- He pastored New Park Street Chapel in London from the age of nineteen till his death.
- He preached up to thirteen times per week.
- Liberalism had spread across England just like America. Spurgeon stood against this "downgrade" and chose to leave his denomination.

> "We have had enough of "The Downgrade" for ourselves when we have looked down upon it. What havoc false doctrine is making, no tongue can tell. Assuredly the New Theology can do no good towards God for man; it has no adaptation for it. If it were preached for a thousand years by all the most earnest men of the school, it would never renew a soul, nor overcome pride in a single human heart . . . The sword and trowel have both been used this year with all our might. We have built up the wall of the city and have both tried to smite the king's enemies. How could we help it? No loyal soldier could endure to see his Lord's cause so grievously wronged by traitors. Something will come of the struggle over the Downgrade."[3] Charles Spurgeon

- He called it the downgrade because the Bible had been downgraded to something man-centered rather than God-centered and inerrancy was denied.
  - Has a "downgrade" happened again in today's church? If so, can you give some examples?

> "Be well instructed in theology, and do not regard the sneers of those who rail at it because they are ignorant of it. Many preachers are not theologians, and hence the mistakes which they make. It cannot do any hurt to the most lively evangelist to be also a sound theologian, and it may often be the means of saving him from gross blunders. Nowadays, we hear men tear a single

---

3. Spurgeon. *The Sword and the Trowel*

sentence of Scripture from its connection, and cry "Eureka! Eureka!" as if they had found a new truth; and yet they have not discovered a diamond, but a piece of broken glass . . . Let us be thoroughly well acquainted with the great doctrines of the Word of God."[4] Charles Spurgeon

"If sinners be damned, at least let them leap to Hell over our dead bodies. And if they perish, let them perish with our arms wrapped about their knees, imploring them to stay. If Hell must be filled, let it be filled in the teeth of our exertions, and let not one go unwarned and unprayed for." Charles Spurgeon

- Discuss the above two quotes from Spurgeon.

INDIFFERENTISTS

Indifferentists sprang from the separation between liberal and fundamental doctrines. They believed in the fundamentals but would not separate from the liberals.

Billy Graham (1918–2018) was the most famous indifferentist.

- Billy Graham started out as a fundamental evangelist. Later he began to include liberals or "non-Christians" as the fundamentalists referred to them in his crusades. This forced fundamentalists to question if they would partner with Graham. Most chose to separate from him.
- Graham preached to nearly 215 million people during his ministry.
- He spoke as though the Bible was his ultimate authority.
    - What is the difference between teaching and preaching?//
- The reason Graham was so successful was because he became an indifferentist and was not clear on any doctrinal issues other than the gospel.

---

4. Spurgeon. *The Sword and the Trowel*

"I think everybody that loves Christ, or knows Christ, whether they're conscious of it or not, they're members of the body of Christ. And that's what God is doing today. He's calling people for 'eh, out of the world for his name whether they come from the Muslim world, or the Buddhist world, or the Christian world, or the non-believing world uh they are members of the body of Christ because they've been called by God. They may not even know the name of Jesus but uh they know in their hearts that they need something that they don't have, and they turn to the only light that they have. And I think that they are saved, and they are going to be with us in heaven."[5] Billy Graham

- Do you agree with Billy Graham on the above statement?

"I used to play God, but I can't do that anymore. I used to believe that pagans in far-off countries were lost—were going to hell—if they did not have the gospel of Jesus Christ preached to them. I no longer believe that. I believe that there are other ways of recognizing the existence of God—through nature, for instance—and plenty of other opportunities, therefore, of saying "yes" to God.[6] Billy Graham

- Why can we not embrace Roman Catholics and Jews as believers?

In a 9/21/57 interview with the San Francisco News, Graham said, "Anyone who makes a decision at our meetings is seen later and referred to a local clergyman, Protestant, Catholic, or Jewish."

At Graham's 1994 Crusades in Minneapolis and Cleveland: 6,000 respondents at each Crusade were referred to the Roman Catholic Church; Graham's 9/96 Charlotte, NC Crusade: 1,700 respondents were referred to the Roman Catholic Church

"When planning for his own funeral, Graham had specified that Catholic prelates including Cardinal Dolan be invited, recalled Passionist Father Jerome Vereb of Pittsburgh, a longtime friend of Graham's who worked with him as a former official of the Pontifical Council for the Promotion of Christian Unity.

---

5. May 31, 1997, on the Hour of Power television program titled "Say 'Yes' To Possibility Thinking," program #1426

6. James Michael Beam, "I Can't Play God Anymore," McCall's [January 1978]: 158, as cited in a pdf by Kurt A. Edwards in a Dissertation for Doctor of Philosophy at the Bowling Green State University

> 'Billy Graham always treasured his many friendships with Roman Catholics,' Father Vereb wrote March 2 in the Pittsburgh Catholic. 'He regarded them not just as ecumenical partners in a diplomatic sense, but as his co-laborers in the vineyard of the Lord.'"
>
> At his crusades, Graham's staff connected people to their local Catholic church, and he always made a point of reaching out to the local Catholic bishop wherever he traveled.[7]

"For some unexplainable or even mysterious reason, Billy Graham is unable to discern the theological, moral, and spiritual soul of Roman Catholicism. Likewise, he has failed to grasp, or worse still, has chosen to ignore the historical character of the entire Vatican system. Instead, he has chosen to become attracted, impressed, and finally to honor and follow the Holy See. The result has been a tragic failure on his part to understand the difference between the truth of God's Word and the utter blackness of Roman Catholicism"[8]

- Though several would disagree with Graham in many ways and the techniques he used, God used him to preach the gospel to millions. Even though there were many false converts, there were also many true converts by the grace of God. We must be careful not to forget polemics when dealing with a celebrity preacher or someone we much admire.

  - Are there any dangers in having an altar call or having someone make a profession of faith?

- Indifferentists believed that fundamentalists separated too quickly and were always looking for a fight.

- The Indifferentists kept the name evangelical and the Fundamentalist separated from evangelicalism.

---

7. Catholic News Herald Article: Thousands gather for Billy Graham's 'last crusade': Feb. 12, 2018

8. Ewin. *The Assimilation of Evangelist Billy Graham Into the Roman Catholic Church.* P. 22

EVANGELICALISM

- Evangelicalism became known as a movement that did not separate from anyone, led by Fuller Theological Seminary and Billy Graham. Unfortunately, this was a fall from orthodoxy and the term "evangelical" does not mean anything anymore.
- Its unwillingness to separate from false teachers and worldliness was driven by a desire for greater influence in society. It is full of every kind of apostate church known now, mixed in with a few solid biblical churches still under the label evangelical.
- Fundamentalism and evangelicalism should have never split. Evangelicals need fundamentalists and fundamentalists need evangelicals. The balance of doctrinal purity and church unity. Without balance the fundamentalist became legalistic and the evangelicals became apostate.

  > Robert Godfrey: "For a long time, I have felt that the cause of biblical Christianity has been undermined in our time by sincere people who engage in unbiblical activities for the sake of being an influence. The sad and ironic result of those actions has been harm to the cause of Christ and little or no good influence has actually occurred. They myth of influence seduces Christians into believing that by compromising important theological truths more people can be influenced for Christ." "The most tragic consequence of the myth of influence is that those who embrace it often end up being influenced by the world rather than being a good influence on the world. For example, Fuller Seminary in its efforts to be more influential by moving beyond its own fundamentalist roots has abandoned basic evangelical doctrines such as the inerrancy of Scripture."[9]

- There are a faithful few in both fundamentalism and evangelicalism that rightfully cling to both doctrinal purity and an attempt to unite the church.
  - What is an important part of discipleship that is missing today, concerning unity? Teaching people how to disagree in love for the purpose of finding truth rather than preference.

---

9. Godfrey. *The Myth of Influence*. Articles: Ligonier. Feb. 20th 2019

D.L. Moody (1837–1899)

- Moody was born in Northfield, Massachusetts and was a well-known evangelist to the United Kingdom. When he returned to America he preached to crowds as large as twenty thousand people.
- He greatly aided foreign missions.
- He started a Bible institute that goes by his name.

Below are some of his well-known quotes:

"There are many of us that are willing to do great things for the Lord, but few of us are willing to do little things."

"He who kneels the most, stands the best."

"The best way to show that a stick is crooked is not to argue about it or to spend time denouncing it, but to lay a straight stick alongside it."

- Moody was not known as a theologian and was largely ignorant of systematic theology. He was more concerned with spreading the gospel.
- Unfortunately, a lack of understanding theology led him to embrace Roman Catholics and share the pulpit with liberal teachers.

> "The ultimate purpose of the evangelical churches was to Christianize the nation—indeed the world. For Moody this task was so great that it demanded an end to internal divisions with the church universal. "I hope,' he exclaimed 'to see the day when all bickering, division and party feeling will cease, and Roman Catholics will see eye to eye with Protestants in this work. Let us advance in a solid column—Roman Catholics, Protestants, Episcopalians, Presbyterians, Methodists—against the ranks of Satan's emissaries.'"[10]

- Why is good theology important for us to understand and what are the repercussions of bad theology?

- Define the following words or terms that not only theologians, but all Christians should know and understand:

---

10. Findlay. American Evangelist. P. 248

i. Gospel
ii. Justification
iii. Sanctification
iv. Repentance
v. Atonement
vi. Propitiation
vii. Imputation
viii. Holiness
ix. Grace vs. Mercy
x. Justice
xi. Original Sin
xii. Incarnation
xiii. Exegesis vs. Eisegesis
xiv. Depravity
xv. Assurance

NOTES

I hope that you have enjoyed going through historical theology. The goal of this study is to help you grow in your knowledge and understanding of who God is in order to glorify him in a greater way in every aspect of your life. One of the things we are called to love God with is our minds.

I pray that your discernment has been sharpened and your understanding of the nature and attributes of God has been propelled. We have a strong heritage in the faith. We must understand that the heroes we read about in church history are not heroes at all, but depraved men and women just like us. The only hero is Jesus Christ who has accomplished what is impossible for us to do and made us to be justified and holy before a thrice holy God because of his righteousness that has been imputed to us who are in him.

I encourage you to continue learning more about historical theology, we only scratched the surface. Pick someone that you learned about who helps your understanding of God grow and get their books or sermons and let them become a mentor. We should all have an old dead guy as a mentor.

Teach what you have learned to others in order to strengthen them in the faith and grow in their knowledge and understanding of who God is and what he has done. Remember that Christians desire to teach others all that we know in order for them to grow to be better and more effective than we are in the ministry that we all are called to. Yes, our goal is for our children, our family, our friends, our students, and our churchmen to be greater than ourselves in the faith by the grace of God.

Below are a few questions concerning what you have studied:

Explain the doctrine of Federal Headship.

What is penal substitutionary atonement?

What attributes of God should be explained in a personal gospel presentation?

What is soteriology?

Who did we study that has a soteriology named after him?

What chapter did you enjoy the most?

What doctrine did you enjoy the most?

What historical church leader did you enjoy the most?

Why is it important to study church history?

Why is it important to study theology?

What is doctrine?

What is Pelagianism and what church father is most known for battling against it?

What is Arianism and what church council dealt with it?

What is Nestorianism and what church council dealt with it?

What is Arminianism?

What is Calvinism?

Name the disciples of the apostles.

What is exegesis vs eisegesis?

Bibliography

Almodiel, Junes. *Tanong Sat Sagot*. Trafford. USA (2012) P. 84
Ambrose. *The Letters of S. Ambrose, Bishop of Milan*. Oxford. James Parker and Co. and Rivingtons. London, Oxford, and Cambridge. (1881) P. 145–56
Aquinas, Thomas. *The Philosophical Theology of St. Thomas Aquinas*. Leo J. Elders. E.J. Brill, Leiden. New York. (1990) P. 120
Athanasius. *The Death of History's Worst Heretic*. Article. The Cripplegate. Nathan Busenitz. 2011
Athenagoras. *A Plea for the Christians*. Translated ty B.P. Pratten. Beloved. Pickerington, Ohio. 2016
Athenagoras. *Embassy for the Christian: The Resurrection of the Dead*. Translated by Joseph Hugh Crehan. Newman. New York. 1955
Augustine. *Exposition 2 of Psalm 31, 2–4*
Augustine. Justification Volume 1. Michael Horton. Zondervan. Grand Rapids. (2018)
Augustine. *On Nature and Grace III*. Boniface Ramsey. *Augustine: Selected writings on grace and Pelagianism*: New City. New York. P. 321
Augustin. *St. Augustine of Hippo Writings in Connection with the Manichaen Controversy*. Apostle Horn. New Apostolic Bible Covenant. (2019) P. 273
Augustine. *The Anti-Pelagian Works of Saint Augustine: On Nature and Grace*. Translated by Peter Holmes. Edinburgh. P. 238
Augustine. *The City of God*. Cited from Peter Toon. *The Puritans, The Millennium and the Future of Israel*. Cambridge. James Clarke. 1970. P. 14–15
Augustine. *The Fathers of the Church: St. Augustine: The Retractions*. Translated by M. Inez Bogan. The Catholic University of America. (1999) P. 90–91
Augustine. *The Life and Writings of Saint Augustine: The Confessions*. Wyatt North. Wyatt North.
Augustine. *The Works of Saint Augustine A Translation for the 21st Century: Sermons*. Translated by Edmund Hill. Edited by John E. Rotelle. New City. New Rochelle, New York. P. 327
Augustine. *Tracing the heart of the Gospel from Christ to the Reformation Long Before Luther*. Nathan Busenitz
Basil. *Nicene and Post-Nicene Fathers The Christian Church Volume VIII: St. Basil: On the Spirit*. Henry Wace and Philip Schaff. Oxford: James Parker and Company. New York. Translated by Blomfield Jackson. P. 36
Bavinck, Herman. *The Last Things*, Edited by John Bolt. Translated by John Vriend. Grand Rapids. Baker. 1999

Baxter, Richard. *A Christian Directory: or, A body of Practical Divinity, and Cases of Conscience*. London (1825)(2007) P. 538

Benware, Paul. *Understanding End Times Prophecy*. Moody. Chicago. 1996, 2006

Bowman, Robert M. Jr. *The Word-Faith Controversy*. Baker. Ada. 2001

Bunyan, John. *A Treatise of the Fear of God*. London. 1679

Calvin, John. *A History of Christian Conversion*. David W. Kling. Oxford University. New York. (2020) P. 218

Calvin, John. *A Treatise on Relics*. Outlook. (Reproduction) Frankfurt am Main, Germany (2018). P. 13

Calvin, John. *Commentary on the Minor Prophets*.

Calvin, John. *Institutes of the Christian Religion 1536 Edition*. Translated by Ford Lewis Battles. William B. Eerdmans. 1975

Calvin, John. *Institutes of the Christian Religion Book III*. Translated by Henry Beveridge, ESQ. P. 386

Calvin, John. *John Calvin's Exegesis of the Old Testament*. David L. Puckett. Westminster John Knox. Louisville, Kentucky. (1995) P. 107

Clement (of Alexandria). *The Instructor: Book 1*. CreateSpace. 2015

Clement (of Rome). *The Epistles of Clement: The First Epistle of Clement to the Corinthians, 1–9*. Edited by Anthony Uyl P. 36–48

Calvin, John. *The John Calvin Bible Commentaries: Psalms 1–35*. Jezzybee Verlag Jurgen Beck. Createspace, North Charleston SC.

Chamberlin, Eric Russell. *The Bad Popes*. Barnes & Noble. New York. 1969

Chrysostom, John. *Nicene and Post-Nicene Fathers First Series Volume XIV: Chrysostom: Homilies on Hebrews*. Edited by Philip Schaff.(1889) P. 367

Chrysostom, John. *Selected Homilies and Treatises St. John Chrysostom: Against Marcionists and Manichaeans*. Jazzybee Verlag Jurgen Beck. Createspace. North Charleston, SC. P. 157

Cyprian. *Invitation to Church History World*. John D. Hannah. P. 88

Cyprian. *The Ante-Nicene Fathers; The Writings of the Fathers down to A.D. 325: Volume 5: Treatise 1*. Edited by Alexander Roberts and James Donaldson. P. 422

Edwards, Jonathan. *Sermons of Jonathan Edwards*. Hendrickson. Peabody, Massachusetts. (2005) P. 15–16

Edwards, Jonathan. *Sinners in the hands of and Angry God*. Printed and Sold by S. Keenland and T. Green. Boston. 1741

Edwards, Jonathan. *The Preaching of Jonathan Edwards*. Banner of Truth. 2008

Edwards, Jonathan. *The Works of Jonathan Edwards*. A Reprint of the Worcester Edition Vol III. Leavitt & Allen. New York. (1851) P. 217

Edwards, Sarah. *The Printer and the Preacher*. Randy Petersen. Nelson. Nashville, TN. (2015) P. 169

Ephraim. *Rapture, The Bride Redeemed*. Paul Lehr. Independent. 2017

Erasmus, Desiderius. *The Praise of Folly*. Translated by John Wilson. Good. 1668

Erickson, J. Millard. *Christian Theology*. Baker Academic. Grand Rapids, Michigan. 1983, 1998, 2013

Eusebius. *The Book of Eusebius #3 The Proof of the Gospel being the Demonstratio Evangelica*. Arne Horn. New Apostolic Bible Covenant. (2016) P. 399

Ewin, Wilson. *The Assimilation of Evangelist Billy Graham into the Roman Catholic Church*. Quebec Baptist Missions. (1992) P. 22

Findlay, James. *American Evangelist: Dwight L. Moody*. University of Chicago. 1969

Geisler, L. Norman and Joshua M. Betancourt. *Is Rome the True Church?*. Crossway. 2008

Geree, John. *The Character of an Old English Puritan, or Non-Conformist*. Printed by W. Wilson for Christopher Meredith. London. 1646

Godfrey, Robert. *The Church and the State After Constantine*. A Survey of Church History. Ligonier Resources. 2019

Godfrey, Robert. *The Myth of Influence*. Articles: Ligonier. Feb. 20th 2019

Goldsworthy, Graeme. *Gospel-Centered Hermeneutics*. IVP Academic. Downers Grove, Illinois P. 170

Graeme, Goldsworthy. *Gospel Centered Hermeneutics*. Downers Grove, IL. (2006) P. 170-71

Henry, Matthew. *An Exposition of the Old and New Testament: Volume 1: Genesis. Exodus, Leviticus, Numbers, Deuteronomy*. Edinburgh. (1790) P. 55

Henry, Matthew. *The Power of Transformation*. Pauline E. Lewinson. iUniverse. Bloomington, IN. (2011) P. 167

Hermas. *The Shepherd of Hermas*. Translated by J. B. Lightfoot. Crossreach. 2014

Hoekema, Anthony. *The Meaning of the Millennium: Four Views*. Edited by Robert G. Clouse. Downers Grove, IL. (1977) P. 172

Hus, Jan. *Vyklad Viry. Opera Omnia*. Quoted in Thomas A. Fudge. *Jan Hus: Religious Reform and Social Revolution in Bohemia*. I.B. Tauris. 2017

Ignatius. *Ancient Christian Writers: To the Magnesians*. Edited by Johannes Quasten, S.T.D. and Joseph C. Plumpe P. 72-74

Irenaeus. *An Exposition of the Thirty-nine Articles*. E. Harold Browne. London. (1864) P. 140

Irenaeus. *Ante-Nicene Fathers:Against Heresies*. Alexander Roberts and James Donaldson. P. 417

Irenaeus. *Irenaeus and Paul*. Edited by Todd d. Still and David E. Wilhite. Bloomsbury. London, WC. (2020) P 262

Irenaeus. *The Ante-Nicene Fathers*. Alexander Roberts and James Donaldson. Charles Scribner's Sons. (1905) P. 560

Irenaeus. *The Early Church at Work and Worship; Volume 1: Against Heresies*. Everett Gerguson P. 255

Irenaeus. *The Early Church at Work and Worship Vol. 1*. Everett Ferguson. Cascade. Eugene, Oregon. (2012) P 255

Jerome. *Historical Theology*. Gregg R. Allison. Zondervan Academic. 2011

Jerome. *The Letters of Saint Jerome: Letter LIII To Paulinus*. Translated by The Hon. W. H. Fremantle with assistance of G. Lewis and W.G. Martley. Aeterna. 1892

Johnson, Bill. *When Heaven Invades Earth*. Destiny Image. Shippensburg, 2009

Justin (Martyr). *2000 Years of Christ's Power*. Needham, Nick. Christian Focus. 2016

Justin (Martyr) *Dialogue with Trypho*. New Apostolic Bible Covenant. (2018) P. 56

Justin (Martyr). *Lost Orthodoxy: Heart of the Gospel*: Jonathan R. P. 439

Justin (Martyr) *The Writings of Justin Martyr and Athenagoras: Dialogue with Trypho*. Translated by Marcus Dods, George Reith, and B.P. Pratten P. 160

Koontz, Terri. Mark Sidwell. S.M. Bunker. *World Studies for Christian Schools*. Bob Jones University. Greenville, S. Carolina. 2000

Lefevre, Jacques. *Lefevre; Pioneer of Ecclesiastical Renewal in France*. Philip Hughes. Wm B. Eerdmans. 1984

Liardon, Roberts. *God's Generals*. Whitaker House. New Kensington, PA. 1996

Luther, Martin. A *Commentary on St. Paul's Epistle to the Galatians*. Erasmus Middleton, B.D., 1807. P. 85

Luther, Martin. *Critical Thinking Using Primary Sources in World History*. Wendy S. Wilson and Gerald H. Herman. Walch. Portland, Maine. (2004) P. 25

Luther, Martin. *History of Interpretation*. Frederic W. Farrar. Bampton Lectures. Baker. Grand Rapids. 1961 P. 329

Luther, Martin. *History of the Christian Church, Volume VII. Modern Christianity. The German Reformation*. Philip Schaff. Logos. Oak Harbor, WA. 1998

Luther, Martin. *Pistis and the Righteous One*. Desta Heliso. Mohr Siebeck. Tubingen, German. (2007) P.7

Luther, Martin. *Preface to the Complet Edition of Luther's Latin Writings: Volume 34. Career of the Reformer IV*. Concordia (1960). P. 336–37

Luther, Martin. *The Ideas that Have Influenced Civilization: Vol. V*. Oliver J. Thatcher. Roberts—Manchester. Boston, New York (1901) P. 119

MacArthur, John *Charismatic Chaos*. Zondervan Academic. Grand Rapids, Michigan. 1992

MacArthur, John. *Christ's Prophetic Plans*. Moody. Chicago. IL. 2012

MacArthur, John. From the Sermon: *Jesus, the Firstborn Among Many Brethren*. 2020

MacArthur, John. From the Sermon: *The Grim Reality of the Last Days*. March 20, 2011

MacArthur, John, *New Testament Commentary on James*. P. 122

MacArthur, John. *Slave*. Thomas Nelson. Nashville, Dallas, Mexico City, Rio De Janeiro. 2012

Manton, Thomas. *The complete Works of Thomas Manton: Vol X*. James Nisbet & Co. Ballantyne and Company. London (1872) P. 309

Masselink, William. *Why Thousand Years?*. Eerdmans. Grand Rapids. (1930) P. 31

Mathison, Keith. As quoted in: *Christ's Prophetic Plans*. John MacArthur and Richard Mayhue. Moody. Chicago. 2012

Mauro, Philip. *Life in the Word: The Fundamentals*. Testimony. Chicago. 1909

McMillan, John. *Annuals of the American Pulpit*. William B. Sprague. Robert Carter & Brothers. New York. (1858) P. 350–351

Murray, Iain. *Revival and Revivalism*. Banner of Truth. Edinburgh. 1994

Napier, K.B. *Azusa Street: The Birth of a Lie*. Article. Bible Theology Ministries. 1994

Naselli, Andy. *Let Go and Let God?*. Lexham. Bellingham, WA. 2010

Needham, Nick. *2000 Years of Christ's Power*. Christian Focus. 2016

Niebuhr, Richard. *The Kingdom of God in America*. Wesleyan University. Middletown, Connecticut. 1988

Origen. *Commentary on Matthew, Chapters 10–11*. Eerdmans. Grand Rapids. 1951

Origen. *The Ante-Nicene Fathers: Translations of the Writings of the Fathers down to A.D. 325 Vol. 4*. Edited by Alexander Roberts and James Donaldson. American Reprint of the Edinburgh Edition. Charles Scribner's Sons. New York. (1907) P. 641

Origen. *The Sacred Writings of Origen*. Translated by Frederick Crombie. P. 581

Owen, John. *Nature and Causes of Apostasy from the Gospel*. Edited by Anthony Uyl. Devoted. Woodstock, Ontario. (2018) P. 6

Owen, John. *Of the Mortification of Sin in Believers*. CreateSpace. 2012

Owen, John. *The Doctrine of Justification by Faith, Through the Imputation of the Righteousness of Christ; Explained, Confirmed, and Vindicated*. Devoted. Woodstock, Ontario. 2016

Bibliography

Owen, John. *The Works of John Owen. Vol. VII.* Edited by William H. Goold. Edinburgh. New York. Robert Carter & Brothers. 1852

Packer, J.I. *Knowing God.* InterVarsity. 1973

Papias. *Ancient Christian Doctrine 5.* Edited by Angelo Di Berardino P. 165

Papias. *Nicene and Post-Nicene Fathers of The Christian Church; The Church History of Eusebius.* Philip Schaff and Henry Wace. P. 172

Papias. *The Apostolic Fathers: Volume II.* Edited and Translated by Bart D. Ehrman. Harvard University. London. 2003

Papias. *The More Excellent Way 2000 Years of Jesus' New Way of Life.* Harold F. Roelling. P. 126

Pink, Arthur. *The Attributes of God.* Sovereign Grace. Lafayette, IN. 2002

Polycarp. *The Apostolic Fathers Vol. 1: Epistle Concerning the Martyrdom of Polycarp: The Encyclical Epistle of the Church at Smyrna.* Chronologically arranged by A. Cleveland Coxe, D.D. P. 39-42

Polycarp. *The Apostolic Fathers Vol. 1: The Epistle of Polycarp.* Chronologically arranged by A. Cleveland Coxe, D.D. 33-36

Prosper. *The Shepherd As Theologian.* John MacArthur. Harvest House. (1995) P. 97

Savonarola, Girolamo. *Selected Writings of Girolamo Savonarola.* Jeremy Bentham. Yale University. 2011

Schaff, Philp. *History of the Christian Church.* Charles Scribner's Sons. New York. (1884) P. 614

Schleiermacher, Friedrich. *The Universalist Quarterly and General Review Volume 25.* Thomas B. Thayer. Universalist. Boston. (1868) P. 397

Sproul, R.C. *The Christian and Science (Part2).* Article. Ligonier. Revell. 1986

Spurgeon, Charles. *Lectures to My Students.* Zondervan. Grand Rapids. 1954

Spurgeon, Charles. *The Downgrade Controversy.* Preface: From 1887 Sword and Trowel Annual Volume. Lexington, KY. 2018

Synan, Vinson. *The Holiness Pentecostal Movement in the United States.* Eerdmans. Grand Rapids. 1981

Tatford, Fred.

Tertullian. *On Modesty Volume IV.* Eerdmans. Grand Rapids. (1951) P. 99

Tertullian. *The Sacred Writings of Tertullian Volume 1: The Prescription Against Heretics.* Translated by Peter Holms and Sidney Thelwall P. 285

Titian. *Address to The Greeks.* Translated by J. E. Ryland. Beloved. Pickering. Ohio. 2016

Tucker, Ruth. *Another Gospel.* Zondervan. Grand Rapids. (2004) P. 155

Tyndale, William. *The Church Historians of England: Reformation Period: The Acts and Monuments of John Foxe.* Fleet Street and Hanover Street. (1857) P. 184

Unknown. *Christian Writing Decoded: The Didache.* Wyatt North. 2012

Unknown. *The Epistle of Barnabas.* Translated by J.B. Lightfoot

Unknown. *The Justification Reader: Epistle to Diognetus.* Thomas C. Oden. William B. Eerdmans. Grand Rapids, Michigan / Cambridge, U.K. (2002) P. 65

Wagner, C. Peter. *The New Apostolic Churches.* Regan. Ventura, CA. 2020

Wagner, C. Peter. *Wrestling with Alligators, Prophets and Theologians.* Regal. Ventura, CA. 2010

Watson, Thomas. *A Body of Divinity.* Banner of Truth. 1958

White, Alma. *Demons and Tongues.* Pillar of Fire. Zarephath, New Jersey. 1949

Whitefield, George. *Readings in Historical Theology.* Robert F. Lay. Kregel Academic & Professional. Grand Rapids. (2009) P. 339

Whitefield, George. *The Works of the Reverend George Whitefield: Vol 1*. Pembroke College. Oxford. London (1771) P. 212

Wilbur, Earl Morse. *Our Unitarian Heritage*. Beacon. Boston, MA. 1963

Wood, Leon J. P. *The Bible & Future Events*. Zondervan. Grand Rapids, Michigan. (1973) P. 35

Wycliffe, John. *Light from Old Times or Protestant Facts and Men*. John Charles Ryle. Wycliffe House. London. (1898) P. 4–5

Zwingli. *Radical Reformation*. George Huntston Williams. Truman State University. Kirksville. Missouri. 1992

Zwingli, Ulrich. *Zwingli A reformed Theologian*. Jaques Courvoisier. WIPF & STOCK. Eugene, Oregon. (2016) P. 33 Previously published by John Knox Press, 1957

Zwingli, Ulrich. *Zwingli & Bullinger*. G.W. Bromiley. Westminster John Knox. Louisville, KY. (1953) P. 68–69

Index

Adoptionism, 34, 38
Amillennialism, 105-8, 110-11, 113, 234
Amyraldism, 227
Annihilationism, 64, 279, 296
Antisemitism, 83, 193
Apocrypha, 95-96, 137, 177
Apollinarianism, 41, 118-20,
Apologetics, 1, 10, 47-49, 65, 167
Apostasy, 40. 74, 146, 185, 317, 324
Arianism, 22, 42, 43, 80-81, 90-93, 96, 118, 281
Aristotelianism, 161-62, 167
Arminianism (Semi-Pelagianism), 43, 44, 100, 102-3, 105, 119 185, 215, 219, 226-31, 233, 245, 248, 252, 261, 262-64, 294
Asceticism P. 66, 96
Assurance, 232, 318
Astral Projection, 242, 292
Atonement (Also see Penal Substitutionary), 34, 120-22, 125 165, 213, 228, 230, 232, 233, 264-65, 279
Attributes of God
    Aseity of God, 161, 165
    Faithfulness of God, 244
    Holiness of God, 88-90, 261-62, 272
    Immutability of God, 88, 282
    Incomprehensibility of God, 88
    Justice of God, 186, 255, 259
    Omnipotence of God, 40, 299
    Omniscience of God, 232-33
    Providence of God, 27, 55, 56, 206, 208, 246, 310, 312

Sovereignty of God, 1, 8, 43, 86, 89, 156, 194-95, 229, 232, 247-48, 251, 253, 266, 285, 305
Auricular Confession, 182

Baptism, 2, 30, 31, 34, 40, 42, 71, 78, 80, 95, 153, 191, 198-99, 201, 208, 249, 256
Baptismal Regeneration, 172, 179, 277

Calvinism, 99, 105, 208, 217, 227, 229-32, 247-48, 260, 263-64
Charismatic, 39, 284, 289-90, 292-93, 296, 299-300, 313
Chrismation, 153
Christology, 118, 122, 152
Complementarianism, 291
Consubstantiation, 192
Cosmological, 162
Covenantalism, 233-34

Dead Orthodoxy, 239
Deism, 96, 243, 279, 307
Depravity, 15, 30, 100, 102, 185-86, 213, 228-29, 232, 317
Diet of Worms, 189
Dispensationalism, 106, 109, 130, 235-36,
Divine Proofs, 162, 167
Docetism, 35, 36, 118
Dominonism, 106, 307
Donatism, 42, 80
Double Truth Theory, 168
Dualism, 39, 305
Dyophysite, 123, 147

Ebionism, 34, 118
Edict of Milan, 77
Edict of Thessalonica, 77
Eisegesis, 2, 296,
Emotionalism, 176, 240
Empirical Method, 161, 167
Epistemology, 167–68,
Eschatology, 2, 26, 105, 108, 110, 113, 130, 234, 236, 279, 308
Evangelical, 70, 204, 244, 246, 315, 323–24
Evolution, 316, 319
Evolutionary Godhead, 242
Exegesis, 2, 96, 236, 261, 307

Federal Headship, 43, 101–2, 265
Filioque Clause, 152
Five Points of Calvinism, 227–28
Five Points of Remonstrance, 227–28
Fundamentalism, 274, 315–19, 321, 323–24

Gap Theory, 319
Global Unity, 242
Gnosticism, 36, 37, 39, 41, 62, 112, 118 156, 277, 279, 313

Habits, 55–56
Half-Way Covenant, 243, 256
Heresy, 1, 22, 33–45,59–60, 65, 67, 90, 99, 100, 118, 121–22, 124 140, 157, 185, 207, 276–77, 289–90, 301, 305, 308,
Hermeneutics, 105–6–107, 110, 114, 137, 233–34
    Allegorical, 29, 65, 110, 111, 113–14
    Grammatical, Historical, 97–98,106, 113, 235–36
Hypostatic Union, 119, 122–23
Hypothetical Universalism, 227

Iconodules/Iconoclast, 125, 146–48, 153
Idolatry, 29, 33, 177, 211
Imperatives, 299–300
Imputation, 43, 101, 102, 214,
Incarnation, 86, 118, 120, 301
Indicatives, 299–300
Indifferentist, 274, 321, 323

Indulgences, 172, 174, 179–80, 182, 195–96
Inerrancy, 138, 274, 318
Infallibility, 138, 274, 302
Infralapsarianism, 226–27
Inner Light, 291
Intercession of the Saints, 196

Jehovah's Witnesses, 35, 43, 53 82–83, 281, 290, 316
Judaizers, 10, 17, 34, 71, 279
Justification, 14, 17, 18, 70–74, 103,182, 183–84, 186–87, 202, 208, 225, 246, 247, 258, 261, 284–86

Kenosis, 308–9
Kingdom Now Theology, 106, 307–8
Kundalini Spirit, 292–93

Latin Vulgate, 95
Legalism, 39,59, 240
Liberalism, 59, 268, 274, 317, 319–21
Libertines, 206
Lordship Salvation, 14, 98, 287
Lord's Supper (Communion), 182, 192, 205, 208, 256

Manichaeism, 39, 40
Marcionism, 37, 138
Mass, 169, 179, 196, 198
Mennonite, 201
Middle Knowledge, 232–33
Millennium, 26, 105, 108, 111, 113, 317
Modalism, 38, 299
Modernism, 240–241, 316, 319
Molinism, 231–32
Monarchianism, 34, 38, 118
Monergism, 70, 183–84
Monophysitism (Eutychianism), 44, 119, 121,123, 141, 147
Monothelitism, 119, 124–25
Montanism, 39, 59
Moravians, 246
Mormonism, 36, 37, 129, 277–78, 290, 296, 316
Mysticism, 156, 158, 171, 242, 285, 311

Natural Theology, 162
Nepotism, 150

Nestorianism, 45, 118, 120–21, 123, 141, 178
New Age Movement, 36, 241–42, 310
New Apostolic Reformation, 119, 307–8, 311
Nonconformist, 221–23
Normative Principle, 196, 217
Novatianism, 40, 42

Ontological, 164
Original Sin, 34, 100, 208, 317

Pacifism, 201
Pantheism, 241
Penal Substitutionary Atonement, 73, 84, 165–66, 214–15, 318
Pelagianism, 43, 44, 96, 99–101
Penance, 71, 95, 146, 153, 186
Persecution, 8, 9, 14, 40 , 41, 47, 48, 66, 77, 80, 219
Perspicuity, 234
Philosophy, 49, 51 ,55, 58–59, 79, 112, 160, 168, 241–43
Pietism, 239–41, 246
Platonism, 35, 49, 52, 55, 111, 160, 162, 167
Polemics, 1, 10, 34, 47, 83, 96, 99, 201–2, 239, 289–90
Polytheism, 48, 65, 79
Postmillennialism, 105–6
Postmodernism, 240–241
Predestination, 100, 175, 180, 208, 219–20, 228
Premillennialism (Chiliasm), 29, 105–8, 111–13 130, 234–35, 317–18
Perseverance, 3, 191, 228, 231, 249
Preterism, 106
Purgatory, 22, 154, 172, 176, 188, 196

Quakers, 290, 304
Quietism, 285, 290

Rationalism, 240–241
Regulative Principle, 196, 201
Repentance, 15, 16, 18, 28, 66, 95, 203, 229, 256
Restorationist, 34, 276, 290, 312, 316

Resurrection, 22, 25–26, 30–31, 49, 53, 82, 106, 108, 109, 112, 129, 136, 153, 280, 281, 318
Revival, 250, 253, 258–60, 263, 266, 297, 309
Revivalism, 157, 259
Romanticism, 241–42, 271

Sanctification, 17, 42, 56, 57, 153, 183, 249, 284–87, 294, 298
Savoy Declaration, 237
Seventh Day Adventist, 34, 279, 316
Shakers, 290–291, 296
Socinianism, 214
Social Gospel, 157, 272, 315–16
Socinianism, 191
Soteriology, 105, 202, 217, 202, 219, 248 278, 281, 294
Soul Sleep, 22, 279, 281
Supersessionism, 110, 234
Supralapsarianism, 226–28
Synergism, 70, 103, 183

Teleology, 163
Theistic Evolution, 319
Theocracy, 150
Theodosian Code, 80
Theosis, 152–53
Tongues, 249, 290, 293–98, 300, 311, 313
Transubstantiation, 176–77, 179, 192
Transcendentalism, 241
Trinity, 4, 12, 22, 34, 38, 42, 51, 53, 58, 64, 80, 86–90, 92, 168 207–8, 220, 233, 245, 291, 317

Unitarianism, 38, 264
Unity, 30,66–67, 157–58, 274, 277, 324
Universalism, 65, 213

Visible and Invisible Church, 157, 166, 181, 208

Wisdom, 17, 27, 48, 72, 78, 98, 100, 143, 159–60, 189, 221–22, 246, 264, 282
Word of faith, 265, 300

Zoroastrianism, 39, 40

Index of Quotes

Aquinas, Thomas, 163
Athenagoras, 53–54
Augustine, 73, 100, 112, 144, 268

Bavinck, Herman, 107
Baxter, Richard, 222
Benware, Paul, 112
Bunyan, John, 223

Calvin, John, 17, 74, 78 114, 203–4, 268
Chamberlin, Eric Russell, 148
Clement (of Alexandria), 55–58
Clement (of Rome), 14–15, 72
Chrysostom, John, 98
Cyprian, 67–68

Edwards, Jonathan, 251–56, 289
Ephraim of Nisibis, 109
Erasmus, Desiderius, 184–85
Erickson, Millard J., 113
Eusebius, 84, 143

Geisler & Betancourt, 74
Godfrey, Robert, 78, 324
Goldsworthy, Graeme, 107
Gregory of Nazianzus, 120
Grerre, John, 221

Henry, Matthew, 223–24
Heraclitus, 161
Hoekema, Anthony, 107
Hus, Jan, 181,

Ignatius, 24–25
Irenaeus, 62–63, 110

Jerome, 97
Justin Martyr, 50, 109

Knox, John, 211–12
Kozar, Steven, 308, 311

Lefevre, Jacques, 183
Luther, Martin, 17, 175, 186, 187, 189–91, 268

MacArthur, 18, 83, 131–32, 133, 175
Manton, Thomas, 249
Masselink, William, 107
Mathison, Keith, 112
Mauro, Philip, 318
McMillan, John, 259–60
Moody, D.L., 325
Murry, Iain, 264–66

Naselli, Andy, 286
Niebuhr, Richard, 274

Olson, Roger E., 108
Origen, 65–66, 142
Owen, John, 224–25, 285–86

Packer, J.I., 5, 273
Papias, 26, 109
Pink, Author, 36, 174, 244, 246, 261–62, 282
Piper, John, 231
Polycarp, 23, 72
Prosper, 74

Savonarola, Girolamo, 182

Schaff, Philp, 108
Slick, Matt, 152
Sproul, RC, 45, 165, 262
Spurgeon, Charles, 247–48, 315, 320–21

Tatford, Fred, 111
Tatian, 51–52
Tertullian, 59, 142
Tucker, Ruth, 280

Tyndale, William, 209

Watson, Thomas, 226
Whitefield, George, 249–50
Wood, Leon J., 108
Wycliffe, John, 180

Zwingli, Ulrich, 194–96

www.ingramcontent.com/pod-product-compliance
Lightning Source LLC
Chambersburg PA
CBHW071933240426
43668CB00038B/1345